POSTIMPERIALISM

T

POSTIMPERIALISM

International Capitalism
and Development in the
Late Twentieth Century

David G. Becker · Jeff Frieden
Sayre P. Schatz · Richard L. Sklar

Lynne Rienner Publishers · Boulder & London

Published in the United States of America in 1987 by
Lynne Rienner Publishers, Inc.
948 North Street, Boulder, Colorado 80302

Library of Congress Cataloging-in-Publication Data

Postimperialism: international capitalism and develop-
    ment in the late twentieth century.

    Bibliography: p.
    Includes index.
    Contents: Why postimperialism? / David G. Becker and
Richard L. Sklar—Postimperialism, a class analysis
of multinational corporate expansion / Richard L. Sklar—
Development, democracy, and dependency in Latin America;
"Bonanza development" and the "new bourgeoisie" / David
G. Becker—[etc.]
    1. International business enterprises—Developing
countries.   2. Industry and state—Developing countries.
3. Elite   (social sciences)—Developing countries.
I. Becker, David G., 1938-   II. Title: Post-
imperialism.
HD2932.P67   1987   338.8'881724   87-4455
ISBN 1-55587-046-5 (lib. bdg.)
ISBN 1-55587-047-3 (pbk.)

Printed and bound in the United States of America

The paper used in this publication meets the
requirements of the American National Standard
for Permanence of Paper for Printed Library
Materials Z39.48-1984. ⊗

Contents

Tables and Figures

Tables

Figure

Preface

Postimperialism is an idea about the political and social organization of international capitalism. It is an intellectual response to two empirical findings that contradict standard theories of capitalist imperialism. The first such finding is a growing separation of national interests from the interests of dominant classes in the industrial capitalist countries; the second is a growing congruence of national interests and dominant-class interests in the "third world." These findings are incompatible with the belief that capitalism drives nation-states to dominate and exploit one another. They are, however, consistent with the evident spread of industrialization to all regions of the world, and with the coalescence of dominant social classes across national and continental frontiers. Everywhere, dominant classes embrace supranational and global values while subordinate classes are relatively more nationalistic and less mobile.

The concept of postimperialism grew out of two bodies of thought: political theories of the modern business corporation, and class analyses of political power in the "third world." Along with Adolf A. Berle, postimperialist thinkers affirm that business corporations are political institutions—more precisely, "nonstatist" political institutions. As such, they rival and check statist political power both within national societies and, increasingly, in world politics.

In "third world" societies, dominant classes have arisen out of varied political and administrative, as well as economic, foundations. In the least industrialized societies, political organization has a far greater impact on class formation than does economic organization. By comparison, in the more industrialized "third world" societies the political and economic determinants of class formation are more evenly balanced. These observations underlie an unorthodox, power-based theory of class structure. In postimperialist thought, capitalism versus socialism is no longer the prime issue of class analysis; it yields pride of place to the question of liberty versus dictatorship. Not only does postimperialism fly in the face of *Marxisant* dependency theory; it owes little, if anything, to dependency theory in any form. Far from being a reaction to dependency theory, it stems directly from earlier analyses of corporate power in the Western world and class formation in the "third world."

Six of the chapters that follow were originally published between 1976 and 1984. In Chapter 1, written for this volume, Becker and Sklar argue the case for postimperialism as an approach to the study of transnational corporate expansion. Chapters 2, 3, and 4 were written from a postimperialist standpoint. Chapters 5, 6, and 7 are by Frieden and Schatz, who agreed to join this project because their own essays on transnational investment and bank lending are complementary to, and consistent with, the postimperialist approach. Chapters 8 and 9, written by Frieden and Schatz for this volume, present separate critiques of the Becker-Sklar thesis. In Chapter 10, Becker responds to their concerns and to criticisms that have appeared elsewhere.

Acknowledgements are due to the following journals for permission to reprint six articles as noted in the text: *Comparative Political Studies, Comparative Politics, International Organization, Third World Quarterly,* and *World Development.*

David G. Becker
Richard L. Sklar

Why Postimperialism?

DAVID G. BECKER and RICHARD L. SKLAR

Imperialism connotes the domination of one people, nation, or country by another. An inherently coercive relationship, imperialism
nonetheless can be maintained by forms of power—notably, economic
power—that originate with civil society rather than with the state's
"monopoly of legitimate force." Theories of capitalist imperialism lo-
cate the causes of this domination in the nature and effects of business
enterprise. Such theories postulate a need for business to expand into
foreign markets in order to deflect the threatened breakdown, actual
or potential, of a domestic enterprise system. Lenin captured the spirit
of these theories in his declaration that imperialism is the "highest," or
ultimate, stage of capitalism.[1]

   Yet the world capitalist system has continued to evolve and adapt
to changing political conditions. During the current era of bipolar
hegemonic rivalry, the link between capitalism and imperialism has
been tested by the dissolution of colonial empires. Meanwhile, corporate forms of enterprise, rooted in both individual and institutional
shareholding, have transcended their national horizons by establishing
subsidiary companies abroad. The magnitude of this transnational
leap by modern business is reflected in the fact that "[w]ell over one-
third of the world's industrial output comes from large business enterprises whose producing facilities are spread out over several countries."
Today, "any list of the world's business leaders, ranked according to
their power or their status, would be headed mainly by the leaders of
multinational enterprises."[2]

   Some analysts find nothing qualitatively new in the transnational
corporation. They note that business firms with branches in more than
one national territory are contemporaneous with both the advent of
capitalism and the rise of the nation-state; that private investors helped

1

impel the original outward expansion of capitalism and were involved intimately in all aspects of colonial exploitation.[3] Transnational enterprise, however, is a late-capitalist phenomenon whose resemblance to earlier institutional forms is superficial. It is conventionally defined with reference to the following criteria:

1. The enterprise is composed of a parent company and daughter or subsidiary companies located in two or more countries. The parent usually has a historical association with a metropolitan country but may be located elsewhere, for example, in an overseas tax haven.
2. The subsidiaries earn the bulk of their profits from the production of goods or services; international trade is for the subsidiaries an ancillary activity. The productive efforts of the whole enterprise are oriented toward more than one national market.[4]
3. The various national components of the enterprise are mutually supportive and subject to central direction. The managerial apparatus of each is designed to promote the overall interests of the group as a unit. Central direction extends beyond the broad coordination of business strategies; embraces coordination or supervision of routine operations; and depends upon modern technologies of organization, communications, and data management.
4. Because of their dependence on elaborate managerial technologies, transnational firms on the average are more likely than others to be under effective managerial control.[5]

The degree and efficacy of centralized direction are what principally distinguish the transnational firm from older forms of international business enterprise. Centralized direction strives to head off each subsidiary's tendencies toward "suboptimization," which can be detrimental to the efficiency and profitability of the whole enterprise. But there is another side to the coin—local concerns may be given short shrift. If, for instance, the corporate group's overall profitability would be enhanced by transferring an operation from one country to another, the *disposition* to make the shift probably will prevail within managerial circles—particularly if the counterarguments heard by management are "political," in the sense of being based on considerations other than those of economic efficiency. Even though the eventual outcome may depend more on bargaining among various interests in the host country and elsewhere than on managerial fiat, the tendency to elevate central corporate concerns over local ones seems to suggest dominance by the more developed country in which the corporation's head office is domiciled. A question then arises—if the parent company always benefits, does it not follow that transnational enterprise tends to perpetuate the domination of wealthy industrial countries, where the parents are usually headquartered, over countries that are non- or semi-industrial and relatively poor? Is not transnational enterprise a new form of imperialism, tailored to suit the postcolonial era?

Let us consider three alternative responses to this question. The first two project varieties of the neoimperialist view; the third may be termed postimperialist.

According to one neoimperialist thesis, international capital, centered in the metropolitan "core" of the world economy, imposes hierarchical, externally rooted structures of control upon the less developed "periphery" so that it may be more readily exploited. Exploitation consists in the extraction of surplus from the national economies of the "periphery," which cripples locally focused development. The less developed countries thus are compelled by economic necessity to import capital, machinery, and technology, thereby becoming dependent upon foreign suppliers, financial institutions, and transnational corporate managements. What is more, much of the imported technology, having been invented with a view toward the needs of the developed countries, is said to be inappropriate to those of the less developed countries. Local bourgeoisies further impoverish their "superexploited" co-nationals in order to accumulate capital of their own; they turn into privileged, "denationalized" elites whose members share few if any interests with the people at large. Elites of this kind can neither establish positions of moral-ideological leadership nor legitimize bourgeois-democratic regimes; the economic success of the local bourgeoisies has to be purchased at the price of political failure. "Peripheral" capitalism, therefore, takes on a characteristically anti-democratic political form in which the local "dominant" class remains in power on the strength of metropolitan economic or military backing.[6]

This thesis remains popular among those Marxists and radicals for whom capitalism is the root of all the world's evils. However, Marxist thought has produced its own anti-populist critique of the "development of underdevelopment" idea, cogently expressed in Bill Warren's documentation of relatively rapid capitalist development in the "periphery" as a direct outcome of imperialism.[7] Although Warren may be said to have rediscovered early Marxist realism with regard to the "progressive character of imperialist expansion,"[8] he had little to say about the changing distribution of power among nations and peoples—the heart of the question of imperialism itself. The grateful reception of his iconoclastic book by realists of Marxist persuasion is a measure of the depths to which "radical" scholars and movement romantics have plummeted in their flights of revolutionary fancy.

The second neoimperialist thesis was worked out by Latin Americans who knew at first hand that the "development of underdevelopment" thesis did not apply to the dynamically industrializing countries of their region. The thesis is epitomized in the writings of the "historical dependency" school associated with Fernando Henrique Cardoso.[9] Cardoso and his fellow *dependencistas* agree with Warren that capitalist development has led to increased industrial output, gross national product, and aggregate national income in many of the "peripheral" economies. But inasmuch as these economies do not produce their own capital goods or technologies, they are "structurally incomplete" and must maintain a "dependent articulation" with a world economy dominated by transnational corporations in order to function at all. Under capitalism, the transnationals are the only source of the "missing" inputs to the productive process and therefore have the monopoly power to decide what shall be produced, and how. The decisions of the transnationals result in a form of local industrialization that overemphasizes the manufacture of goods that, although massively consumed in the metropoli, are luxuries in the "periphery." Thus, the transnationals' interests are best served by economic policies that concentrate income, even at the cost of precluding the advance of mass consumption levels.[10]

Local bourgeois supremacy falls into the hands of a power bloc[11] made up of state officials and business executives who are associated closely with foreign direct investment. The power bloc uses its control of the local state to impose the requisite policies of income concentration. In other words, imperialist domination is transformed by the "dependent" country's class structure into an apparently local domination residing largely "in the social practices of local groups and classes which try to enforce foreign interests, not precisely because they are foreign, but because they may coincide with values and interests that these groups pretend are their own."[12] The resultant political dynamic is not the simple elite-mass dichotomy implied by the "development of underdevelopment" idea; it is, Cardoso and Faletto contend, a complex process whereby selected subordinate groups are incorporated into the networks of political representation while others are excluded. The process is ridden with conflict because those targeted for exclusion can be expected to resist their fate.

Cardoso and Faletto insist that the class dynamics of "dependent development" are historically specific to each country and cannot be deduced from "general laws of motion of dependent capitalism." Nevertheless, Cardoso and Faletto's theory can be shown to hinge on two broad generalizations about capitalist systems in newly industrializing countries. One is economic—"structural incompleteness" (inability to produce capital goods) and a bias toward the production of luxuries, it is claimed, create bottlenecks and crises that interfere with the expanded reproduction of capital. Because of the narrowness of internal markets and the deficiencies of a domestic capital goods sector that is "not strong enough to ensure continuous advance of the system, in financial as well as in technological and organizational terms,"[13] the difficulties can be surmounted only when the forces of metropolitan capital, acting in their own interest, intervene to restructure the model of accumulation.[14]

The other generalization is political—however deep its domestic roots may seem to have struck, capitalism is at bottom a foreign import and responds, ultimately, to the "needs" of the international market in place of those of the country's people. The local bourgeoisie, consequently, is deprived of its image of industrial leadership and the local state of its ability to project plausibly "national" interests; although the state is not a mere puppet of foreign interests, neither is it fully sovereign. These circumstances essentially rule out the establishment of a stable bourgeois-democratic political order. The alternatives are a quasi-authoritarian populism or, increasingly, bureaucratic authoritarianism under the aegis of military officers and civilian technocrats.[15]

Many Marxists, for whom the "development of underdevelopment" is either simplistic or unacceptably populist, have seized upon Cardoso's interpretation of "dependency," praising it for its supposedly faithful adherence both to Marx's realistic appreciation of capitalist development and to his class-analytical mode of explanation.[16] The praise is misplaced. Cardoso and Faletto's argument for "dependency" rests on a gross underestimate of newly industrializing societies' capacity for, and experience with, technological innovation and adaptation; the argument also overestimates the technological self-sufficiency of most advanced industrial economies. Cardoso and Faletto's survey of the varieties of capitalist development in Latin America, although a significant contribution to the economic historiography of the region, describes a "circulation of elites," not a conflict of classes.[17] Cardoso and Faletto take *intra-class* conflict due to differences of immediate, parochial interest between nationally and internationally oriented sectors of domestic bourgeoisies as evidence of a fundamental, systemic contradiction between national concerns and those of transnational corporations. The portrait of bourgeois "denationalization" painted by Cardoso and Faletto is arbitrary, reflecting their apparent distaste for the cosmopolitanism embodied in transnational enterprise. Their standard for measuring the economic and political attainments of "peripheral" capitalism—total autonomy, together with a state that truly embodies a popular will[18]—is not realistic.

Cardoso and the *dependencistas* who are indebted to him have advanced beyond the ingenuousness of the "development of underdevelopment" thesis. But their theoretical edifice sits atop a flawed foundation: the erroneous premise that international capitalist expansion is necessarily and ineluctably imperialist.

The third alternative thesis, postimperialism, abandons that premise. It begins with the observation that global corporations function to promote the integration of diverse national interests on a new transnational basis. In particular, transnational firms offer the "third world" countries[19] access to capital resources, dependable markets, essential technologies, and other services. The postimperialist viewpoint suggests that beneath the usual differences regarding distribution of rewards there lies a mutuality of interest between politically autonomous countries at different stages of economic development. At the deepest level, their interests are not fundamentally antagonistic and do not entail automatically the intensified domination of the less developed countries by the more developed.[20]

Certainly, the leaders of "third world" countries, almost without exception and regardless of ideological orientation, act as if this were their interpretation of current capitalist reality. Everywhere they evince a desire to establish stable relationships with transnational firms. A virtually universal condition for the existence of viable relationships is the localization, or indigenization, of both labor and management. Corporate policy moves toward full acceptance of indigenization out of economic self-interest; where corporate policy does not, the local state must have, and typically does have, an effective policy for imposing indigenization.[21] A second, widely affirmed condition is local participation in equity ownership. Consequently, the transnational presence often takes the form of joint ventures in which a local partner, frequently an arm of the state apparatus, acquires a percentage of the shares.[22]

Those two conditions abet the organizational revolutions that seem to occur as a matter of course in "third world" countries. Organizational revolutions, in their turn, bring into being new institutions and an entirely new social infrastructure. In many of these countries today, a major source of high-level employment is the parastatal sector of the economy. Highly bureaucratized parastatal entities employ many university graduates. Members of the intelligentsia so employed form part of an elite social stratum. They tend to embrace elitist ideologies, including the value systems of transnational business groups with which they may be associated, and are inclined to promote the growth of private enterprise at home. Even though parastatal elites may begin by promoting local private enterprise for instrumental reasons such as perceptions of efficiency and limitations on state resources, these elites often acquire a dedication to private property as soon as they detect opportunities for supplementing their incomes in the private sector. In most Latin American countries, where the process of modern class formation is older, the results are still more far-reaching. Burgeoning technocratic-industrial elites, their class interests and ideological world view transformed by a thorough indoctrination in the panoply of modern management techniques and by intimate contact with the transnationals, at last have displaced the "oligarchic" landed-financial-commercial dominant classes of yore.[23]

Together the state management sector and the large private enterprise sector that it protects and nurtures give rise to a new social class. Richard L. Sklar has termed this class the *managerial bourgeoisie*.[24] Let there be no misconception as to what is meant here. The term *does not connote a "class" of managers or a state elite*; managerial bourgeoisie is not an occupational or functional concept. It is a socially comprehensive category, encompassing the entrepreneurial elite, managers of firms, senior state functionaries, leading politicians, members of the learned professions, and persons of similar standing in all spheres of society. It is a *class* because its members, despite the diversity of their parochial interests, share a common situation of socioeconomic privilege and a common class interest in the relations of political power and social control that are intrinsic to the capitalist mode of production.[25] The term is used because it specifically is reminiscent of the business-entrepreneurial tradition; at the same time, the term reflects the *primary* disposition of this class in many "third world" countries to manage state agencies and large-scale enterprises that have been nationalized or created in collaboration with foreign investors.[26]

Within a host country for foreign investment, the managerial bourgeoisie consists of two distinct wings. The *local wing* is composed of those privileged host-country nationals who occupy the roles enumerated in the preceding paragraph; note that the class positions and interests of these privileged individuals derive from political and educational as well as economic sources. The *corporate international* wing is made up of foreign nationals who manage businesses and other transnational institutions. The local wing of the managerial bourgeoisie is also the upper stratum of a much larger and more complex national bourgeoisie consisting of a variety of local notables whose interests are circumscribed more closely and confined to the domestic scene. In some of the more industrialized "third world" countries, domestic private corporate enterprise already has achieved political and cultural preeminence and a degree of economic power that approaches or equals that of the state management sector. The upper stratum of the local bourgeoisie has evolved a cadre of class leaders who are themselves dependent on the corporate form of organization and whose interests and world views are already very close to those of the wing associated with international capital. David G. Becker has introduced the term *corporate national bourgeoisie* to describe this kind of locally dominant class.[27] Many radical commentators are wont to impugn the nationalist integrity of the managerial bourgeoisie, but their criticism is both misleading and unfair. The local wing of the managerial bourgeoisie is intensely and parochially nationalistic, although the intensity and parochialism of the corporate national variant are tempered somewhat by the effects of a closer involvement with transnational cosmopolitanism.

Managerial-bourgeois nationalism in "third world" countries often takes a populistic form whereby national leaders proclaim the political unity of the whole people and repress dissent in the name of defense against the threat of foreign domination. In that circumstance, which is commonplace today, the political values and attitudes of the managerial bourgeoisie's local wing are likely to be at odds with those of the corporate international wing. With few exceptions, the political values of transnational business executives are neither illiberal nor statist; but it would be naive to minimize the political opportunism of these men and women, their ability to set aside ideology for expediency.

Conflict stemming from discordant political values is less of a problem, argues David G. Becker in Chapter 3, where a corporate national bourgeoisie is locally ascendant. Democratic governance, often of a corporatist instead of a traditional, liberal variety, serves the interest of that kind of dominant class in much the same way, and for many of the same reasons, that it serves the class interest of the bourgeoisies of the metropoli. In addition, the dialectic of development gives rise to better organized subordinate classes whose members insist on political incorporation and opportunities for social mobility in return for their acquiescence in capitalist socioeconomic arrangements. Transnational business executives, for their part, have no cause to object to local democratic governance, so long as its presence is compatible with the stable economic environment that corporate planning requires. Such, increasingly, is the case. On the other hand, the usual conflicts of immediate interest that are endemic to any bourgeois group can lead to friction about key issues of economic policy: the corporate national bourgeoisie, motivated as it is by developmental nationalism, generally favors a more economically active local state and a more "mercantilist" policy of industrial protection and subsidization than transnational managers would prefer.

In short, transnational business relationships, whether or not punctuated by divergent political values, are subject to recurrent clashes between intense local nationalism and the cosmopolitan internationalism that is the *Weltanschauung* of the corporate international bourgeoisie. A potential for such conflict also is implicit in the inclination of transnational enterprise managers to subordinate local interests to those of the enterprise or corporate group as a whole. The postimperialist thesis posits that conflict between the local and corporate international wings of the managerial bourgeoisie is mitigated regularly or resolved through the medium of an ideological and behavioral disposition of the latter, a disposition that is captured in the idea of the *doctrine of domicile*.[28] According to this doctrine, local subsidiaries of transnational business groups should and do undertake to adapt, to operate in accordance with the policies of states in which the subsidiaries are domiciled. This adaptation, of course, has as its chief aim and purpose the promotion of the interests of the whole enterprise or group.

The doctrine of domicile should not be misconstrued as a guarantee of good corporate citizenship.[29] Properly understood, the doctrine is a tenet of ideological belief, a maxim of corporate action for those who plan and rationalize the transnational expansion of corporate enterprise. This tenet of business ideology is significant mainly because it smooths the relationship between the corporate bourgeoisies of the industrial capitalist countries and the bourgeoisies of those "third world" countries that are newly developing but as yet are narrowly industrialized. It is also a guide to the self-conceptions of transnational business managers. Inasmuch as the doctrine of domicile is concerned with an ideological and behavioral predisposition of transnational business, it draws attention to the action of societal groups whose cohesion and sense of common purpose are ideologically determined. What is implied, for the analyst, is a social rather than systemic or institutional frame of reference: a preference for looking "beyond" reified systems and their abstract "laws of motion," but also "behind" corporations and governments, to the group and class bases of the actions of these institutions. David G. Becker shows, in Chapter 4, how the doctrine of domicile has operated in the instance of natural resource development in Peru.[30]

Hence, the postimperialism thesis is specifically class analytic. It propounds the idea of transnational class formation based upon the coalescence of dominant class elements across national boundaries. This conception is particularly plausible within regions consisting of countries that have broadly similar cultures. But transcultural bourgeois class coalescence, too, has become an ever more reasonable expectation. The processes of transnational and transcultural bourgeois class coalescence are promoted powerfully by the operations of transnational enterprises.[31] In this regard, the creation of partnerships between elements of the corporate international bourgeoisie and the local managerial bourgeoisie is especially significant. Such partnerships, or "marriages," are sanctified by the vow of good corporate citizenship that underlies the doctrine of domicile—an affirmation of the capacity and intention of the transnational subsidiary to operate as required by local state policies. That vow is valued highly by the leaders of "third world" countries who wish to forge stable relationships with international business organizations. Like a real marriage vow, it occasionally may be breached when expediency beckons; the point is that both partners, although not always faithful, take care to avoid a divorce.

Neither cultural nor ideological barriers have prevented the formation of business partnerships between dominant class elements on a transnational basis. With increasing frequency, ideological reservations to collaboration with transnational corporations are set aside in deference to the practical imperatives of economic policy. All "third world" countries, regardless of their ideological preferences, need to import *some* capital and technology from abroad, even though in most cases local sources account for the bulk of capital formation. "Primitive accumulation," whether on the Soviet model or in the fashion of Dickensian England, entails a social and political price that the people of today's newly developing societies cannot and will not pay. The most reliable, if not the only, sources of the capital that must be imported are direct and indirect foreign investments by transnational business firms and banks.

Direct private foreign investment (the principal mode of large-scale metropolitan investment in the "periphery" from the end of World War II until the surge of bank loans and indirect investments during the 1970s) poses a dilemma for "third world" leaders who want to import capital and technology but who worry about a loss of their ability to exercise sovereign control of their countries' internal affairs. As Sayre P. Schatz observes in Chapter 5, there has been an intense debate between the advocates of open-arms acceptance of direct foreign investment and those, including many Marxists, who favor rejection whenever possible. But the attitudes and policies of "third world" leaders clearly are converging around a satisfying, nonideological middle course of "assertive pragmatism" toward direct foreign investment. Several leaders also have concluded that the answer to their dilemma is relatively heavier reliance on indirect investment. The consequences of that choice are examined in Jeff Frieden's four-nation case study, which is presented in Chapter 6.

The surge of development loans to newly industrializing "third world" countries was made possible by the transnationalization of the metropolitan banking system as well as by the flood of OPEC "petrodollar" deposits that entered the system beginning in the early 1970s. However, these "push" factors were complemented by a "pull" factor: the borrowers' nationalist developmentalism, their determination to proceed with broadly based industrial development under local entrepreneurial control. In each of the four cases studied by Frieden, the political outcome was the reinforcement of state capitalism, but in a manner that also strengthened the private industrial bourgeoisie.[32] The economic outcome in each of these cases was a major advance of industrialism—in aggregate output, in increased technological content, and in larger ratios of manufactured to total exports. Importantly, the results were independent of official ideology; much the same effects were observed, for example, in "socialist" Algeria as in "ultra-capitalist" South Korea.

It would be innocent and illusory to suppose that partnership agreements with transnational corporations and banks, even when arrived at for pragmatic and instrumental reasons, are ideologically or politically neutral. These partnerships transmit capitalist values to the host countries through the alliances that are cemented with the local wing of the managerial bourgeoisie. Such partnerships also foster, as we have seen, the organizational revolutions that facilitate bourgeois class consolidation.[33] Even so, traffic in ideas and attitudes does not pass between the partners of a dominant-class alliance on a one-way street. Members of the corporate international bourgeoisie are as likely to be sensitized to the developmental values of their host country partners as the other way around. Would it be unduly optimistic to anticipate a renewal of confidence in the ability of humankind to avert severe nationalistic and ideological strife?

In addition to the transformation of imperialistic relationships between industrial and nonindustrial countries, there is a question about the impact of transnational enterprises on interstate relations within particular regions. By adhering to the doctrine of domicile, the subsidiaries of transnational corporations can survive and flourish in all but the most intemperate of political and ideological climates. How will the presence of these subsidiaries in the rival states of turbulent regions, such as Southeast Asia, southern Africa, and the Middle East, where the fabric of peace is torn by national and ideological antagonisms, affect the causes of war? Will that presence help to create outlooks and attitudes that would render the old squabbles obsolete?

The answers to these questions carry grave implications for socialists everywhere. Ever since Marx, socialists have believed that the capitalist system is riven by a basic contradiction between the social character of production and the private, anarchic character of the regulation of production. They also have believed that the contradiction shortly would appear incarnate in the system's ultimate crisis. Ever since Lenin, socialists have professed to glimpse this crisis in the nationalist protest of peripheral regions against the domination and exploitation to which they have been subjected by metropolitan powers. Yet the system has withstood the waves of decolonization and protest and seems even to have prospered from them. "Third world" nationalism has become the ideological vehicle, not of socialism emergent, but of a bourgeoisie triumphant. If the socialist project is to thrive instead of stagnate, socialists will have to reexamine and bring up to date their theories of capitalist development on a world scale. This is a task that Sayre P. Schatz undertakes in Chapter 7.

Schatz accepts Marx's view of the contradiction between social production and directive anarchy. Schatz nonetheless avers that capitalism has evolved an adaptive process that enables it to alleviate the effects of the contradiction before they can rupture the continuity of the system. When confronted by a major problem that resists resolution using customary tools and methods, the system responds by forging a greater degree of conscious, centralized control. There are two key limitations: changes in the modalities of control usually are restricted to those that are minimally necessary to overcome the immediate manifestations of the crisis; and changes always lag behind the crisis in time because they are instituted only in reaction and never in anticipation. The contradiction, consequently, is never finally resolved; new crises erupt periodically, to be followed in each instance by partial, incremental adjustments.

With the advent of postcolonial capitalism, Schatz continues, the process of "socializing adaptation" transcends the national political framework, to which it heretofore has been confined, and becomes global. The impetus is the disjuncture between economic interdependence, on which the survival of all major capitalist institutions now depends, and the self-serving decisions of transnational corporations and metropolitan state authorities. When such decisions do serious damage to "third world" development, they engender a hostile reaction from countries that no longer are willing to endure in silence and that are both economically and militarily capable of inflicting telling damage in return. Worse still, if dissatisfaction with the fruits of capitalist development becomes widespread, the result could be to unleash political cataclysms that might in turn lead to "third world" defections from capitalism. The newly emergent global socializing adaptation aims to forestall these eventualities. It is characterized by growing conscious coordination on a world scale and involves a slow but perceptible accommodation by the chief institutions of international capitalism to the most urgent demands of the "third world" countries. It is encouraged strongly by transnational class formation. For, besides sensitizing those who hold power to the need for adaptation, transnational class formation has created a broadly based international class interest in undertaking the requisite adaptive measures.

In this connection it is worth underscoring that *postimperialism is not a theory of economic development per se.* One can properly infer from it that the current global division between developed and less developed territories is fluid rather than fixed—but not that capitalism will develop the latter uniformly. On the contrary, there is every likelihood that capitalist development will continue to be uneven, as in the past, although the present national boundaries may cease to serve as adequate delineations of that unevenness. The supersession of nationalist and ideological dissension, if it occurs, may not put an end to all quarrels about the rewards of development; the roots of discord simply may shift to a dimension other than the territorial one. Sayre P. Schatz's prediction is that we can look forward to further cycles of sharpening systemic contradiction, each ameliorated for a time, yet only for a time, by a new accommodation.

This does not resolve the issue of the prospects for socialism. There remains the irreducible conflict of class interest between bourgeoisie and proletariat—between those who exercise political and social control and those who, lacking control of the means of production, consumption, and exchange, are compelled by economic necessity to devote the bulk of their hours to tasks selected and structured by others. Until now, capital has been far more mobile internationally than has labor. But one of the striking features of the postimperialist age is that change now can be seen here as well. Tendencies toward international *proletarian* class formation can be observed in, for example, the spread of "guest worker" programs and other kinds of legal and illegal labor migration; and in the increasing prominence of international working-class organizations, ranging from the ILO to the AFL-CIO's American Institute for Free Labor Development to the Socialist International. These tendencies warrant further investigation.

Although there are grounds for optimism about the prospects for bourgeois democracy at the national level, it must be emphasized that *postimperialism is a theory of international oligarchy.* Should the nation-state be increasingly or decisively marginalized as an economic institution by "Cosmocorp,"[34] and should the nationalistic vendettas with which we are all too familiar be overcome, it is not certain that the result would be the Utopia foreseen by the ideologists of corporate capitalism. A world dominated by an international bourgeois oligarchy offers little that would appeal to progressives. Its institutions of political power and accountability might be even more remote from those affected by them than is the case today. What is more, the dominant oligarchy may resort to openly coercive forms of social control if it has to face a sullen or hostile proletariat without the legitimation afforded by nationalism.

Postimperialism implies the beginning of a new postnationalist age. In this phase of social construction, the bourgeoisie, true to its historic mission, has taken the lead. The transnational corporation itself, along with the financial system and the other institutions of international capitalism, should be analyzed from the standpoint of transnational class development. They are the chief instrumentalities of the corporate international bourgeoisie in the historic drive by that class to transcend the restrictive system of nation-states. To the extent that the drive succeeds, imperialism—the domination of one people by another—will be (is being) superseded by transnational class domination of the world as a whole. The implications of this transformative movement for social structure and social theory are but dimly understood.

Notes

The authors wish to thank Sayre P. Schatz, whose critical reading of an earlier draft of this chapter caused us to rethink and, we hope, to clarify several of our ideas. Such errors of omission and commission that may remain are, of course, our responsibility alone.

1. V.I. Lenin, *Imperialism, the Highest Stage of Capitalism* (New York: International Publishers, 1939).
2. Raymond Vernon, *Storm over the Multinationals: The Real Issues* (Cambridge: Harvard University Press, 1977), p. 15.
3. This appears to be the position of those who perceive a capitalist "world-economy" dating from the sixteenth century or before; see, e.g., Immanuel Wallerstein, *The Modern World-System* (New York: Academic Press, 1974).
4. A subsidiary of a transnational bank, for example, accepts deposits and makes loans in the currency of the country in which it is domiciled; it also does business with local firms and individuals insofar as such business is permitted. The transnational bank is very different from an older form of international financial institution, whose overseas branches existed mainly to service the foreign trade of home-country enterprises.
5. On the concept and limitations of managerial control, see Edward S. Herman, *Corporate Control, Corporate Power* (Cambridge: Cambridge University Press, 1981); Maurice Zeitlin, "Corporate Ownership and Control: The Large Corporation and the Capitalist Class," *American Journal of Sociology* 79

(1974):1073–1119; and Maurice Zeitlin and Samuel Norich, "Management Control, Exploitation, and Profit Maximization in the Large Corporation: An Empirical Confrontation of Managerialism and Class Theory," in Paul Zarembka (ed.), *Research in Political Economy*, vol. 2 (Greenwich, CT: JAI Press, 1979), pp. 33–62. Like these authors, we deny that the fact of managerial control constitutes managers as a class apart from the propertied bourgeoisie. However, managerialism does make a difference with respect to the nature of class formation and the structures of political power and social control.

6. This version of the neoimperialist thesis is found, with relatively minor variations, in Paul A. Baran, *The Political Economy of Growth* (New York: Monthly Review Press, 1957); André Gunder Frank, *Capitalism and Underdevelopment in Latin America* (New York: Monthly Review Press, 1969); Samir Amin, *Accumulation on a World Scale* (New York: Monthly Review Press, 1974); and Samir Amin, *Unequal Development* (New York: Monthly Review Press, 1976). Positions similar to theirs have been staked out by Marxists such as Stephen Hymer, "The Multinational Corporation and the Law of Uneven Development," in Jagdish N. Bhagwati (ed.), *Economics and World Order from the 1970s to the 1990s* (New York: Macmillan, 1971), pp. 113–140; and Michael Barratt-Brown, *The Economics of Imperialism* (Harmondsworth, Eng.: Penguin Books, 1976). Their thinking also has influenced non-Marxists such as Richard J. Barnet and Ronald E. Müller, *Global Reach* (New York: Simon & Schuster, 1974).

7. Bill Warren, "Imperialism and Capitalist Industrialization," *New Left Review*, 81 (1973):3–44; and Bill Warren, *Imperialism, Pioneer of Capitalism* (London: New Left Books, 1980).

8. Warren, *Imperialism*, p. 47.

9. Fernando Henrique Cardoso, "Dependency and Development in Latin America," *New Left Review*, 74 (1972):83–95; also Fernando Henrique Cardoso and Enzo Faletto, *Dependency and Development in Latin America* (Berkeley and Los Angeles: University of California Press, 1979).

10. Cardoso and Faletto, *Dependency and Development*, pp. xx–xxii. They mention "cars, televisions, refrigerators" as examples of the sorts of goods in question. Although transnational subsidiaries in newly industrializing countries indeed predominate in the manufacture of these and other consumer durables, on the whole these subsidiaries offer an exceedingly wide range of goods and services—many of which are mass-consumption items even by local standards.

11. Nicos Poulantzas, *Political Power and Social Classes* (London: New Left Books, 1973). Although Cardoso and Faletto do not use the term *power bloc*, it readily captures their meaning.

12. Cardoso and Faletto, *Dependency and Development*, p. xvi. "Pretend" is a mistranslation of *pretender* in the original Spanish, which connotes a sincerely stated claim or endeavor, rather than a pretense.

13. Cardoso and Faletto, *Dependency and Development*, p. xxi.

14. The forces of metropolitan capital *must* do so, in Cardoso's schema, for the usual Leninist reason—"the imperialist economies need external expansion for the realization of capital accumulation." They *can* do so for the

reason that their preeminence in capital goods production serves "as a form of maintenance of control" as well as "a necessary step in the process of capital accumulation" (Cardoso, "Dependency and Development in Latin America," pp. 90–91).

15. Guillermo A. O'Donnell, *Modernization and Bureaucratic-Authoritarianism: Studies in South American Politics* (Berkeley: Institute of International Studies, University of California, 1973); and Guillermo A. O'Donnell, "Reflections on the Patterns of Change in the Bureaucratic-Authoritarian State," *Latin American Research Review* 13, 1 (1978):3–38. O'Donnell holds that the populist solution was common during an earlier stage of Latin American industrialization, which was based on mass-consumption goods and therefore benefited from controlled political incorporation of the masses. In the next stage of industrial "deepening" (shifting of the product mix toward more expensive durable goods), the acceptance, or active promotion, of income concentration necessitated the political exclusion of these same masses (see also Cardoso and Faletto, *Dependency and Development*, p. 163). This was the political service that bureaucratic-authoritarianism appeared to perform for the captains of Latin American industry. However, bureaucratic-authoritarianism is plagued by internal tension and is subject to pressures for democratization, as is shown by recent events in Argentina and Brazil.

16. On the connection between Marxism and *dependencismo*, see Gabriel Palma, "Dependency: A Formal Theory of Underdevelopment or a Methodology for the Analysis of Concrete Situations of Underdevelopment?" *World Development* 6, 7–8 (1978):881–924.

17. Of the 215 pages of text in *Dependency and Development in Latin America*, just ten refer in any way to subordinate groups other than the middle class. Popular elements, largely undifferentiated, are accorded subjectivity only insofar as they exert unspecified "pressures" on behalf of equally vague "demands."

18. Cardoso and Faletto, *Dependency and Development*, pp. 162, 202. They look with favor on political authoritarianism and economic statism, if that is the price to be paid for preserving national autonomy while industrial development proceeds (see p. 162).

19. After weighing the options, we settled on "third world" as our descriptive adjective for societies at early or intermediate stages of industrialization. It avoids unwanted connotations associated with "developing" and "less developed" and, we hope, leaves no uncertainty as to what countries are meant. By placing the term within quotes and not capitalizing it, we signal our disagreement with any effort to divide the globe into separate "Worlds" on the basis of political as well as economic criteria. In our usage, "third world" embraces China and other less industrialized socialist societies.

20. This does not signify that *every* experience of capitalist development is on balance helpful to a country. Much less does this signify that all social classes and groups always benefit. But where capitalist development is hurtful to a country, it is so today because of contingent circumstances, not because of systemic features of the world economy. Although exposés of the visible, short-run harm done to subordinate social groups by capitalist development are both

useful and necessary, a theory of development ought not to neglect the dialectics of the long term: the possibility that development itself ultimately arms subordinate groups politically, so that by their own efforts they can obtain redress for some of the harm done to them earlier on. *e.g. Korea, Taiwan*

21. Transnational corporations have learned that local citizens placed in subsidiary enterprises in positions of trust soon acquire the same degree of identification with corporate goals as do "home"-country personnel. Even if the salaries of local citizens match those of expatriates, the former do not demand the "hardship" allowances, housing subsidies, and other special benefits that expatriates receive; local citizens thus are cheaper to hire and maintain. The transnationals' residual reluctance to hire locals derives from concern about their skill levels and the costs of training programs to overcome deficiencies; it is in countering this residual reluctance that state indigenization policies have much of their impact.

22. A sign of the importance of corporate joint ventures to both local states and transnational firms is the considerable variety of imaginative arrangements for constituting such partnerships at minimal out-of-pocket cost to the local partners: built-in "fadeout" provisions, automatic reinvestment of profits accruing to the local partners' account, and so forth. Another sign is the frequency with which government officials take the lead in promoting joint ventures that link the state, transnational firms, and, where possible, local private capital. See, e.g., Peter Evans, *Dependent Development* (Princeton: Princeton University Press, 1979).

23. The "oligarchic" order in Latin America was capitalist, not "semifeudal." Its transformation reminds us that renewing organizational revolutions are possible *within* capitalism and can signal a transition from an early, commercial capitalist phase to a late-capitalist phase featuring industrialism, oligopoly, and corporatism.

24. Richard L. Sklar, *Corporate Power in an African State* (Berkeley and Los Angeles: University of California Press, 1975), pp. 198–199.

25. A mode of production is composed of "the relations of control, the modes of cooperation and the technology that govern material production"; Richard W. Miller, *Analyzing Marx: Morality, Power and History* (Princeton: Princeton University Press, 1984), pp. 8–9. Miller continues: "Surely, systems of control and the conflicts to which they give rise are, in a broad sense, political as well as economic."

26. Richard L. Sklar, "The Nature of Class Domination in Africa," *Journal of Modern African Studies* 17, 4 (1979):531–552; see pp. 546–547.

27. David G. Becker, *The New Bourgeoisie and the Limits of Dependency* (Princeton: Princeton University Press, 1983), pp. 330–335. Strictly speaking, the managerial bourgeoisie is the dominant class of societies in which state capital plays a paramount role in production but does so in a way that nurtures the growth and development of private enterprise. Becker regards the corporate national bourgeoisie as a variant of the managerial bourgeoisie; although the state management and private elements of a corporate national bourgeoisie are symbiotically related, the latter is relatively independent of state power and may have its own historical roots. Other types and variants can be defined in

accordance with the evolution of a society's key economic institutions. For example, *state bourgeoisie* describes the dominant class of centrally planned economies where state capital is monopolistic; *entrepreneurial bourgeoisie,* the dominant class of market economies where state capital's role in production is distinctly minor in comparison to that of private capital.

28. Sklar, *Corporate Power,* pp. 182–188.

29. Wherever they operate, *including in the metropoli,* business corporations attempt to evade expensive regulations imposed upon them by the political authorities, if corporate managements conclude that the savings thus achieved outweigh the risks and penalties of discovery. To the extent that government administrators in "third world" countries are less capable or efficient than their metropolitan cohorts in overseeing corporate activities, they face a correspondingly greater likelihood of evasion. However, they have risen to the challenge with remarkable rapidity—partly with the assistance of international institutions such as UNCTAD, partly by means of managerial expertise *transferred to them by the transnational corporations themselves.* Besides, there is much evidence that transnational firms, due to their smaller numbers and far greater visibility, are *more* law abiding, on the average, than are locally owned private enterprises.

30. Another interesting case of the operation of the doctrine of domicile in natural resource development is that of Zambia, analyzed by Sklar in *Corporate Power.*

31. Awaiting the researcher's attention are the new transnational enterprises that are headquartered in "third world" countries and that are concentrating, thus far, on investment in neighboring countries. Locally headquartered transnationals are already a fact of life in Latin America, where their development has been stimulated by regional economic institutions. (These institutions are backed, at the political level, by a bourgeois desire for a greater measure of political assertiveness in international affairs and by an understanding in the same quarter that a regional approach offers a better prospect than a national one for attaining it.) In Asia, South Korea and one or two ASEAN countries have begun to spawn transnational enterprises of their own.

32. Algeria is the exception because no private industrial bourgeoisie existed there. However, private entrepreneurs shared in the bounty through the borrowed capital that was channeled to them by state development banks. Instead of regarding the tremendous expansion of the economically active state as a threat, local entrepreneurs saw the state as a partner and its growth as an alternative preferable to additional transnational corporate competition.

33. Which is not to claim that direct foreign investment is a *necessary* condition for organizational revolution in "third world" countries.

34. George W. Ball, "Cosmocorp: The Importance of Being Stateless," in Courtney C. Brown (ed.), *World Business: Promise and Problems* (New York: Macmillan, 1970), pp. 330–338.

CHAPTER TWO

Postimperialism:
A Class Analysis of Multinational
Corporate Expansion

RICHARD L. SKLAR

New frontiers for substantive research frequently give rise to theoretical challenges. More often than not, these will in fact be old challenges revived or rediscovered in a new context. Political scientists may well discover a fertile field for research in the phenomenal expansion of multinational business enterprise. Yet the challenges they encounter may not differ in principle from those that have been presented in the past by the growth of corporate enterprise in particular nations. Indeed, the failure of political science to comprehend the modern business corporation is well enough known. As Grant McConnell has written, "The existence of the modern corporation does not accord with long-standing conceptions of political organization, and no theory exists by which it can be reconciled with such conceptions."[1] The unmistakable relevance of transnational corporations to basic issues of political development and international relations creates a new opportunity for political scientists to face challenges that have been posed but, largely and lamentably, ignored in the past.

In this essay, three issues that arise from the problem of corporate power in political theory are identified with reference to pioneering works on corporate power in modern industrial society. These issues, involving economic oligarchy, managerial authority, and class formation, are then transposed to the transnational plane of study. Recent works on transnational enterprise and the problems of development in nonindustrial societies indicate that these questions may now be studied on a broader scale than heretofore, at possibly deeper levels of theoretical comprehension.

This article originally appeared in *Comparative Politics* 9, 1 (1976):75–92. Reprinted with permission.

I

No challenge to political science excites a more defensive reaction than that implied by Adolf A. Berle's view that the business corporation is "essentially, a nonstatist political institution."[2] This idea casts doubt upon the separation of economic power from political power for analytical purposes, a presupposition that is widely accepted in standard political science.[3] It also severely restricts the claim of democracy that can be made on behalf of political orders in societies that rely upon oligarchic forms of economic organization. As this observation implies, there may be an ideological basis for the characteristic attribution of economic and political power to different causes or generative activities by the vast majority of Western political scientists. Yet the pioneers of scientific political analysis did not uniformly balk at the challenge to conceive their subject as a unified field of power. Upon that provocative premise George Catlin has proclaimed the conceptual identity of political science and sociology, envisioning from that point of view a transdisciplinary domain which, as Charles Hyneman observed, might be extended to encompass much of the discipline of economics as well.[4] It may not be amiss to suggest that Berle's apparent iconoclasm is, essentially, traditional common sense.

The classic analysis of corporate power in the modern era was published by Berle and Gardiner C. Means in 1932.[5] This work set forth a theory of managerial autonomy within the modern business corporation based upon the authors' debatable finding that the evolution of corporate organization entails the divorce of ownership from control and the lodgement of decisive power in the hands of managers rather than owners. By 1940, other authoritative studies had shown, contrary to Berle and Means, that large nonfinancial corporations in the United States were likely to be controlled by their leading owners.[6] Nevertheless, the age of managerial authority, whether it be inseparable from legal ownership or coexistent upon separate foundations, had been proclaimed. It was a short step from there to announce the appearance of a managerial class, created by the organizational imperatives of the corporation itself. Thus, in 1941, James Burnham, recently estranged from Trotskyite Marxism, declared that a managerial ruling class, nurtured by the corporation, was emerging in the United States and other industrial countries.[7]

As a rule, those who conceive social class to be a function of property ownership have rejected the notion of a bureaucratic or managerial "class" in capitalist societies.[8] However, the managers of business enterprise and those who serve business in a professional capacity, in addition to their professional and social counterparts in other employment sectors, are often classified with property owners to constitute the bourgeoisie as a whole.[9] As a recruitment agency to the ranks of "middle management," bureaucratic organization promotes the growth of a social stratum that identifies firmly with the interests of property. Andrew Hacker has argued that the American corporation has produced a "new middle class" of junior and senior executives. This class is "large, national, and propertyless." Following William S. White, Hacker labels the species "*homo Americanus,*" or the "Consensus American." Its mode of social thought is cosmopolitan (within national limits) rather than narrowly sectional; its political style is passive and nonpartisan rather than earnestly participative and staunchly partisan, as the old middle class had been.[10]

Apart from Hacker, H.H. Wilson, and a few others, political scientists have been remarkably reticent about inquiring into political aspects of the corporate presence in modern industrial societies.[11] Among the many questions that bear investigation, three issues to which I have alluded in connection with the pioneering works of Berle, Means, and Burnham appear certain to capture the attention of those who study the multinational corporation. First, Berle's conception of the corporation as "a nonstatist political institution" points, as we have seen, toward oligarchy as the probable political future of the industrial capitalist societies. This may be contested by those who visualize a significant redistribution of corporate power from managers to employees,[12] and by those who are satisfied to define democracy as a system of imperfect competition between opposing groups. of politicians.[13] For Berle himself, the legal separation of corporate from state power was a virtue of paramount importance, since it would allow for the perfection of libertarian institutions under modern industrial conditions.[14] At the supranational level, the impression of oligarchy as a consequence of corporate enterprise may be intensified by the absence of an international state which might countervail oligopolistic corporate power. Richard J. Barnet and Ronald E. Müller refer to the leading executives of multinational corporations as "World Managers."[15] Do the actions of multinational corporate executives serve to secure and perpetuate the domination of some countries by others? In other words, the issue of oligarchy entails the question of imperialism.

Second, at the supranational level, the old issue of autonomous managerial authority becomes crucial to calculations about the potential exercise of corporate statesmanship in world affairs. In particular, it relates directly to the often vaunted ability of corporate managers to act in accordance with broad political and social values in addition to their normal economic objectives. John K. Galbraith has argued that the principled pursuit of noneconomic goals by a "mature corporation" is entirely consistent with its concurrent pursuit of overriding economic and technological goals. In fact, he contends, social goals for the corporation are needed to maintain the loyalty and morale of the many mental, as distinct from manual, workers who serve it.[16] This theme has been amplified by various expositors of multinational enterprise. Thus, Howard V. Perlmutter believes that the senior executives of the leading multinational corporations are the most important "social architects" of the new era. He postulates the "geocentric man" as the ideal executive for the "geocentric corporation"—a multinational enterprise whose national affiliates operate on the basis of economic equality.[17]

Third, beyond the issue of managerial autonomy, we may conceive the formation of a transnational class comprising at its core those who manage multinational corporations. To substantiate this thesis, it would be necessary to show that the members of any such presumed class tend to think and act as a collective entity. Social classes are sustained and strengthened by many different generators of vitality. A transnational ruling class would be especially difficult to overthrow inasmuch as its power would be fortified by the appropriation of diverse resources in many countries. Its significance as a power group might transcend the conception of imperialism. These three issues—imperialism, managerial autonomy, and transnational class domination—will be discussed in relation to the penetration of nonindustrial countries by multinational corporations.

II

The multinational corporation (or enterprise or firm) may be suitably defined according to these criteria: it consists of a parent company and subsidiary companies, the latter of which are located in a few or more countries and are engaged in the performance of basic economic, typically productive, activities in addition to trade. The various national components of the enterprise are mutually supportive and subject to central direction. The management of each component is designed to promote the overall interests of the group as a whole.[18] If, for example, it should appear to be in the interest of the enterprise as a whole to move certain productive operations from one country to another in quest of cheaper labor or lower taxes, the inclination to do so is likely to prevail. Inevitably, it will be suggested that the interests of the whole normally coincide with the interests of the controlling part. Since the parent company does have a specific national identity and since it is normally controlled by directors of a specific nationality, or a small set of nationalities, the spread of multinational enterprise appears to result in the perpetuation and intensification of hegemonic domination by the industrial capitalist powers. In short, the national and organizational loyalties of transnational business executives may be expected to fuse with imperialistic force. This argument has been made from a Marxist-Leninist standpoint as a matter of doctrine:

> Capital without a state is . . . unthinkable. But in the world as it is constituted today only nations have states: there is no such thing as a supranational state. . . . If, for example, the state of the nation to which it belonged were to collapse, capital would lose its indispensable protector. It would then either be incorporated into the capital of another nation or it would cease to be capital by coming under the jurisdiction of a revolutionary regime dedicated to the abolition of the entire set of relations of production of which capital is one part. . . . [T]he historic course of the global capitalist system is leading to one of two outcomes: world empire or world revolution.[19]

An empirically based demonstration of the thesis that multinational corporations promote imperialism by economic means has been presented by Stephen Hymer.[20] The basis of his argument is his insistence upon the differing effects of the technological and organizational determinants of economic development. In his view, technological diffusion alone does not produce or serve to perpetuate imperialist domination. This condition is plainly the result of corporate organization, which typically distributes the functions of planning, coordination, and routine operation according to the principle of hierarchy. The result is a proliferation of subsidiary firms, whose actions are coordinated at regional levels by higher subsidiaries of parent corporations, themselves located in the major geographic centers of corporate power and planning.[21]

Marxists in general assume that domination (of the underindustrialized countries by the industrial capitalist countries) and exploitation go hand in hand—that in the course of multinational corporate expansion, relatively poor and weak countries are compelled by various means to pay for the benefits that accrue to the advanced capitalist countries.[22] Few people today would bother to challenge this assumption by resuscitating the late Victorian doctrine of beneficient, paternalistic imperialism.[23] However, another somewhat paradoxical thesis to the effect that imperialism is not only injurious to subjugated peoples but also harmful to the imperialist nations themselves—John A. Hobson's distinctive viewpoint[24]—has been reiterated by antiimperialists of diverse ideological orientations. Thus, Barnet and Müller hold that by means of "transfer pricing" and other exploitative/manipulative devices, multinational corporations systematically cheat, and thereby retard the economic development of, poor countries. At the same time, they contend, in the spirit of Hobson, that such corporations are directly responsible for retrogressive tendencies in their industrial "home" countries, especially the United States, as shown by symptoms of economic, political, and social decay that are reminiscent of conditions in underdeveloped countries. American workers, they state, are especially liable to suffer from the transfer of productive and distributive operations from the United States to low wage "host" countries.[25]

These observations suggest that the domination of one people or nation by another, which, strictly speaking, defines the concept of imperialism, should not be confused with the calculation of benefits and costs that result from such domination. Benefit/cost calculations involve an assessment of outcome rather than power. Until the mid-twentieth century, it was widely assumed that exploitative economic relations between countries at different levels of economic development were established and maintained by means of imperial domination. With the advent of colonial freedom in Asia and Africa, and the emergence of communist powers comparable in strength to their capitalist adversaries, it became reasonable to expect that the causes of economic exploitation would be clearly identified and progressively eliminated. Proponents of multinational enterprise do hold that this, in fact, is the direction of movement within the noncommunist sphere. Responding to the charge of exploitation, they say that multinational corporations diffuse modern skills, technologies, and urgently needed capital resources to the nonindustrial countries, that they contribute handsomely to governmental revenues in such countries, and that they provide secure access to world markets for their exports. Since there are both benefits and costs on either side of all international economic relationships, the calculation of *relative* benefit and cost is crucial to this argument. If it can be shown, contrary to the case for transnational enterprise, that the economic position of given industrial nations is enhanced relative to (or at the expense of) particular non- or less-industrial nations, the relationships in question may be deemed to promote or perpetuate imperialist domination. In fact, the debate about relative benefit and cost in relationships mediated by multinational corporations has been intense; it is also likely to be interminable and inconclusive, as powerful arguments are marshalled on both sides.[26]

Advocates of the exploitation-imperialism thesis have had to assume an added theoretical burden in addition to the weight of their evidence on costs. They need to explain the persistence of exploitation despite the passing of colonialism and other overtly imperialistic forms of political control.[27] Obviously, it will not suffice merely to infer domination from a (usually rebuttable) demonstration of exploitation. To this author's mind, the elements of controversy about imperialist domination (whether and why it persists) have not been identified with anything like the clarity that recent studies have shed upon the question of relative benefit and cost. For want of satisfactory formulations of specific matters of controversy relating to the question of domination, the debate about imperialism in the age of multinational enterprise has not been properly joined.

III

Whereas the benefit/cost calculation, upon which a finding of "economic" imperialism[28] depends, does not directly bear upon the bases and exercise of power, the issue of managerial authority is directly and indubitably pertinent to the study of corporate power. Managers exercise authority. But the heralds of managerial autonomy misperceived the evolving relationship between management and ownership-interest as a case of divorcement. Recent evidence relating to the major American "global" corporations has been summarized by Barnet and Müller thus: "in the upper reaches of America's corporations there is no 'technostructure' made up of managers with interests distinct from those of owners. Increasingly, the managers are the owners, deriving an increasing proportion of their income not from their managerial skills but from the stock they own in their own corporations."[29] Paradoxically, the thesis of managerial autonomy may be revived in connection with multinational corporate expansion mainly as a result of conditions in the nonindustrial and newly developing countries, where corporate enterprise has been established upon foundations of foreign capital.

To be sure, the detection of managerial rule in nonindustrial societies would not mark the first removal of this idea from its original setting. Heretofore, expositors of the "managerial revolution" have cited developments in socialist countries, especially the Soviet Union, to corroborate their thesis.[30] Trotsky's harsh judgment, in *The Revolution Betrayed*,[31] has been repeated and refined by Marxist critics of "bureaucratic" autocracy in the Soviet Union, some of whom identify a "new class," comprising a party-bureaucratic formation,[32] while others, who are equally critical, do not.[33] Charles Bettelheim uses the term "state bourgeoisie" to describe and condemn the ruling stratum in the Soviet Union, holding, in a Maoist vein, that its existence actually portends nothing less than the restoration of capitalism.[34]

As in the socialist countries, bureaucratic cadres in the nonsocialist, newly developing countries have increasingly come to the forefront of public affairs. Typically, the bureaucratic elites of such countries enjoy incomes and social privileges far beyond the dreams or expectations of all but a few of their relatively impoverished compatriots. In his moving critique of social inequality and poor economic performance in newly independent African states, the French agronomist, René Dumont, observes that "a new type of bourgeoisie is forming in Africa . . . a bourgeoisie of the civil service."[35] The concept of a "bureaucratic bourgeoisie" as the new ruling class has been applied effectively in African studies.[36] But it does not appear to match the social realities of countries such as Nigeria, where an entrepreneurial bourgeoisie is well established; nor has this term been widely adopted by students of those Asian and Latin American societies where private enterprise is the principal economic form.

As in the study of industrial societies, so also in the study of nonindustrial societies the relationship between bureaucratic and entrepreneurial class power becomes a matter of serious controversy. The theoretical problems are compounded by widespread uncertainty as to the approximate degree to which the private enterprise sectors of most newly developing countries are dependent upon state patronage and support. Invariably, a degree of dependence that is deemed to be either too great or too small will automatically activate theoretical defense mechanisms against the specter of an indistinct analytical boundary between the bureaucratic and entrepreneurial spheres of life. In this circumstance, a complex idea is needed to comprehend business executives, members of the learned professions, leading politicians, and upper level bureaucrats as members of a single class. Perhaps the term "managerial bourgeoisie" will suggest an idea of merit. Inasmuch as this term clearly refers to the private business elite as well as to the managers of public enterprises and to high government officials, it may be preferred to either "bureaucratic" or "state" bourgeoisie. Moreover, this term, in contrast with the term "entrepreneurial bourgeoisie," reflects the apparent disposition of bourgeois elements in the nonindustrial and newly developing countries[37] to manage the production and distribution of wealth rather than to create new wealth-producing enterprises.[38]

In many postcolonial and nonindustrial countries, as C.B. Macpherson has observed, the state is conceived and appraised mainly in terms of its contribution to development.[39] Development itself is a value-laden idea, connoting progress toward the achievement of desired goals.[40] The political aspect of development, as distinct from those value premises that involve political goals, may be understood to signify the improvement of a society's ability to control the rate and direction of change. The concept of control is crucial to this definition, since it implies the ability to formulate and implement strategies for solving problems and achieving goals. In newly developing countries, drastic changes in the organization of authority—organizational revolutions[41]—are frequently required to facilitate the effective exercise of social control. These political transformations are themselves contingent upon the recruitment of unprecedented numbers of trained people to staff the new and rejuvenated state agencies. To this end, certain democratic and egalitarian devices, such as equal educational opportunity, are useful if not indispensable. However, the new organizational men and women, taken together with their immediate families and social peers, constitute a minor fraction of the population, about 5 to 10 percent. The organizational revolution, spurred by material incentives, is a forcing house for class formation and privilege.

In all societies, "revolutions from above" are prone to develop deeply conservative tendencies. In newly developing countries, modern conservatism, as distinct from traditionalism, normally connotes a disposition to arrest the transformation of organizational revolutions into social revolutions or shifts in the class content of power. Typically, the managerial bourgeoisie, virtually born (as a class) to authority, takes care to contain radicalism and maintain its position as the predominant class. Insecure as it is and not strongly committed to liberal principles, this class has shown a marked disposition to take refuge in various forms of political monopoly, such as the one-party state and the "caesarist" military regime. Populist and socialist rhetoric may be "poured on" to obscure and excuse this imposition of political monopoly. Normally, however, this kind of arrangement serves to protect and consolidate the rule of the bourgeoisie.[42]

To what extent does empirical evidence sustain the hypothesis of widespread class domination of the nonindustrial countries by the managerial bourgeoisie, as herein defined? The evidence is not inconsiderable, although Maurice Zeitlin has correctly noted the present need for studies of "dominant classes" in underdeveloped countries.[43] Regional studies would be especially valuable. In African studies, the hypothesis in question is supported by a formidable body of literature[44]; in Asian studies, a few works on India and Iran have corroborative value[45]; and in Latin American studies, evidence relating to Brazil is particularly relevant.[46]

It would not be correct to hold that the presence of a managerial bourgeoisie as the dominant class necessarily means that a given country will be receptive to capitalist principles of development. Anticapitalist—including Marxist—strategies of development may be chosen, as in the case of Tanzania.[47] Thus far, however, the vast majority of such governments have chosen to adopt mixed economy strategies in conjunction with various forms of foreign investment. Increasingly, "partnerships" between state investment agencies and multinational corporations serve to promote the organizational revolution and, by extension, the class interests of the managerial bourgeoisie. Leading members of the bourgeoisie are constantly tempted to imbibe the capitalistic and managerial attitudes of their foreign business associates. Some of them may aspire to careers in the wider business world. Given the obviously bourgeois life styles of individuals in this elite social stratum, they may be expected to embrace an elitist ideology. The influence of international capitalism functions to reinforce immanent tendencies toward embourgeoisment of the state bureaucratic elite.

No one should assume that a policy of partnership with the agencies of international capitalism portends the abandonment of nationalist principles on the part of governments in the nonindustrial countries. It is the singular failing of many "radical," including Marxist, analyses of such countries to underestimate the strength and historic importance of bourgeois class formation as well as the nationalist integrity of that class. Too often, the generic term "bourgeoisie" is casually qualified with the contemptuous adjective "comprador," a synonym for "puppet"—entirely dependent and subservient.[48] It is thereby suggested that the emergent bourgeoisie is a "clientele" class that betrays the national interest of its own country to foreign capitalist powers. This notion is fundamental to the closely related doctrines of "dependency" and "neocolonialism."[49] Indeed, these doctrines purport to supply a theory of postcolonial domination that cannot be derived from the traditional economic theories of imperialism. Beholden as they are to Marxism, these doctrines are disabled, as is standard Marxism itself, by the inadequate conception of class upon which they are founded. As Stanislaw Ossowski has observed, in his Marxist criticism of the Marxist conception of class, the relevant determinants of class include relationships of the means of production, consumption, *and* compulsion.[50] Given its control over the means of consumption and compulsion, the managerial bourgeoisie, as herein identified, must be comprehended, contrary to the doctrines of dependency and neocolonialism, as an autonomous social force—the veritable ruling class in most of those countries that comprise the so-called "third world." The identity of this class becomes more firmly established with each passing year.[51] Its ardent desire for autonomy is unmistakable. And it yields to no other class in the intensity of its nationalism.

Intense nationalism on the part of the managerial bourgeoisie poses an historic challenge to the leaders of international capitalism. Will they be able to harmonize their practices with the nationalistic values of bourgeois governments in the newly developing countries? Only, we may answer, if it is in their perceived interest to do so. Adam Smith taught successive generations that business executives who pursue their own interests serve the general interest as well. The business creed comprehends this even more plausible corollary: One who serves another benefits oneself.

Is it not logical to expect the subsidiaries of a multinational business group to harmonize their policies with the interests of various host governments insofar as they seek to survive and prosper in the host countries concerned? Corporate policies of precisely this nature are described in my study of multinational mining companies that operate in the several states of central and southern Africa. In particular, I have observed that South African and American controlled mining corporations domiciled in the Republic of Zambia complied faithfully with Zambian national policies of economic disengagement from the white-ruled states of southern Africa even before the Zambian Government acquired majority ownership of those companies in 1970. They did so at considerable cost to themselves and despite the fact that the Zambian policies in question were largely inconsistent with economic values and policies espoused by the directors of the parent companies in South Africa and the United States. On the other hand, these companies made no apparent concession to the Zambian point of view in implementing their policies of equally good corporate citizenship on the part of subsidiaries domiciled in other states, including the white-dominated states of southern Africa.[52]

These observations suggest a corporate doctrine of domicile, meaning that individual subsidiaries of an international business group may operate in accordance with the requirements of divergent and conflicting policies pursued by the governments of their respective host states. Ultimately, the aim of local adaptation is to promote the interests of the enterprise as a whole. Meanwhile, the policy of good corporate citizenship will appeal to the leaders of newly developing host countries who would like to establish stable relationships with international business organizations. Positing a mutuality of interest, the doctrine of domicile justifies transnational corporate expansion while it also legitimizes large-scale foreign investments in the eyes of the host country. Furthermore, it commands subservience to the local authority of the managerial bourgeoisie.

My formulation of the doctrine of domicile as a tenet of corporate ideology is based upon political and logistical evidence from a turbulent and, in many ways, atypical region. It will be tested again within that region by relations between the giant corporations and the newly independent, avowedly anticapitalist governments of Angola and

Mozambique. In southern Africa, as elsewhere, it would be far more difficult to make out a prima facie case for compliance with host country interests at the expense of corporate group interests with evidence derived from routine business practices. Having surveyed the "transfer pricing" practices, "cross subsidization" strategies, and sundry exploitative devices to which multinational enterprises normally resort, Barnet and Müller conclude that comprehensive regulatory policies by the governments of the capitalist states themselves will be required to discipline and humanize the global corporations.[53] Other commentators, more sympathetic to multinational enterprise, have discerned a greater capacity for the exercise of corporate statesmanship in the quest for policies that will satisfy transnational corporate managers and the nationalist governments of newly developing countries at one and the same time.[54] Joint ventures, involving the transfer of substantial, even majority, ownership to agencies of host states, have become increasingly familiar. Rarely do such schemes silence the cry of exploitation; nor do they settle the question of control, since minority owners may yet retain effective control of a given venture, while the reality of self-management by the host state is contingent upon many circumstances, including the attainment of technical competence in diverse fields. Nonetheless, joint ventures do facilitate the "revolution from above," and thereby help to produce the institutional conditions and climate of opinion that enhance the authority of the bourgeoisie and promote its growth as a class.

IV

Within its sphere of control—specifically, a newly developing, nonindustrial, and nonsocialist country—the managerial bourgeoisie rises above a larger, normally far larger, national bourgeoisie, the diversity and extent of which depend mainly upon the size of the country and its level of economic development. In effect, the managerial bourgeoisie is the ruling stratum of the national bourgeoisie.[55] Its distinctive identity as a subclass is manifest behaviorally in the collective actions and attitudes of its members. The action which, more than any other, sets this subclass apart from the bourgeoisie as a whole is its tendency to coalesce with bourgeois elements at comparable levels of control in foreign countries. To the extent that the doctrine of domicile becomes a maxim of corporate action, it helps to reconcile the staunch nationalism of the managerial bourgeoisie with the cosmopolitan values of bourgeois leaders abroad who have global interests and perspectives. Thus, it functions to promote transnational class cohesion.

It may be enlightening to think of the worldwide corporate and managerial bourgeoisie as a class in formation that now comprises three overlapping entities, as shown in Figure 2.1. The corporate bourgeoisie, based mainly in the industrial capitalist countries, includes a corporate international segment. The managerial bourgeoisie of the newly developing, nonsocialist countries also overlaps with the corporate international bourgeoisie. These transnational extensions of, and linkages between, comparable segments of the bourgeoisie depend upon the creation and perfection of transnational institutions. The multinational corporation is probably the most effective institution for this purpose. It should, therefore, be analyzed and understood in terms of transnational class development. In this process, the

Figure 2.1 Structure of the Worldwide Corporate and Managerial Bourgeoisies

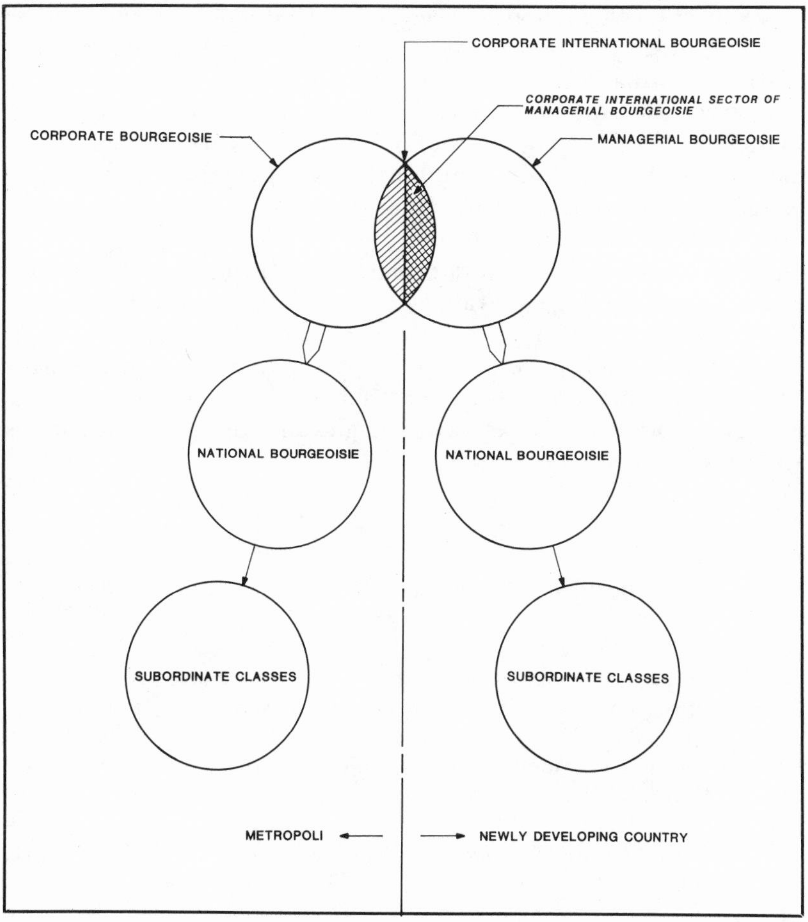

bourgeoisie, true to its epoch-making tradition, has taken the lead.

Corporate internationalism is a social movement and a rising class interest. With its advent as a major social force, the working classes of the world confront a corporate bourgeoisie in industrial capitalist countries, and a managerial bourgeoisie in newly developing countries.[56] Where the transition of a given developing country to the stage of industrial capitalism is sustained, indigenous elements of the corporate bourgeoisie will emerge. In the long run, if capitalism in that country is preserved, the corporate bourgeoisie may be expected to supersede the managerial bourgeoisie as the ruling class. This essay presents a short-term analysis. It draws attention to the coalescent relationship between two dominant classes—the managerial bourgeoisie and the corporate international bourgeoisie. In so doing, it seeks to make the hypothesis of transnational class formation credible.[57]

Wars of redistribution between rival capitalist powers, specified by Lenin as the distinctive product of imperialism,[58] may yet disrupt and abort the transnational evolution of the bourgeoisie. But that danger is counteracted by the emergence of the managerial bourgeoisie as a cohesive ruling class in newly developing countries in conjunction with the growth and spread of multinational enterprise. Increasingly, power in world affairs comes to be organized in accordance with class rather than national interests and values. Imperialism, as a stage of capitalism, gives way to corporate international capitalism. We may anticipate severe ideological strain between the doctrinaire liberalism of the corporate bourgeoisie[59] and the paternalistic authoritarianism of the managerial bourgeoisie. However, the fate of the bourgeoisie— corporate and managerial—will probably be determined by domestic struggles, not by anti-imperialist struggles that pit insurgent nations against foreign powers.

Notes

I am grateful to Professor William Tordoff for many valuable discussions and for his ever constructive criticisms of my work during the term of my appointment as Simon Visiting Professor at the Victoria University of Manchester, where this essay was written. Acknowledgments are due also to Edward Merrow and Martin J. Sklar.

1. Grant McConnell, *Private Power and American Democracy* (New York: Knopf, 1966), p. 129.

2. Adolf A. Berle, Jr., *The Twentieth Century Capitalist Revolution* (New York: Harcourt, Brace, 1954), p. 60; and *Power Without Property* (New York: Harcourt, Brace, 1959), pp. 17–24.

3. Systems theorists, in particular, normally separate the economic and political spheres of life for analytical purposes. See, for example, David Easton, *A Framework for Political Analysis* (Englewood Cliffs, NJ: Prentice-Hall, 1965), p. 60; Easton, *A Systems Analysis of Political Life* (New York: Wiley, 1965), pp. 21–23; and Karl W. Deutsch, *The Nerves of Government* (New York: Free Press, 1966), pp. 119–124. For an example of this bent in "group theory," see David B. Truman, *The Governmental Process*, 2d ed. (New York: Knopf, 1971), pp. 257–260.

4. George E. Gordon Catlin, *Systematic Politics* (Toronto: University of Toronto Press, 1962), pp. 34–38, 45–47; and Charles S. Hyneman's important defense of the "power" approach to political science espoused by Catlin and Harold D. Lasswell, in Hyneman, *The Study of Politics* (Urbana: University of Illinois Press, 1959), pp. 142–150.

5. Adolf A. Berle, Jr. and Gardiner C. Means, *The Modern Corporation and Private Property*, rev. ed. (New York: Macmillan, 1968).

6. These studies have been reviewed by Maurice Zeitlin, "Corporate Ownership and Control: The Large Corporation and the Capitalist Class," *American Journal of Sociology* 79, 5 (1974):1073–1119 (see p. 1084). A vigorous debate persists on the issue of management- versus owner-control of large American corporations. See the exchange between Michael Patrick Allen and Zeitlin in *American Journal of Sociology* 81, 4 (1976):885–903.

7. James Burnham, *The Managerial Revolution*, new ed. (Bloomington: Midland Books, Indiana University Press, 1960); note esp. the author's preface to this edition.

8. H.H. Gerth and C. Wright Mills, "A Marx for Managers," *Ethics* 52, 3 (1942):200–215. Franz L. Neumann, a leading political scientist in the Marxist tradition, held that in capitalist societies economic power is translated "into social power and thence into political power." He doubted the alleged shift of political power from social groups to bureaucracies; he also distinguished bureaucratic behavior from class action. Neumann, "Approaches to the Study of Political Power," *Political Science Quarterly* 65, 2 (1950):161–180. On the "problem of bureaucracy" in Marxist social thought, see Daniel Bell, *The Coming of Post-Industrial Society* (New York: Basic Books, 1973), pp. 80–99.

9. The theoretical basis for this view is Stanislaw Ossowski's exposition of "synthetic gradation" in his *Class Structure in the Social Consciousness*, trans. Sheila Patterson (New York: Free Press, 1963), pp. 44–57. Representative statements include Leonard Reissman, *Class in American Society* (Glencoe, IL: Free Press, 1960), pp. 217–218; and Zeitlin, "Corporate Ownership," pp. 1078–1079. For an alternative view, see Gerhard Lenski, *Power and Prestige* (New York: McGraw-Hill, 1966), pp. 352–361.

10. Andrew Hacker, "Politics and the Corporation," in Hacker (ed.), *The Corporation Take-Over* (New York: Harper & Row, 1964), pp. 239–262. The similarly baleful and convincing portrait of recruits to the managerial vocation

drawn by William H. Whyte, Jr., *The Organization Man* (New York: Simon & Schuster, 1956), should also be cited.

11. My own appreciation of the need for political studies of the business corporation derives from the inspired teaching of Professor H.H. Wilson at Princeton University in the mid-1950s. Among the pioneering analyses of corporate power by political scientists and sociologists, two are particularly noteworthy: C. Wright Mills, *The Power Elite* (New York: Oxford University Press, 1956); and Earl Latham, "The Body Politic of the Corporation," in Edward S. Mason (ed.), *The Corporation in Modern Society* (Cambridge: Harvard University Press, 1959), pp. 218–236. The relevant literature has been reviewed by Edwin M. Epstein, *The Corporation in American Politics* (Englewood Cliffs, NJ: Prentice-Hall, 1969). More recent studies of particular significance include Richard J. Barber, *The American Corporation* (New York: Dutton, 1970); and Karen Orren, *Corporate Power and Social Change* (Baltimore: Johns Hopkins University Press, 1974).

12. Peter Bachrach, *The Theory of Democratic Elitism* (Boston: Little, Brown, 1967), pp. 102–105.

13. Joseph A. Schumpeter, *Capitalism, Socialism, and Democracy,* 2d ed. (New York: Harper & Row, 1947), pp. 269-273, 283.

14. This appears to be the main basis of Berle's preference for the American corporate system to the Soviet system; see Berle, *Power Without Property,* pp. 141–158. Similarly, Raymond Vernon, a foremost authority on multinational enterprise, has declared: "The challenge in social organization is to ensure that the large units on which our future societies are likely to be based act as countervailing political powers, not as mutually reinforcing ones." See his *Sovereignty at Bay* (New York: Basic Books, 1971), p. 273.

15. Richard J. Barnet and Ronald E. Müller, *Global Reach* (New York: Simon & Schuster, 1974).

16. His original term for this element is the "technostructure." Efficiency of operation, he contends, depends upon the congruence of corporate and social goals with the personal values of most individual members of the technostructure according to the "principle of consistency." John Kenneth Galbraith, *The New Industrial State* (Boston: Houghton Mifflin, 1967), pp. 169–188.

17. Howard V. Perlmutter, "The Tortuous Evolution of the Multinational Corporation," in Courtney C. Brown (ed.), *World Business: Promise and Problems* (New York: Macmillan, 1970), pp. 66–82 (see pp. 81–82).

18. These criteria are derived from the following works, which mention all of them, but vary in their emphases: Jack N. Behrman, *National Interests and the Multinational Enterprise* (Englewood Cliffs, NJ: Prentice-Hall, 1970), pp. 1–2; John H. Dunning, "The Multinational Enterprise: The Background," in Dunning (ed.), *The Multinational Enterprise* (London: Allen & Unwin, 1971), pp. 15–48 (see pp. 16–17); Vernon, *Sovereignty at Bay,* p. 4; and Isaiah A. Litvak and Christopher J. Maule, "The Multinational Firm: Some Perspectives," in Gilles Paquet (ed.), *The Multinational Firm and the Nation State* (Don Mills, Ont.: Collier-Macmillan, 1972), p. 22. Samuel P. Huntington contends that "transnational corporation" is a more suitable term for the business organization with these characteristics. His clarifying definitions of "transnational," "interna-

tional," and "multinational" organizations should be consulted; see Huntington, "Transnational Organizations in World Politics," *World Politics* 25, 3 (1973):333–368 (esp. p. 336). Barnet and Müller, *Global Reach,* pp. 17–18, prefer to use the term "global corporation."

19. Paul M. Sweezy and Harry Magdoff, "Notes on the Multinational Corporation," *Monthly Review* 21, 5 (1969):1–13 and 21, 6 (1969):1–13 (quoted from 5:9 and 6:13). One way for the polemicist to live with an awkward phrase that has "caught on" is to define it so that it suits an approved purpose. "Third world" is a case in point. This term has been provocatively (and to my mind sensibly) defined by Marxist-Leninists for partisan purposes to designate "that large and in many ways diverse collection of colonies, semi-colonies, and neo-colonies which form the base of the global capitalist pyramid [ibid., 5:2–3]."

20. Stephen Hymer, "The Multinational Corporation and the Law of Uneven Development," in Jadgish N. Bhagwati (ed.), *Economics and World Order from the 1970s to the 1990s* (New York: Macmillan, 1971), pp. 113–140.

21. Although Hymer's standpoint is avowedly Marxist, his thesis on corporate organization and the location of subsidiaries is derived from non-Marxist sources and implies an un-Marxian organizational determinism. Similar views are set forth in two significant essays: Norman Girvan, "Multinational Corporations and Dependent Development in Mineral Export Economies," *Social and Economic Studies* 19, 4 (1970):490–526; and Johan Galtung, "A Structural Theory of Imperialism," *Journal of Peace Research* 8, 2 (1971):81–117.

22. See the excellent summation of this view by Michael Barratt-Brown, *The Economics of Imperialism* (Harmondsworth, Eng.: Penguin Books, 1974), pp. 201–255.

23. See the analyses of this outlook by Bernard Semmel, *Imperialism and Social Reform* (Cambridge: Harvard University Press, 1960), pp. 53–72; and by Richard Koebner and Helmut Dan Schmidt, *Imperialism: The Story and Significance of a Political Word, 1840–1960* (Cambridge: Cambridge University Press, 1964), pp. 166–220. See also the dispassionate survey of benefits and costs by John Plamenatz, *On Alien Rule and Self-Government* (London: Longmans, 1960).

24. John A. Hobson, *Imperialism: A Study,* rev. ed. (London: Allen & Unwin, 1938). Also see Bernard Semmel's keen summation of "the Hobson-Schumpeter theory," in his *The Rise of Free Trade Imperialism* (Cambridge: Cambridge University Press, 1970), pp. 222–226.

25. Barnet and Müller, *Global Reach;* see their chapters entitled, "The Latinamericanization of the United States," and "The Obsolescence of American Labor." See also the trenchant critique of American foreign investment as an alternative to domestic investment and foreign trade, written to clarify "the American national interest," in Robert Gilpin, *U.S. Power and the Multinational Corporation* (New York: Basic Books, 1975).

26. The following statements exemplify these opposing positions. The case for exploitation is argued from a Marxist standpoint by Barratt-Brown, *Economics of Imperialism;* and from a non-Marxist standpoint by Ronald E. Müller, "The Multinational Corporation and the Underdevelopment of the Third World," in Charles K. Wilbur (ed.), *The Political Economy of Development and Underdevelopment* (New York: Random House, 1973), pp. 124–151. The case

against exploitation is put by Peter F. Drucker, "Multinationals and Developing Countries: Myths and Realities," *Foreign Affairs* 53, 1 (1974):121–134; and by Mira Wilkins, who presents a succinct summary of the positive effects of U.S. direct investment in less developed countries, in her *The Maturing of Multinational Enterprise* (Cambridge: Harvard University Press, 1974), pp. 398–401. See also the carefully balanced assessments by Raymond F. Mikesell, "Conflict in Foreign Investor-Host Country Relations: A Preliminary Analysis," in Mikesell et al., *Foreign Investment in the Petroleum and Mineral Industries* (Baltimore: Johns Hopkins University Press, 1971), pp. 29–55; Paul Streeten, "Costs and Benefits of Multinational Enterprises," in Dunning (ed.), *The Multinational Enterprise*, (fn. 19), pp. 240–258; and Vernon, *Sovereignty at Bay*.

27. The recent doctrines of dependency and neocolonialism are addressed to this problem. They will be commented upon at a more relevant point in this essay.

28. I place the word "economic" in quotes because I take "imperialism" to be a political conception, implying the domination of one people, nation, or country by another. (I think that John Strachey's definition is sound; see his *The End of Empire* [New York: Random House, 1960], pp. 7–8, 319–342.) This may be effectuated by various means, including buying, selling, and lending, as well as by coercion and influence. To my mind, the institutions involved in these processes are "political," as is the resulting relationship among peoples. See also Benjamin J. Cohen, *The Question of Imperialism* (New York: Basic Books, 1973), pp. 15-16.

29. Barnet and Müller, *Global Reach*, pp. 246, 294, 458.

30. Burnham, *Managerial Revolution*, p. vi.

31. Leon Trotsky, *The Revolution Betrayed*, trans. Max Eastman (Garden City, NY: Doubleday, 1937).

32. Milovan Djilas, *The New Class* (New York: Praeger, 1957).

33. Herbert Marcuse, *Soviet Marxism* (New York: Random House, 1961).

34. Paul M. Sweezy and Charles Bettelheim, *On the Transition to Socialism* (New York: Monthly Review Press, 1971), p. 43. See also Sweezy's appreciative discussion of Bettelheim's recent book about class struggle in the Soviet Union: Sweezy, "The Nature of Soviet Society," *Monthly Review* 26, 11 (1974):1–16; and 27, 1 (1975):1–15. The extrapolation of class relationships from the situation of bureaucratic control is, at best, tangential to the Marxist tradition of class analysis. Its theoretical basis is Ralf Dahrendorf's doctrine to the effect that class relationships are essentially relationships of authority rather than of property; see his *Class and Class Conflict in Industrial Society* (Stanford, CA: Stanford University Press, 1959), pp. 137, 165.

35. René Dumont, *False Start in Africa*, 2d ed., rev., trans. Phyllis Nauts Ott (New York: Praeger, 1969), p. 81; also Frantz Fanon, *The Wretched of the Earth*, trans. Constance Farrington (New York: Grove Press, 1963), p. 179.

36. For example, Ian Clegg, *Workers' Self-Management in Algeria* (New York: Monthly Review Press, 1971). A study of similar import is Claude Meillassoux, "A Class Analysis of the Bureaucratic Process in Mali," *Journal of Development Studies* 6, 2 (1970):97–110.

37. I classify a country as industrial if a large part of its population—well over half—is engaged in occupations that depend upon a nonhuman and no-

nanimal power-driven machine technology. The basic measures of industrialization include the following: per capita consumption of standard energy units;
percentage of labor force employed outside of agriculture; and possession of
an engineering capacity to produce tool-making tools. According to these
criteria, countries like India and Brazil are classified as nonindustrial despite
the large industrial sectors of their economies. Most Indians and Brazilians do
not live and work within the industrial sectors of their countries. Among nonindustrial countries, the range of difference between the least industrialized and
those that are considered to be entering the industrial stage is immense.

   38. This passage is partly derived from Richard L. Sklar, *Corporate Power
in an African State* (Berkeley and Los Angeles: University of California Press,
1975), p. 199, where these ideas are substantiated by a case study. See also Martin Kilson's interesting perspective on the "emergent African bourgeoisie" in
his "African Political Change and the Modernization Process," *Journal of Modern African Studies* 1, 4 (1963):425–440 (esp. p. 439).

   39. C.B. Macpherson, *The Real World of Democracy* (London: Oxford University Press, 1966).

   40. See Gunnar Myrdal, *Asian Drama* (New York: Pantheon, Random
House, 1968), v. 1, pp. 49–69.

   41. Cf. Harold D. Lasswell and Abraham Kaplan, *Power and Society* (New
Haven: Yale University Press, 1950), pp. 272–273.

   42. Two classic expositions of this idea are Karl Marx, *The Eighteenth
Brumaire of Louis Bonaparte* (New York: International Publishers, 1963) (Marx
did not like the analogy between nineteenth century bonapartism and classical
caesarism); and Fanon, *Wretched of the Earth*, pp. 148–205. See the keen comparison of Marx and Fanon with reference to this matter in Colin Leys, *Underdevelopment in Kenya* (Berkeley and Los Angeles: University of California Press,
1974), pp. 207–212.

   43. Zeitlin, "Corporate Ownership," p. 1112.

   44. Evidence pertaining to class relationships between the party political,
state bureaucratic, and entrepreneurial leaders of Nigeria has been sum-
marized by Richard L. Sklar and C.S. Whitaker, Jr., "The Federal Republic of
Nigeria," in Gwendolen M. Carter (ed.), *National Unity and Regionalism in Eight
African States* (Ithaca, NY: Cornell University Press, 1966), pp. 7–150 (see pp.
27–30, 65–67, and 110–115). See also Richard L. Sklar, *Nigerian Political Parties*
(Princeton: Princeton University Press, 1970); and Sayre P. Schatz, *Nigerian
Capitalism* (Berkeley and Los Angeles: University of California Press, 1977).
For a penetrating class analysis of Ethiopian politics, see John Markakis,
Ethiopia: Anatomy of a Traditional Polity (Oxford: Oxford University Press,
1974). Comparable studies of other African countries include Leys, *Underde-
velopment in Kenya;* Michael F. Lofchie, "The Political Origins of the Uganda
Coup," *Journal of African Studies* 1, 4 (1974):464–496; Robert Molteno and William Tordoff, "Independent Zambia: Achievements and Prospects," in William Tordoff (ed.), *Politics in Zambia* (Berkeley and Los Angeles: University of
California Press, 1974), pp. 363–401; Sklar, *Corporate Power*, pp. 192–216; the
convincing thesis on "caesarist bureaucracy" in Zaïre by Jean-Claude Williame,
Patrimonialism and Political Change in the Congo (Stanford, CA: Stanford University Press, 1972); Meillassoux, "A Class Analysis of the Bureaucratic Process in

Mali"; Clegg, *Workers' Self-Management*; Gérard Chaliand and Juliette Minces, *L'Algérie indépendante* (Paris: Maspero, 1972); Manfred Halpern, *The Politics of Social Change in the Middle East and North Africa* (Princeton: Princeton University Press, 1963), pp. 51–78; and Anouar Abdel-Malek, *Egypt: Military Society*, trans. C.L. Markman (New York: Random House, 1968). These references are limited to intensive studies relevant to my identification of the bourgeoisie as the dominant class. There is also an extensive literature of commentary upon and speculation about class conflict in Africa, but it is not especially relevant to the argument of this essay.

45. On the commitment of the bourgeoisie to "state capitalism" in India, see Charles Bettelheim, *India Independent*, trans. W.A. Caswell (New York: Monthly Review Press, 1969). Similarly, Michael Kidron maintains that the rule of the Indian bourgeoisie is consolidated by mutually supportive relationships among the state sector, foreign enterprise, and domestic private enterprise; see his *Foreign Investments in India* (London: Oxford University Press, 1965). James Bill's class analysis of Iran, *The Politics of Iran* (Columbus, OH: Merrill, 1972), should be noted. See also his suggestive essay, "Class Analysis and the Dialectics of Modernization in the Middle East," *International Journal of Middle East Studies* 3, 4 (1972):417–434. Marvin Zonis, *The Political Elite of Iran* (Princeton: Princeton University Press, 1971), is also relevant.

46. On the political and social implications of multinational enterprise as the predominant industrial force in Brazil's economy, see Fernando Henrique Cardoso, "Associated-Dependent Development: Theoretical and Practical Implications," in Alfred Stepan (ed.), *Authoritarian Brazil* (New Haven: Yale University Press, 1973), pp. 142–176. Of the twenty largest enterprises in Brazil, ranked according to the values of their assets, fourteen are state-controlled, five are controlled by multinational corporations, and one by Brazilian private investors (*Expresso* [Lisbon], 7 June 1975). Vernon cites impressive statistics on the heavy recruitment of local managers by U.S.-owned corporations in Brazil and elsewhere in *Sovereignty at Bay*, p. 149.

47. The continuing attempt by noncommunist leaders to build socialism in Tanzania has been extensively studied. Michael F. Lofchie has analyzed the leading issues that arise in several such studies, in his "Agrarian Socialism in the Third World: The Tanzanian Case," *Comparative Politics* 8, 4 (1976):479–499. See also Reginald Herbold Green, "Political Independence and the National Economy: An Essay on the Political Economy of Decolonisation," in Christopher Allen and R.W. Johnson (eds.), *African Perspectives* (Cambridge: Cambridge University Press, 1970), pp. 273–324; John S. Saul, "African Socialism in One Country: Tanzania," in Giovanni Arrighi and John S. Saul (eds.), *Essays on the Political Economy of Africa* (New York: Monthly Review Press, 1973), pp. 237–335; and Issa G. Shivji et al., *The Silent Class Struggle* (Dar es Salaam: Tanzania Publishing House, 1973).

48. A locus classicus is Paul A. Baran, *The Political Economy of Growth* (New York: Monthly Review Press, 1957), pp. 194-196. A characteristic example of the genre is André Gunder Frank, *Lumpenbourgeoisie: Lumpendevelopment: Dependence, Class, and Politics in Latin America*, trans. Marion Davis Berdecio (New York: Monthly Review Press, 1973); also Samir Amin, *Accumulation on a World*

Scale, trans. Brian Pearce (New York: Monthly Review Press, 1974), pp. 20–25, 359–394.

49. For an incisive discussion of neocolonialism that is nonetheless sympathetic to the idea itself, see Barratt-Brown, *Economics of Imperialism,* pp. 256–284. For a comparable discussion of the dependency doctrine, see Susanne Bodenheimer, "Dependency and Imperialism: The Roots of Latin American Underdevelopment," in K.T. Fann and Donald C. Hodges (eds.), *Readings in U.S. Imperialism* (Boston: Porter Sargent, 1971), pp. 155–181. The Chilean origins of this doctrine and certain of its conceptual weaknesses are shown by Theodore H. Moran, *Multinational Corporations and the Politics of Dependence* (Princeton: Princeton University Press, 1974). Aspects of the "dependency" thesis are specifically tested by Charles T. Goodsell, *American Corporations and Peruvian Politics* (Cambridge: Harvard University Press, 1974). For a realistic appraisal of capitalist development in "third world" countries—one that rebuts a basic tenet of the standard dependency thesis from a Marxist standpoint—see Bill Warren, "Imperialism and Capitalist Industrialization," *New Left Review,* 81 (1973):3–44. For an incisively critical appraisal of the dependency doctrine, see Cohen, *The Question of Imperialism,* pp. 189–227.

50. Ossowski, *Class Structure,* pp. 185–186.

51. In an earlier study, mainly concerned with the political implications of class formation in Nigeria, I used the descriptive term "new and rising class," defined with reference to four objective criteria—high status occupation, high income, superior education, and ownership or control of business enterprise—and linked with reality by means of behavioral evidence of class action and incipient class consciousness. See Sklar, *Nigerian Political Parties,* pp. 474–505. Subsequently, I adopted the term "political class," as proposed by Gaetano Mosca, to designate those persons who control the dominant institutions of society, in my "Contradictions in the Nigerian Political System," *Journal of Modern African Studies* 3, 2 (1965):201–213 (see pp. 203–204). For the reasons given in this essay and in Sklar, *Corporate Power,* pp. 198–209, I now think that "managerial bourgeoisie" is the most appropriate term for the modern ruling class of a nonindustrial and newly developing but nonsocialist country.

52. Sklar, *Corporate Power,* pp. 144–148, 164–178, 182–188.

53. Barnet and Müller, *Global Reach,* pp. 363–388.

54. Vernon, *Sovereignty at Bay,* pp. 265–270; Mikesell, "Conflict in Foreign Investor-Host Country Relations," pp. 48–51.

55. This generalization should be qualified with reference to Zeitlin's call for the study of dominant classes in underdeveloped countries (fn. 43). My sketch of a major pattern for ruling class development in nonindustrial countries must be read with the realization that every country has its own mix of bureaucratic, entrepreneurial, and traditionally oligarchic elements.

56. In socialist countries, the working class may well confront a "state bourgeoisie," as Bettelheim contends (fn. 34). Similarly, Immanuel Wallerstein argues that, in effect if not in form, there is but one world economic system which will remain essentially capitalistic until it is transformed as a whole. See Wallerstein, "Dependence in an Interdependent World: The Limited Possibilities of Transformation within the Capitalist World Economy," *African*

Studies Review 17, 1 (1974):1–26; "Trends in World Capitalism," *Monthly Review* 26, 5 (1974):12–18; and "The Rise and Future Demise of the World Capitalist System: Concepts for Comparative Analysis," *Comparative Studies in Society and History* 16, 4 (1974):387–415.

57. See also the suggestive comments by Irving Louis Horowitz, "Capitalism, Communism, and Multinationalism," in Abdul A. Said and Luiz R. Simmons (eds.), *The New Sovereigns: Multinational Corporations as World Powers* (Englewood Cliffs, NJ: Prentice-Hall, 1975), pp. 120–138 (esp. pp. 123, 129–130).

58. See V.I. Lenin's rebuttal of Karl Kautsky's thesis of interimperialist cooperation, *Imperialism, the Highest Stage of Capitalism* (New York: International Publishers, 1939), pp. 88–98. A portion of Kautsky's provocative article of 1914 has been republished in *New Left Review*, 59 (1970):41–46. The contemporary relevance of this debate has been noted by Richard J. Barnet, *Roots of War* (New York: Atheneum, 1972), p. 229; and by Barratt-Brown, *Economics of Imperialism*, pp. 323–325.

59. On the ideology of corporate liberalism in the United States, see James Weinstein, *The Corporate Ideal in the Liberal State, 1900-1918* (Boston: Beacon Press, 1968); and Martin J. Sklar, "Woodrow Wilson and the Political Economy of Modern United States Liberalism," in James Weinstein and David W. Eakins (eds.), *For a New America* (New York: Random House, 1970), pp. 46–100.

CHAPTER THREE

Development, Democracy, and Dependency in Latin America: A Postimperialist View

DAVID G. BECKER

Development, today, is no longer taken to be synonymous with aggregate economic growth. Most of us now acknowledge that the word signifies progress toward desired goals, hence is not value-free. It is entirely appropriate, then, that we think of those values in progressive, humanistic terms, with the result that the concept of development comes to mean an improvement in the quality of life and an enlargement of the ambit of human freedom. As judged by the pronouncements of governments, opposition movements, and professional students of development, agreement on this point is widespread.

Once development has been so conceived, we can deduce that it is a multifaceted process embracing industrialization, equitable distribution of societal goods, and democracy. Industrialization denotes the systematic application and innovation of labor-saving technology in the productive process, together with the implantation of social relations of production that spur technology utilization. Industrialization must be coupled to an equitable scheme of distribution in order for people to be freed of the compulsion of having ceaselessly to labor for their subsistence. Clearly, there is no freedom without democracy. At a minimum, democracy consists in the accountability of the governing authority to the people at large; in a more substantive vein, it includes the right of participation in the making of decisions that are authoritatively binding on the collectivity. Although the matter can be debated, in my view democracy is not fully realized until all adult citizens enjoy both a right of formal political participation and a right to associate freely, without the application of any ideological test, for nonviolent political purposes.

Industrialization and distributional equity pertain to the material

An earlier version of this paper appeared in *Third World Quarterly* 6, 2 (1984):411–431. Reprinted with permission.

(economic) aspect of development. There is also an interdependent but conceptually distinct political aspect, consisting in "the improvement of a society's ability to control the rate and direction of change" and entailing "the ability to formulate and implement strategies for solving problems and achieving goals."[1] An awareness that development has a political aspect directs our attention to issues of power and control. They are amenable to a class analysis.

Capitalism and Democracy

From a developmental perspective, a superior political order would presumably be what appeared in the lexicography (but not in the practice) of Peru's "revolutionary" military regime (1968–80) as *democracia social de participación plena*: fully participatory social democracy. (In a social democracy, egalitarian public control of the institutions responsible for economic growth assures that industrialization will proceed in a climate of distributional equity.) Perhaps a selfless, farsighted leadership, operating within a social space left open by an absence of intense, institutionalized class conflict, could design and implement such a political order. Richard L. Sklar believes that in parts of Africa the opportunity to do so is there for the taking.[2] In Latin America, however, no such opportunity currently exists or is likely soon to present itself: class structures and institutions embodying them, in all cases the products of lengthy sequences of historical evolution, are everywhere firmly embedded throughout the social order. Cuba and Nicaragua aside, the Latin American reality is one of solidly established capitalism tightly linked to the world economy. But "established" must not be read as "static." Latin American capitalism, like the international capitalism that helps shape it, is a dynamic order and has been undergoing major changes for many years. The nature and probable near-term course of its present stage—"late" or "organizational" oligopoly capitalism—are of central concern to the analyst.

 Capitalism can in principle be compatible with both industrialization and democracy. To be sure, capitalist democracy fails fully to guarantee freedom; for, in defining as nonpolitical key structures and institutions of economic power, it places them arbitrarily beyond the reach of democratic norms and, thereby, enables them to go on functioning as mechanisms of domination, exploitation, and accumulation of class privilege. Nevertheless, late-capitalist democracy provides institutionally for some political control of economic life; the right of political association, meanwhile, allows elements of the subordinate classes to acquire autochthonously a capacity for self-definition and pursuit of their class interests. Their efforts can bear fruit when they are limited to issues of immediate concern. The reason is that a bourgeoisie whose social control is secure has much to gain—*inter alia,* social peace and stability—from respecting the indigenous political institutions and accommodating to the most urgent demands of lower-class groups.[3] Under capitalism, as under any socioeconomic order, democracy provides the only meaningful assurance that the question of distributional equity will be addressed. Equity is never the reliable product of the altruism of those in power.

However, Latin American capitalism has not previously been hospitable to democracy. Civilian governance, when it has existed, has often taken the form of oligarchic exclusionism[4] or of populist authoritarianism. More recently the region has witnessed a spate of capitalist "developmental dictatorships"[5] led by the military and civilian technocrats—so-called bureaucratic-authoritarianism—that have devoted themselves to advancing their countries' industrialization by means of strategies that deliberately bypass both equity and democracy.[6] Particularly worrisome was the fact that the wave of "bureaucratic-authoritarianism" that crested in the 1960s and 1970s managed to sweep away civilian governance from Chile and Uruguay, which had long been considered Latin America's most stable democracies.

The *Dependencista* Perspective

Latin Americans have assiduously sought to elucidate these circumstances as a first step toward changing them. They have rejected proffered explanations that are ethnocentric or racist—e.g., those that emphasize the peculiarities of the "Iberic-Latin tradition"[7] or the lack of a "Protestant ethic" in the outlook of the bourgeoisie. But, perhaps because they have been beguiled by the overweening U.S. preeminence in the hemisphere, they have tacitly accepted the Anglo-Saxon experience as the norm of capitalist development. That is, they have assumed that thoroughgoing capitalist development must be the product of a dynamic and socially transformatory, or Schumpeterian, bourgeoisie.[8] Consequently, they have defined their problem as arising from a bourgeois "deficiency." Having properly refused to blame their own culture for that supposed deficiency, they have attributed it to the manner of their nations' articulation with international capitalism. Thence the idea of *dependencismo.* This term signifies an internally coherent paradigm of dependency that embraces both an elucidation of economic structures of dependence and a political explanation, couched in the language of class analysis, for the persistence of those structures. From here on I shall be concerned primarily with the latter.

There are two principal varieties of *dependencismo*. Each begins with the notion that capitalist democracy is inconceivable without an ideologically hegemonic bourgeoisie: not only one that is able to make the accommodations described earlier, but also one whose world view can win universal acceptance and thus portray its class interests and privileges as incidental to the "national interest."[9] According to the first variant, local capitalism is little more than a hose at the end of a pump—the capitalist system of the metropolis—that sucks economic surplus out of the country. The domestic bourgeoisie is therefore a "comprador" class (in André Gunder Frank's colorful terminology, a "lumpenbourgeoisie"), an agent of economic imperialism with no nationally based class interests save for a narrow preoccupation with state power, needed to keep it securely atop the social structure. Such a bourgeoisie is too evidently self-serving to aspire to hegemony; its apparent dominance (the *real* dominant class, we are forced to conclude, is the foreign bourgeoisie that controls metropolitan capital) has to be backed by raw coercion.[10] A sub-variant, associated with the writings of Immanuel Wallerstein, holds that domestic bourgeoisies of "peripheral" countries opt for coercive forms of labor control[11]; for that reason they are debarred from legitimizing their class position by appealing to an ideologically produced societal consensus.

This version of *dependencismo* cannot any longer be sustained in the face of the facts.[12] As Bill Warren saw some time ago, the facts in question include the rapid industrialization, under transnational corporate auspices, of many developing countries and the coincident spread of capitalist relations of production.[13] In Latin America as a whole, activities belonging to the modern capitalist sector (manufacturing, public utilities, transport and communications) have become the linchpins of the economy; in addition to the stimulus they provide to other sectors, they now account directly for over one-third of gross domestic product. Manufacturing has also come to weigh heavily in export trade: 20 percent of merchandise exports are now manufactured goods, up from an average of 10 percent in 1960–68.[14] Argentina, Brazil, Mexico, and Peru currently derive 60, 64, 43, and 70 percent of their export earnings, respectively, from sales of manufactured goods (including factory-processed mine products). Literacy rates and school attendance ratios, which correlate closely with the extent of capitalist relations of production, have risen dramatically in most of the countries of the region.[15]

The second variant of *dependencismo* places less stress on broad generalizations inferred from postulated system-maintenance requisites and admits that capitalism in the "periphery" can lead to industrialization. But it holds (i) that the nature of industrial technologies and products, dictated by the profit maximization strategies of transnational corporations, is such as to demand and reinforce a highly skewed distribution of wealth and income; and (ii) that the domestic bourgeoisie's reliance on international capital for technology, financing, and principles of enterprise organization saps it politically, depriving it of the hegemonic assets of an indigenous dynamism and a "national-popular" value orientation. Here, too, "peripheral" capitalism is said to be incapable of universalizing capitalist relations of production throughout the society; in this instance the reason given is that the capital-intensive, "inappropriate" technologies acquired from the transnationals do not provide employment opportunities in proportion to need. Once again, a weak bourgeoisie is regarded as unable to become hegemonic, as compelled to take political shelter behind authoritarian rule.[16]

Unlike the first version, this newer and more sophisticated variety of *dependencismo* cannot be refuted by data on industrialization. Neither can it be negated by observations on local state assertiveness in dealings with transnational corporations and international financiers; for the modern Marxian theory of class and state specifically provides for a state that is "relatively autonomous" and that need not act in the service of short-term bourgeois interests.[17] My critique of the "dependent development" school of *dependencismo* will consider instead its implications for development strategy and the accuracy of its political analysis.

Anti-Democratic Implications of *Dependencismo*

If "dependent development" in the sense defined above (not merely in the indisputable sense that development is conditioned by the world economy) is Latin America's reality, then capitalist democracy is ruled out, and maldistribution of wealth cannot be mitigated within a capitalist framework. And *dependencista* class analysis, which is undialectical, finds no counterforces generated by "dependent development" that might modify its character over the long haul.[18] Hence, the conclusion can only be that real development will not occur until and unless there has been a clean break with capitalism at both the national and international levels.

But such a break cannot come at the hands of a majoritarian, class-conscious, radically internationalist working class—Marx's revolutionary proletariat—inasmuch as "dependent development" precludes its emergence. As a result, the needed revolution is confined to a Leninist scenario: a radical movement of national liberation on a multiclass foundation, led by an intellectual elite claiming the right to "represent" the working class without consulting it.[19] After sixty-five years, progressives ought to have lost any remaining illusions about Leninism; its undeniable accomplishments in the realm of distributional equity are more than offset by its second-rate industrialization performance and its stultifying elitism, which, together, diminish the scope of freedom instead of enlarging it.

What is more, *dependencismo* postulates rather than demonstrates that the temperament of the popular classes is potentially or actually revolutionary. The assumption is belied by experience in Latin America and elsewhere; it has been proven time and again that poverty and marginalization, alone, do not a revolutionary make. Later on I will evaluate the practical political consequences of a radical ideology whose prescription for bringing about change must remain unfilled for lack of the requisite social forces. For now I shall simply suggest that, even where a revolutionary temperament exists, authoritarian socialism ranks no higher in comparison to authoritarian capitalism than a lesser evil.

Although there are probably conjunctures—as in parts of Central America today—where the nature of contending class forces allows for no other alternative, why should progressives be so quick to jettison our ideals and to grant that the lesser evil is satisfactory *anywhere* in the "third world"? There is, I feel, another way. Were we firmly to abandon the teleology and stasis of system-maintenance ideas, along with the tendency to deduce class action from axiomatic first principles, and were we to attend more closely to an empirical study of class forces designed so as to reveal the dialectics of change within "third world" capitalism, we might discover better alternatives—or, at the very least, become more thoroughly convinced than we can be at present that none is available.

The Evidence Reevaluated

The first thing that empirical investigation lays bare is that the wave of authoritarianism has spent its force and is receding. Latin America's current political panorama is the following: In Colombia, Costa Rica, Mexico, and Venezuela, capitalist democracy has functioned without interruption for ten or more years.[20] In Argentina, Brazil, the Dominican Republic, Panama, and Peru, processes of transition from authoritarianism to capitalist democracy are under way or have recently been completed. In Chile and Uruguay, military authoritarianism persists[21] but is under increasing challenge from a wide spectrum of forces, including many members of the bourgeoisie and middle class. In El Salvador, Guatemala, Haiti, and Paraguay, capitalist authoritarianism of the traditional, antidevelopmental oligarchic type remains. In Cuba and Nicaragua, nationalist-popular rebellions have led to the implantation of authoritarian socialism (not yet consolidated in the latter). And in Bolivia, Ecuador, and Honduras, fragile and unstable capitalist democracies rest uneasily on largely backward socioeconomic underpinnings.

In sum, capitalist democracy is entrenched or nascent in nine of the twenty Latin American republics. These nine have a combined population of 290 millions and a combined land area of 16.7 million square kilometers—each about 82 percent of the regional total. Their combined gross domestic product amounts to 82.2 percent of the regional total; and their combined GDP per capita is $1,640 (1980 datum), as compared to $1,060 for the rest (Cuba, which does not publish economic statistics, is excluded). Manufacturing generates 24 percent of their combined GDP, compared with 18.5 percent of the others'; and 6.6 percent of their total exports is accounted for by machinery and equipment, versus 4.3 percent for the others. Thus, the nine are characterized by a higher prevailing level of industrialization than is found in the remaining countries of the region.

Additionally, democratic institutions in these nine countries have undergone important changes. The last of the old-line populist leaders, Peru's Víctor Raúl Haya de la Torre, departed the scene in 1979; there have been no younger replacements. Political parties have become more programmatic and more often rest on stable aggregations of interests than on charisma. While one or two parties often predominate, one finds in all of the nine countries a multiplicity of licit parties that cover a wider ideological range than ever before. In Brazil, the military gave up its ten-year-long effort to impose an *oficialista* two-party system and acquiesced in the restoration of the local multiparty tradition. In Mexico, the political monopoly of the Partido Revolucionario Institucional (PRI) has been weakened somewhat by measures that allow for a larger number of independent parties and that guarantee them minimum representation in the national parliament. In Peru, parties span the full spectrum from U.S.-style conservatism to Marxism-Leninism and Trotskyism; Marxists have been elected to major offices (including the mayoralty of Lima, the capital, and of Arequipa and Cuzco, the second- and third-largest cities) and enjoy significant representation in the Chamber of Deputies. In Argentina, the recent presidential election showed that Peronism had lost its appeal for the electorate. In Colombia, Costa Rica, the Dominican Republic, Panama, and Venezuela, power has been transferred peaceably to electoral oppositions.

I stated previously that a hallmark of capitalist democracy is toler-ance of autonomous lower-class political institutions, of which the most prominent are labor unions. One of the classic failings of Latin Ameri-can capitalist orders has been their intolerance of free labor movements: labor unions have been severely restricted by law (Peru), controlled di-rectly by ministries of state (Brazil), or manipulated by political parties (Argentina, Mexico, and Peru to an extent). This is now changing. In Argentina, Peronist labor bosses have been steadily losing their control over the movement. In Brazil, the military regime permitted the old system of state-run labor unions to fall into disuse but was unable to prevent the rise, for the first time in the nation's history, of a truly in-digenous labor movement, constructed from the grass roots upward by workers intent on organizing themselves to defend their common interests. A still stronger "bottom-up" labor movement has surged to the fore in Peru and has made common cause with a variety of popular struggles.[22] Even in Mexico, sectors of labor have demonstrated in-creasing independence from PRI domination. Many of these labor movements regularly indulge in radical political rhetoric (although none is revolutionary in any real sense). Some of them, recognizing that the economic interests of the working class are greatly affected by infla-tion and the means chosen to cope with it, have engaged in general strikes and other forms of political action intended to influence directly the orientation of government policy. Yet, the bourgeoisies of the nine countries do not seem to feel threatened by these developments, since they have staunchly supported democratic institutions and have not called for a renewed repression of organized labor.

The legitimacy of late-capitalist democracy depends in part on the presence of state apparatuses that are strong and effective enough to restrain the most extreme abuses of corporate oligopoly power, espe-cially—of critical importance in an age of nationalism—when such power is wielded by foreign corporations. (Restraining those abuses need not interfere with the ability to accumulate capital and can be shown to be in the long-term interest of the entire bourgeois class.) The record reveals that all nine of the democratic or redemocratizing coun-tries have strong state apparatuses, which have been used to monitor and regulate the activities of both local and foreign enterprises.[23] Meaningful economic planning has become the rule rather than the ex-ception; it almost always incorporates reliable statistical data and effec-tive administration, the results of the increased competence and ex-perience of state personnel.

The newfound ability of Latin American state apparatuses to em-body and project plausibly "national" interests is also seen in the area of foreign policy. On key issues of regional import (such as the Malvinas war, the Central American and Caribbean crises, defense of the 200 mile limit of territorial waters, investment disputes, the campaign for a New International Economic Order, protection of the sovereign right to obtain military assistance from any source), the states of Latin America no longer defer routinely to the preferences of the hemisphere's hegemonic power. Indeed, the Organization of American States has been largely transformed from an institutional expression of U.S. hegemony to a forum in which the "Yanquis" can be called to account; and one hears frequent mention of the possibility that the OAS may one day be reconstituted as a purely Latin American institution.

Concurrently, the stock of direct foreign investment in Latin America has increased by leaps and bounds; it has reached a total value in excess of $40 billion. Over two-thirds of the increase during the past two decades has involved the manufacturing sector. Transnational corporations, often operating through joint ventures with parastatal or private domestic enterprises, have figured prominently in the "deepening" of Latin American industrialization—that is, the relative shift of the product mix away from nondurable wage goods and toward consumer durables and producer's goods: chemicals, plastics and synthetic fibers, basic metals, motor vehicles, production machinery, and so forth. As I have pointed out, not every variant of *dependencismo* is confounded by this investment trend. However, all *dependencista* paradigms anticipate and predict a negative correlation between it and democratic capitalism.

What do the data show? From 1967 to 1975 (the latest year for which complete data could be obtained), the Latin American countries which today are, or are on the way to becoming, capitalist democracies saw a 60 percent increase in direct foreign investment—a 28 percent increase in per capita terms. At the end of the period their combined stock of direct foreign investment amounted to $103 per capita. The other countries of the region experienced a 30 percent increase, only 2 percent on a per capita basis; at the period's end, their combined stock of direct foreign investment was worth $50 per capita. The correlation between direct foreign investment and the potential for capitalist democracy thus turns out to be positive—exactly the opposite of the *dependencista* prediction.

To raise the possibility, nowadays, that relationships between transnational enterprises and newly developing countries can be mutually beneficial is to be suspected of apologetics in the service of capital. This is another symptom of our habit of thinking about those relationships in system-maintenance rather than in dialectical terms. Consider, in contrast, what a dialectical perspective might suggest: (a) The challenge of economic denationalization posed by the transnationals' presence is likely to call forth, sooner or later, a nationalist reaction; it usually takes the form of a strengthening of the regulatory and economic policymaking organs of the state.[24] (b) The transnationals, themselves, unwittingly help to nourish the domestic manageriat and technocracy that, out of self-interest, bring about the reaction; they do it by means of staff training, technical assistance, and demonstration. (c) Due to their greater profitability, home-country experience, and political sensitivity to a foreign and potentially hostile environment, transnational firms are frequently less resistant to unionization of their workers than are domestic employers.[25] The domestic bourgeoisie often views this tendency with equanimity, at first; for if the transnationals are made to pay higher wages, their competitive advantages are somewhat reduced. But the eventual outcome is usually a stronger labor movement across the board, especially if better-paid workers in the transnationals' employ prove willing to tax themselves in order to subsidize the organization of their less fortunate comrades in the employ of local firms. That degree of working-class solidarity is not uncommon in Latin America.

Empirical investigation encourages us to examine three additional propositions about the role of transnational corporations in development:

1. The transnationals are indifferent, not antagonistic, to democratic governance. They seek access to natural resources and to markets; stable economic environments; and the advantage of lower prevailing wages than in the metropoli. Their behavior indicates that, whatever the ideological predilections of their representatives on the scene, they have rarely acted as if they believed that a particular set of (presumably, "orthodox") economic policies were necessary to achieve stability. In Chile, monetarist orthodoxy has not attracted much new foreign investment but instead has deindustrialized the economy. On the other hand, transnational corporations have invested heavily in Argentina, Brazil, Mexico, and Peru despite their economic interventionism, expansionary policies, and, in Peru's case, implementation of far-reaching property and social reforms.[26]

2. As Albert Szymanski demonstrates for a cross-section of developing countries, the past twenty-odd years have witnessed a net influx of foreign capital in spite of profit remittances.[27] In any event, it is misleading to think of capital outflows via remitted profits and other transfers as a siphoning-off of economic surplus. What actually happens is that incoming capital investment increases the size of the surplus by introducing new productive activities, after which a small part of this *increase* is taken

out; most of it remains behind in the form of local wages, taxes, and purchases.

3. While direct foreign investment is in part attracted to the "third world" by the promise of lower wages, the fact that transnational firms are capital-intensive means that absolute wage rates are not a crucial consideration for them. A "pull factor" of equal or greater significance is access to local markets, which is controlled by states and must be bargained for.[28] Even though income concentration may be a viable short-term strategy—if the host country has a large population—for expanding the market for the consumer durables in which many transnationals specialize, long-term market growth depends on increasing the numbers and purchasing power of all participants in the cash economy. Thus, the transnationals' wage concerns are partially counterbalanced by an interest in improving the purchasing power of their workers and of other subordinate groups; they may benefit from land reform as well (as they have in Peru), since its tendency to raise food prices, and thence wages, is offset by the fact that in the longer run it converts former subsistence peasants into commodity farmers and consumers of manufactured goods.

Postimperialism and Class Formation

Unless one's approach to the topic is motivated more by doctrine than by science, these observations call inescapably for a new paradigm of Latin American development. The new paradigm need not be a mirror image of *dependencismo,* viewing capitalism as uniformly progressive, nonexploitative, and free of internal contradiction. However, it should conceptualize capitalist domination and exploitation in class, not national, terms. These are features of Sklar's paradigmatic conception, postimperialism.[29]

Postimperialism signifies transnational class domination on a global scale, a stage of world capitalist evolution that is just now making its debut. Transnational enterprises are integrating the world economy, and their action produces and reproduces an international bourgeois class. The members of this "corporate international bourgeoisie" are united by mutual interests transcending those expressed through the states whose passports they happen to carry; they are true cosmopolitans. Although transnational managers and "home"-state authorities remain friendly with each other, the former can no longer count on the imperialist power wielded by the latter to win them the "third world" markets and investment outlets that are necessary to the expanded re-production of capital.

(I hasten to add that postimperialism, having rejected function-alism in all its guises, has no difficulty in acknowledging the continued existence of imperialism. Metropolitan states do not set aside im-perialist policies just because international capital has ceased to "have need" of them. As J.A. Hobson understood,[30] imperialism may persist because it advances the politico-military interests of a governing group, aids certain economic interests that are not fully integrated into the international circuits of capital and that need state protection, etc.)

In a postimperialist world, capital's access to the "periphery" is se-cured by ideological and political means. The international bourgeoisie is motivated by an ideological *doctrine of domicile,*[31] a particular manifes-tation of capitalism's separation of the political from the economic sphere. This doctrine holds that there is no innate antagonism between the global (and economic) interests of transnational corporations and the locally focused (and chiefly political) national aspirations of newly developing host countries; it instructs corporate subsidiaries to behave like "good citizens" of the host country. (A "good citizen" obeys the law, acts in conformity with local behavioral norms, and does not work to contravene well-understood national interests.) A corollary is that transnational firms can be, simultaneously, "good citizens" of *every* country, including the "home" country, where they do business.

The doctrine of domicile is an element of the corporate interna-tional bourgeoisie's hegemonic world view. Like any hegemonic ideology, it "has its basis in the perception of the apparently intelligible order of the social reality." That is, *"it works,* both cognitively and in practice"[32]— whence the possibility of mutually beneficial transnational-host coun-try relations. These relations are, of course, mutually beneficial *in an institutional context;* their dominative and exploitative content is only ex-posed when the tool of class analysis is brought to bear on international capitalism. In contrast, all forms of *dependencista* analysis, based as they are on territorial delineations (whether conceived as individual nations or as "core" and "periphery"), are institutional despite the use that they make of class-analytical rhetoric.

No guarantees can be offered that the host country will invariably benefit from each and every relationship it maintains with a transna-tional firm. The local state must help to propitiate that outcome by adopting and enforcing an authoritative definition of "good corporate citizenship" which does not impinge on the transnationals' central con-cern—the opportunity to make profits—or on their world market strategies and other global interests. Increasingly nationalist local states—sometimes the result of organizational revolutions that institutionalize nationalist tendencies, sometimes the outcome of gradual political evolution—serve the interest of postimperialist international capital (here is the other side of the relationship of mutual benefit) because their profound commitment to development makes it easier for them to contain or deflect anticapitalist class action by popular groups. Moreover, they legitimize the local presence of transnational enterprise to the extent that they resolve ideologically the contradiction between that commitment and global capital accumulation.

Strong, capable, institutionally nationalist states arise not *ex nihilo* but when they are constructed by members of society who have the power to do so and whose class interests will thereby be promoted. Thus, the postimperialist paradigm focuses analytical attention on the question of class formation, viz.,

> the process by which individuals (1) become aware that they share specific interests and a specific orientation toward the existing mechanisms of power and control; (2) form social bonds on the basis of that [awareness]; (3) organize to secure . . . advantages for themselves; and (4) collectively employ their political assets to that end.[33]

A chief aim of the analysis is to determine how class formation processes at work in different sectors of the society affect the nature and actions of the state— particularly, its ability to manage the society's relationships with international capital. As a rule, transnational corporate action in newly industrializing countries tends to condition and facilitate the emergence therein of domestic bourgeois groups which, while holding "junior membership" in the international bourgeoisie, have a class interest in broadly based industrial development at the national level[34]; indeed, this interest *complements* those groups' international concerns, since it ratifies in their class practice their aspiration to *full and equal membership* in the international bourgeoisie. The national "new bourgeoisie" is a state-building class element; but its relationship to state power is dialectical, not causative—another way of saying that its formation is also conditioned and facilitated by state action. In semi-industrial societies like those of much of Latin America, where the process of economic development relies heavily on the corporate form of enterprise (parastatal as well as private), the "new bourgeoisie" is a *corporate national bourgeoisie*.[35] This class stratum is

> the economic and political hinge [point] between local societies and the metropoli. Yet, inasmuch as [it] . . . need not opt for either national or metropolitan concerns, [it] can be nationalist and developmentalist without contradicting [its] international interests. As [its]

dominance is not narrowly self-serving, [that dominance] does not need to rest on coercive force and can be consistent with formal democracy.[36]

A local dominant class of this character has a potential for hegemony. Insofar as transnational enterprise contributes to host-country industrialization, it assists the corporate national bourgeoisie to demonstrate its nationalist *bona fides* and, thereby, to maintain its social control with the consent of the people at large.

At the same time, the corporate national bourgeoisie is an active class subject, not a mere systemically generated object, and has a capacity to influence the action of international capital even while being shaped by it. Therefore, the current international division of labor is not forever fixed; although world capitalist development is uneven, some "third world" countries may one day attain metropolitan status (and some present metropoles may decay to "peripheral" status) without contravening the fundaments of the international order.

Lastly, it must be remembered that the formation of a corporate national bourgeoisie does not take place in a societal vacuum. Processes of proletarian class formation are also under way.[37] Conditioned, too, by transnational enterprise, a new working class is emerging that is technologically literate, industrially disciplined, and organizationally strong. Unlike the violence-prone protoproletariat, easily manipulated by populist demagoguery, that it is replacing, the new working class has a certain economic stake in the social order and considerable confidence in its ability to wring concessions from the state and the dominant class. In consequence, it is not insurrectionary. The corporate national bourgeoisie, for its part, has less reason to fear these demands for accommodation than did its predecessor. Its interest in meeting them combines with other bourgeois interests to create a political atmosphere that is much friendlier to democratic governance than that of a previous era.[38]

Conclusion: Progressive Praxis versus *Dependencismo*

Far from being old liberal wine in new Marxian bottles, as diehard *dependencistas* are wont to charge, postimperialism offers a more telling critique of late-capitalist domination in newly developing countries than *dependencismo* could ever manage. It is able to because it does not distort or wave away observed reality, does not substitute nationalism for class analysis, and does not fall back upon static, teleological explanation. It does not picture capitalism as uniformly progressive; instead its portrait simply includes the fact that *some* of what is happening . . . is . . . still development: painful, wasteful, and ruthless, like early capitalism everywhere, but development nonetheless. . . . In the sufferings of the masses . . . there is also a certain potential for advance. The failure to recognize and grapple with this renders dependency theory misleading and hence impotent in relation to those areas where the advance has occurred.[39]

Postimperialism owes no slavish obedience to doctrine; it regards Marx and other classical thinkers as intellectual precursors rather than Delphic oracles. But it is not blindly eclectic and, in fact, is more faithful than are most strands of *dependencista* thought to Marx's anti-Utopian comprehension of historically evolved social structures as limitations on the course of collective action.

Postimperialism shares the Marxian perspective that theories of development are to be judged in large part according to their contribution to a progressive praxis. It insists that such a praxis must work toward the attainment and perfection of democracy *in addition to* economic equality; and that all forms of democracy are intrinsically more favorable in the long run for popular-class interests than is any form of authoritarianism.

Let us consider in this light the tasks confronting a progressive praxis in Latin America. The socioeconomic reconstruction that led to the ascent of corporate national bourgeoisies did not materially reduce the dependence of the region's local economies on the state of the world economy. Hence, the recession that has afflicted the latter has seriously impaired the health of the former. It is heartening—and a confirmation of the validity of the postimperialist viewpoint—that economic difficulties have not, thus far, brought with them a relapse into military rule. Neither have economic reverses encouraged nationalist or populist demagoguery to anything like the degree that they did some years ago. Still, we cannot be too sanguine about the prospects for democratic survival, given the newness and fragility of participatory institutions as well as the dearth of norms of nonexclusionary, limited government in the political tradition. In this climate of uncertainty, the practices of politically active groups can be determinant. Progressives ought not to underestimate the repressive capabilities of the military and their willingness to use them, with or without bourgeois support, if faced with a danger of social dissolution. And we must not overestimate the ability of the industrial proletariat, which is yet at an early stage of its formation and which does not approach a societal majority, to lead a transition to socialist democracy. A counsel of revolution, the stock-in-trade of Left ultranationalism, is irresponsible and dangerous in the present conjuncture.

(This analysis applies only partially, however, to Chile and Uruguay, where it is vital that a broad political coalition continue its agitation for a military *salida*.[40] Nor does it apply at all to the oligarchic dictatorships of Central America, where the rebellions now in progress probably represent the only progressive option.)

But *dependencismo* remains an *ideological* force to be reckoned with. Paradoxical though it may seem, in insinuating itself into the popular consciousness throughout Latin America, *dependencismo* is performing yeoman service in helping to legitimize the new capitalist order. By plausibly attributing the present economic difficulties to an international economy that no Latin American government can hope to alter by itself, it enables the local dominant classes to avoid being held responsible for them.

A legitimizing ideology does not have to value and justify the status quo in explicit language. Since people normally do not desert a sociopolitical order unless they can conceive of something both better and attainable, ideology can accomplish its purpose surreptitiously if it undercuts or excludes from the agenda a radical critique leading to a feasible strategy for effecting change. In fact, it can be more efficacious when it functions in this manner because its Utopianism is a moral critique, but *only* a moral critique, of the status quo. An order that can tolerate moral criticism advances a claim to eventual self-perfection.

Dependencismo is Utopian because the only alternative it can propose is immediate, universal socialist revolution followed by economic autarky; and because it finds little to praise in political action that works within the bounds of capitalist democracy or that settles for less than absolute goals. Its critique of the corporate national bourgeoisie on ultranationalist grounds, if morally appealing to some, is otherwise unconvincing, as it has no theory of how another kind of social order might resist the overwhelming power of international capital. Equally unconvincing is its implicit Leninist elitism, which today's more sophisticated working classes have seen through and do not admire. Consequently, *dependencismo* disarms popular class action that seeks a middle way between insurrectionism and "economism."

Of course, *dependencismo* is not alone in acting as an ideological prop for a social order quite different from what its teachings seems to advocate. North American evangelical Christian fundamentalism performs a similar service when it puts forth its moral critique of oligopoly power, corporate internationalism, and some aspects of mass consumer society, and when it posits a Utopian alternative: a return to an individualist, market-capitalist, hyper-patriotic society. And David Shipler has recently taken note of the legitimizing role of an ascendant Great Russian nationalism which, though apparently critical of many aspects of Soviet rule, actually upholds it by offering in its stead nothing better than a vaguely outlined religio-political statism.[41]

Progressives need to consider with due care whether an ideology that keeps company such as this is worthy of our allegiance.

Notes

An earlier version of this paper appeared in *Third World Quarterly* 6, 2 (1984):411- n-431. Reprinted with permission.

1. Richard L. Sklar, *Corporate Power in an African State* (Berkeley and Los Angeles: University of California Press, 1975), p. 179.

2. Richard L. Sklar, "Democracy in Africa," presidential address to the Twenty-Fifth Annual Meeting of the African Studies Association, Washington, DC, 5 November 1982.

3. I assume, as is commonly the case, that such an accommodation need not wreck the mechanisms of capital accumulation. To the contrary, it tends to keep them humming efficiently for a longer period of time, so that the short-run decline in the absolute profit rate is compensated by a larger and more secure future cash flow. Under late-capitalist conditions, where oligopolistic corporations are not rigidly constrained by market forces but can plan strategically for profit maximization, this tradeoff is an attractive one.

4. Marcelo Cavarozzi, "Elementos para una caracterización del capitalismo oligárquico," *Revista Mexicana de Sociología* 40, 4 (1978):1327–1352.

5. A. James Gregor, *Italian Fascism and Developmental Dictatorship* (Princeton: Princeton University Press, 1979).

6. Guillermo A. O'Donnell, *Modernization and Bureaucratic-Authoritarianism: Studies in South American Politics* (Berkeley: Institute of International Studies, University of California, 1973). On the economic policies of the Brazilian military regime, until its last years an archetypical "bureaucratic-authoritarianism," see Thomas E. Skidmore, "Politics and Economic Policy Making in *Authoritarian Brazil,* 1937–71," in Alfred Stepan (ed.), Authoritarian Brazil (New Haven: Yale University Press, 1973), pp. 3–46.

7. Howard J. Wiarda, "Toward a Framework for the Study of Political Change in the Iberic-Latin Tradition: The Corporative Model," *World Politics* 25, 2 (1973):206–235. Wiarda's study is blameless; it is a careful analysis of the historical shaping of a political culture. Although the "Iberic-Latin tradition" cannot be held responsible for Latin America's late start toward democratization, it is highly relevant to questions of the character of ideological legitimation.

8. Joseph A. Schumpeter, *The Theory of Economic Development* (Cambridge: Harvard University Press, 1935); and *Capitalism, Socialism, and Democracy* (New York: Harper & Row, 1942). I consider Schumpeter's work a locus classicus of "economism" in development theory: the systematic undervaluation of the political dimension of organized social life.

9. Antonio Gramsci, *Selections from the Prison Notebooks* (New York: International Publishers, 1971); and *Letters from Prison* (New York: Harper & Row, 1973). The Introduction to the latter work, by Lynne Lawner, contains a useful exposition of the Gramscian conception of hegemony. See also Walter L. Adamson, *Hegemony and Revolution: Antonio Gramsci's Political and Cultural Theory* (Berkeley and Los Angeles: University of California Press, 1980); Joseph V. Femia, "The Gramsci Phenomenon: Some Reflections," *Political Studies* 27, 3 (1979):472–483; and Bob Jessop, *The Capitalist State* (New York: New York University Press, 1982), pp. 148–149.

10. Paul A. Baran, *The Political Economy of Growth* (New York: Monthly Review Press, 1957); André Gunder Frank, *Capitalism and Underdevelopment in Latin America* (New York: Monthly Review Press, 1969), and *Lumpenbourgeoisie: Lumpendevelopment: Dependence, Class, and Politics in Latin America*, trans. Marion Davis Berdecio (New York: Monthly Review Press, 1973); Samir Amin, *Accumulation on a World Scale*, trans. Brian Pearce (New York: Monthly Review Press, 1974), and *Unequal Development*, trans. Brian Pearce (New York: Monthly Review Press, 1976). (Editorial note: Since the original publication of this paper in *Third World Quarterly*, it has come to my attention that the coiner of the term "lumpenbourgeoisie" was not Frank but Baran; see *Political Economy of Growth*, p. 173.)

11. Immanuel Wallerstein, *The Modern World-System: Capitalist Agriculture and the Origins of the European World-Economy in the Sixteenth Century* (New York: Academic Press, 1974); also his "Dependence in an Interdependent World: The Limited Possibilities of Transformation within the Capitalist World-Economy," *African Studies Review* 17, 1 (1974):1–26; and his "The Rise and Future Demise of the World Capitalist System: Concepts for Comparative Analysis," *Comparative Studies in Society and History* 16, 4 (1974):387–415. Well-targeted critiques of Wallerstein's thesis and conclusions have been put forward by Robert Brenner, "The Origins of Capitalist Development: A Critique of Neo-Smithian Marxism," *New Left Review*, 104 (1977):25–92; and by Theda Skocpol, "Wallerstein's World Capitalist System: A Theoretical and Historical Critique," *American Journal of Sociology* 82, 5 (1977):1075–1090.

12. Yet a few proponents seem untroubled by the failure of the facts to support their position. See, for instance, Samir Amin, "Expansion or Crisis of Capitalism?" *Third World Quarterly* 5, 2 (1983):361–380.

13. Bill Warren, "Imperialism and Capitalist Industrialization," *New Left Review*, 81 (1973):3–44. Recently, Immanuel Wallerstein, "Nationalism and the World Transition to Socialism: Is There a Crisis?" *Third World Quarterly* 5, 1 (1983):95–102, has taken a position in agreement with Warren's view of the spread of industrialization and capitalist relations of production into the "periphery." It would have been useful, however, if he had seen fit to reconcile the contradiction between his new perspective and his previous insistence that coercive labor control is a key variable that determines the structure of the "world-economy." Perhaps he is still holding to the misconception that the universalization of wage labor constitutes socialism.

14. These and other economic data in this paper have been drawn from various publications of the Inter-American Development Bank. The IDB's data show that the 1971–78 average annual growth rate of foreign exchange

earnings from Latin America's manufactured exports was 10.7 percent; when traditional exports of processed foodstuffs and nonferrous metal products are excluded from the calculation, the rate rises to 14.7 percent. Both computations are based on constant 1980 prices.

15. My rough computation yields a 60 percent school attendance ratio as of 1980 for the age group 6–23 years and for Latin America as a whole; and a corresponding ratio of 37 percent for 1960.

16. Fernando Henrique Cardoso, "Dependency and Development in Latin America," *New Left Review*, 74 (1972):83–95; and his "Associated-Dependent Development: Theoretical and Practical Implications," in Stepan (ed.), *Authoritarian Brazil* (fn. 6), pp. 142–176. See also Fernando Henrique Cardoso and Enzo Faletto, *Dependency and Development in Latin America*, trans. Marjory Mattingly Urquidi (Berkeley and Los Angeles: University of California Press, 1979). A useful discussion of the relationship between Cardoso's work and other Marxian currents of development analysis is contained in Gabriel Palma, "Dependency: A Formal Theory of Underdevelopment or a Methodology for the Analysis of Concrete Situations of Underdevelopment?" *World Development* 6, 7–8 (1978):881–924.

17. Ralph Miliband, *The State in Capitalist Society* (New York: Basic Books, 1969); Nicos Poulantzas, *Political Power and Social Classes* (London: New Left Books, 1973); David A. Gold, Clarence Y.H. Lo, and Erik Olin Wright, "Recent Developments in Marxist Theories of the Capitalist State," *Monthly Review* 27, 5 (1975):29–43 and 27, 6 (1975):36–51.

18. Dynamic, ideologically hegemonic bourgeoisies are as much the *products* of capitalist development as they are its producers. Anthony Brewer, *Marxist Theories of Imperialism* (London: Routledge & Kegan Paul, 1980), argues (p. 289) that the question is whether an independent national bourgeoisie is eventually formed: "Independence in this sense does not require that development be financed locally and under local control. . . . I see no reason why an independent capitalist class should not be formed on the basis of export led industrialisation or copying of technique; in an interdependent world economy a considerable degree of specialisation and large scale exchanges of goods, capital and technology are to be expected." See also Bill Warren, *Imperialism, Pioneer of Capitalism* (London: New Left Books, 1980), pp. 42–43; as he puts it, the classes that begin the process of industrialization "may themselves be industrial bourgeoisies or may be displaced by the industrial Frankensteins they have created or they may become fused with them."

19. The claim is grounded in ideological dedication and in an assertion that the "meaning and purpose" of history are known to initiates. Marx, of course, "inverted" rather than abandoned the Hegelian metaphysic, that human history has a comprehensible meaning and is directed toward a foreseeable end point. It is time, I believe, to let go of this metaphysic, which more properly belongs to a nineteenth-century world view. Stephen Jay Gould's critique of the same metaphysic in Darwinian natural history is relevant here as well; see Gould, *The Panda's Thumb* (New York: Norton, 1980).

20. There has appeared during the last decade or so a considerable literature that emphasizes the authoritarian features of Mexico's "one-and-a-half party" system of "guided democracy." But this literature also makes plain that

a fair degree of pluralism—not, of course, of a sort that allows all interest groups an equally effective representation—exists within the official party, the PRI; and that there are political institutions, most notably the tradition of presidential campaigning, that operate to provide a measure of accountability.

21. Since this was originally written, in 1983, civilian governance has been reinstated in Uruguay.

22. Alan Angell and Rosemary Thorp, "Inflation, Stabilization and Attempted Redemocratization in Peru, 1975–1979," *World Development* 8, 11 (1980):865–886; and Evelyne Huber Stephens, "The Peruvian Military Government, Labor Mobilization, and the Political Strength of the Left," *Latin American Research Review* 18, 2 (1983):57–93. See also David G. Becker, "Modern Mine Labour and Politics in Peru since 1968," *Boletín de Estudios Latinoamericanos y del Caribe* 32 (1982):35–60.

23. On Brazil see Peter Evans, *Dependent Development* (Princeton: Princeton University Press, 1979). On Peru see David G. Becker, *The New Bourgeoisie and the Limits of Dependency* (Princeton: Princeton University Press, 1983).

24. One of those who have recognized this relationship is Alfred Stepan, *The State and Society: Peru in Comparative Perspective* (Princeton: Princeton University Press, 1978), pp. 235–236. See also the discussions by Sayre P. Schatz in chs. 5 and 7 of this volume.

25. A counterargument is that transnational corporations "superexploit" local labor by virtue of technological "deskilling" of the labor force and reliance on newly developing countries' "industrial reserve armies" to keep wages at or below the subsistence level. The argument is without merit and is in any case falsified by comparative wage data within any newly developing country. "Deskilling" means that artisan skills, which can only be mastered through long experience and which are thus the "property" of the worker, are replaced by routinized skills which can in principle be taught to anyone. But the mechanical skills at issue are still considerable by the standards of societies at an early stage of industrialization. For this reason, workers who are skilled enough to be trusted with complex machinery are relatively scarce in newly developing countries; when they go on strike, as they often do, they cannot be replaced by any unemployed person hauled in off the street.

26. See John F.H. Purcell's interesting discussion of the actions and attitudes of transnational corporate managers with respect to Nicaragua's Sandinista regime: Purcell, "The Perceptions and Interests of U.S. Business in Relation to the Political Crisis in Central America," in Richard E. Feinberg (ed.), *Central America: International Dimensions of the Crisis* (New York: Holmes & Meier, 1982), pp. 103–123, esp. pp. 107–108; also his comments on business ideology, pp. 111–113, and his description of the "adaptive and reactive" character of transnational firms' responses to political events, pp. 117–118.

27. Albert Szymanski, "Capital Accumulation on a World Scale and the Necessity of Imperialism," *The Insurgent Sociologist* 7, 2 (1977):35–53.

28. The argument does not apply in the case of export-platform industrialization, which usually concentrates on precisely those labor-intensive operations that can no longer be profitably performed at metropolitan wage rates. But industrialization of this sort, though it exists in places (e.g., in

Mexico's northern frontier zone), is not the norm in Latin America.

29. See ch. 2 of this volume. Postimperialist thought is rapidly gaining ground in African studies: see Richard L. Sklar, "The Nature of Class Domination in Africa," *Journal of Modern African Studies* 17, 4 (1979):531–552; also his *Corporate Power*; and Sayre P. Schatz, *Nigerian Capitalism* (Berkeley and Los Angeles: University of California Press, 1977). Colin Leys, *Underdevelopment in Kenya* (Berkeley and Los Angeles: University of California Press, 1974), pictured the domestic bourgeoisie in *dependencista* terms, as a class "auxiliary" to foreign capital; but in his "African Economic Development in Theory and Practice," *Daedalus* 111, 2 (1982):99–124, he has left that position completely behind in order to embrace a postimperialist view. To my knowledge, the first attempt at a postimperialist analysis of a case of Latin American development is Becker, *New Bourgeoisie*.

30. John A. Hobson, *Imperialism: A Study*, rev. ed. (London: Allen & Unwin, 1938).

31. Sklar, *Corporate Power*, pp. 182–188.

32. John Mepham, "The Theory of Ideology in Capital," in John Mepham and David-Hillel Ruben (eds.), *Marxist Philosophy Vol. III: Epistemology, Science, Ideology* (London: Harvester Press, 1978), pp. 141–169; emphasis in original.

33. Becker, *New Bourgeoisie*, p. 15. I note that class formation as here defined "corresponds generally to the Marxian idea of a transition to the condition of a class *für sich*." On the latter see Karl Marx, *The Poverty of Philosophy* (New York: International Publishers, 1963).

34. These groups constitute the "local wing" of the corporate international bourgeoisie; see Richard L. Sklar, "Postimperialism" (ch. 2 of this volume).

35. Becker, *New Bourgeoisie*, pp. 330–336.

36. Ibid., p. 13.

37. Colin Henfrey, "Dependency, Modes of Production, and the Class Analysis of Latin America," *Latin American Perspectives* 8, 3–4 (1981):17–54, makes the argument that *dependencista* class analysis, despite its Marxist pretensions, has regularly neglected the proletariat and, for that reason, is more properly considered elite analysis. See also Eugene F. Sofer, "Recent Trends in Latin American Labor Historiography," *Latin American Research Review* 15, 1 (1980):167–176.

38. The case for a bourgeois class interest in democracy is made by Bob Jessop, "Capitalism and Democracy: The Best Possible Political Shell?" in Gary Littlejohn et al. (eds.), *Power and the State* (New York: St. Martin's, 1978), pp. 10–51; and by Göran Therborn, "The Travail of Latin American Democracy," *New Left Review*, 113–114 (1979):71–109. Therborn maintains that only under a system of pluralist participation can any bourgeois functional group be assured that its rivals within the class will not capture the ear of the state authorities and, with them, ride roughshod over its particular interests. Since the bourgeoisie is rent by internal conflict over such interests, pluralist democracy alone provides for the consensual aggregation of what will become the whole bourgeoisie's common class interest. But political democracy has its own logic; once established, it cannot be limited to the bourgeoisie and its allies.

39. Leys, "African Economic Development," p. 105; emphasis in original.

40. See fn. 21.

41. David K. Shipler, *Russia: Broken Idols, Solemn Dreams* (New York: New York Times Books, 1983).

CHAPTER FOUR

"Bonanza Development" and the "New Bourgeoisie": Peru Under Military Rule

DAVID G. BECKER

What is the nature and political significance of transnational corporate action in the mineral resource industries of the "third world"? Although waves of nationalization have washed over the minerals industries in recent years, the question is not yet moot. Some nationalizations have been partial; subsidiaries of transnational resource firms remain, with reduced ownership stakes. Where nationalization has been complete, it is not uncommon for the transnationals to go on providing essential services on a fee basis. The products of nationalized resource industries, with very few exceptions, are brought to market internationally through the transnationals' sales networks. In short, the role of transnational corporations in "third world" mineral export development has changed but not disappeared. It will not soon disappear, so long as "third world" governments seek to realize the potential wealth of their mineral reserves and to use it for underwriting national development. Transnational enterprise therefore retains a considerable capacity for influencing development in the newly industrializing countries. This chapter attempts a political analysis and interpretation of that influence.

If a newly developing country is able to generate large export earnings from the minerals trade, its leaders are apt to perceive political and economic options that are foreclosed to countries not so favored. In particular, the flow of export revenues represents a "bonanza," an apparently easy source of development capital, that can seemingly help them solve some of the most pressing problems of early industrialization—including the political problems of legitimation and control that arise in the wake of the changes and dislocations brought about, inevi-

An earlier version of this article appeared in *Comparative Political Studies* 15, 3 (1982):243–288. Used with permission.

tably, by the industrialization process. What results is a distinctive model, or strategy, of development, one that can be appropriately named "bonanza development." I will argue that it is a viable model; and that both its viability and its unique political and social ramifications are closely related to its dependence on transnational corporate participation.

The Class Analysis of Bonanza Development

Development has a political aspect, described by Richard L. Sklar as "the improvement of a society's ability to control the rate and direction of change. The concept of control is crucial to this definition, as it implies the ability to formulate and implement strategies for solving problems and achieving goals."[1] The political significance of bonanza development lies in its effect on the nature of power and social control. An understanding of this effect can best be attained through the use of a class analysis, provided that:

1. The analysis approaches domination and subordination in terms of actual class formation processes and class practices. Class structures and practices cannot be specified a priori on the basis of observations elsewhere or in another epoch, nor can they be deduced in the abstract from "laws of motion of 'dependent' capitalism."[2]

2. It supports any claim of external domination with an analysis of actual class structures and practices that includes an accurate conceptualization of external class formation. The criterion is important because, in the case of a newly developing, "peripheral" society like Peru's, the possibility that domination is effectively external—i.e., that class forces outside of Peruvian society shape its development, foreclose autochthonous choice, and establish an internal system of controls and rewards that mostly serves external needs and interests—ought not to be ruled out in advance. External domination is, of course, the basis of the popular dependency paradigm.[3] But it is not enough, in my view, to rest the case for external domination on structuralist propositions that operate wholly in an abstract economic realm.[4]

3. It deals with the formation, practices, and relations of all significant class actors—including, specifically, the working class, as the latter is essential to the dialectic of capitalist change and transformation. An analysis of bourgeois and middle-class "fractions," alone, is actually an elite analysis. Elite analysis can

display the inequities of capitalist development, but it conceives of power and control solely in terms of a "circulation of elites."[5] It can neither comprehend tendencies toward the amelioration of capitalist excesses that arise with the growth of working-class political cohesion and capability, nor consider the prospects for bourgeois political-ideological hegemony[6]; it *presupposes* an undynamic, nontransformatory capitalism that must be maintained in force by political authoritarianism. The dependency paradigm, despite the notable advances of recent years, has not yet succeeded in incorporating this broader, dialectical class analysis—in large part because it does not deal empirically with subordinate class forces.[7]

There is still another reason why the dependency paradigm is not up to the task of the political analysis of bonanza development. True, the latest advances have carried dependency analysis well beyond the naïve early versions that spoke of "development of underdevelopment" and of domination by "comprador" classes or "lumpenbourgeoisies."[8] But these advances have all been based on the unfolding of the import-substitution model in countries like Brazil and Argentina, whose export bases are largely agricultural and are (or were) under the control of landed classes. It is the dynamics and bottlenecks of this model that are adduced to explain "associated-dependent development"[9]; "technological-industrial dependency"[10]; "national disintegration"[11]; and, in the political dimension, "bureaucratic-authoritarianism."[12] Dependency studies of mineral export-based development have simply not progressed much farther than the formulations of Lenin and Baran: that external force is used to deprive "third world" host countries of a fair return on their mineral wealth, thereby impeding their development while underwriting metropolitan economic development with cheap raw materials.[13] The political consequences are held to be the encapsulation of the minerals sector in an economically disarticulated "enclave"; the reinforcement of anti-developmental agro-export elites, whose control is contested only by an ineffectual populism; and the eventual emergence of a pseudo-autonomous state which, though able in the short run to carry through a few reforms that weaken the grip of the agro-export groups, lacks a societal base and is hence incapable of institutionalizing these reformist tendencies.[14]

The Peruvian case suggests something quite different. Bonanza development tends to propitiate the formation of a certain stratum or subclass of the national bourgeoisie—a group that is frequently referred to as a "new bourgeoisie"[15] and that aspires to become the leading element of a dominant national bourgeois class. The rise of the new bourgeoisie is a consequence of its association with the activities of transnational resource corporations. Paradoxically, however, its power is exerted to combat and reduce foreign domination. The new bourgeoisie does not need to rely on the favors of foreign interests or raw coercion to maintain its power and privileges. Instead, it has the potential to secure its domination peaceably, through the identification of its class interest in development with wider popular aspirations—including those of an organized, politically assertive working class in the mines and smelters.[16] Corroborating evidence comes from observations of class formation and consolidation of a similar sort in two other cases of mineral-export-based development: Nigeria and Zambia.[17]

A Replacement for Dependency?

Richard L. Sklar's alternative paradigmatic conception of capitalist development, "postimperialism," is better suited than dependency to the analysis of bonanza development, yet does not surrender dependency's progressive value orientation.[18]

Transnational corporations, argues Sklar, are integrating the world economy and reducing interimperialist conflict among the metropolitan states. The expansion of corporate horizons from a national to a global frame indicates that a process of international class formation is under way. In other words, transnational corporate action is producing an international bourgeoisie whose concerns transcend the political interests of its members' home states. This international bourgeoisie has learned how to bring its global interests into harmony with the national aspirations of "third world" countries that play host to transnational subsidiaries. The stage is thus set for the appearance in these countries of dominant classes whose leading bourgeois strata have a structural interest in national development but participate, at the same time, as junior partners in the international bourgeoisie. This kind of local dominant class has a capacity for hegemony. It does impose late-capitalist values, culture, and social forms on its society, but in a manner quite different from the dependency conception:

> The leading bourgeois strata interact with both metropolitan and local societies, since they have interests in each. . . . [I]n interacting with the latter they impose metropolitan values *because to do so is in their self-interest.* . . . [T]he leading strata are the economic and political hinge points between local societies and the metropoli. Yet, inasmuch as these strata need no longer opt for *either* national *or* metropolitan concerns, they can be nationalistic and developmentalist without contradicting their international interests. As their dominance is not nar-

rowly self-serving, it does not need to rest on coercive force and can coexist with formal democracy.[19]

What emerges, Sklar contends, is a new, "postimperialist" phase of capitalist development that leaves colonialism[20] behind.

The evolving structure of the world minerals industries lends particular credence to Sklar's assertions. These industries are international oligopolies in which the internationalization of capital and of managerial control are already accomplished facts.[21] Markets are highly integrated at the world level. Without doubt it is over questions of minerals investment where "third world" host countries have become most assertive and, on the whole, most successful in their dealings with transnational firms; the transnationals, for their part, have not generally opposed host-country aims to the bitter end and have not called routinely on the power of their home governments to redress the bargaining balance.[22] On the contrary, they have tacitly acknowledged that wage, taxation, concession, and ownership policies in natural resources lie within the exclusive province of the host state, and that local subsidiaries must conform to such policy dictates like "good corporate citizens." The ability of transnational managers to justify their subsidiaries' conformity to the local policy dictates of host states, without perceiving a sacrifice of their firms' global interests, has been systematized by Sklar as an element of managerial belief, an ideological "doctrine of domicile."[23]

Bonanza Development Defined

One of the aims of this paper is to suggest that, in thinking about "third world" export-oriented development, it is better not to regard primary product exports, agricultural and mineral, as all of a piece. At the economic level, mineral exports do not subject the exporting nations to the secularly declining terms of trade that have been widely reported for agricultural exports.[24] As regards its social and political impact, mining is today an eminently *industrial* activity: it relies on typically industrial modes of labor control, is often quite capital-intensive, and usually embraces considerable pre-export processing of the raw ores. Consequently, my definition of bonanza development excludes export bases that are predominantly agricultural or that depend on directly coercive (i.e., non-wage) forms of labor control.[25]

The bonanza development model has these defining characteristics:

1. The underlying mechanism is the production for export of mineral products, with a substantial part of the earned surplus ear-

marked for the host government. Its share is used for its own financial
support; to develop other economic sectors, some of which may be unrelated to minerals production, in a setting of an official commitment
to industrial promotion; and to provide economic benefits to vocal,
mobilized elements of the population so as to dissuade challenges to the
existing structures of political domination and social control. Mineral
production and export are valued primarily as sources of capital and
scarce foreign exchange; their direct employment and linkage effects
are considered secondary.

2. With minerals extraction becoming a primary generator of new
industrial capital, there is an official concern with productive efficiency
and surplus maximization, to the exclusion of potentially conflicting
noneconomic objectives. This conduces to capitalist relations of production in minerals enterprises, irrespective of the nature and nationality of juridical ownership and, to a large degree, of regime ideology.
It also conduces to a preference for capital-intensive technologies in
the export sector. On the other hand, there is nothing to prevent the
host government from pursuing limited noneconomic objectives that
do not conflict with efficiency goals. One such objective is the indigenization of enterprise management, ideologically justified by nationalism
or antiracialism and useful in that it seemingly increases local control.

3. The emphases on productive efficiency and high technology
combine to encourage the continuing presence in the minerals sector
of transnational firms, even in an era of rising host-country
nationalism.[26] They alone command access to the huge amounts of investment capital required to launch a major high-technology mining
or drilling project. Their organizational and technical expertise is usually indispensable for setting up the project and for staffing it until local
citizens can be trained to the task. If nothing else, they are needed to
supply the machinery and supervise construction and installation.
Finally, their specialized knowledge of international marketing is
irreplaceable.

4. The state's capture and redistribution of a share of the economic surplus from mineral production—the "bonanza"—substitutes
for direct economic linkages to the rest of the domestic political economy and weakens the mineral sector's "enclave" character. The capture
of surplus is accomplished through taxation, royalties, direct claims on
profits (when the state is a joint venturer or the sole juridical owner), or
forced transfer payments. Surplus redistribution to other economic
sectors takes either or both of two forms: direct investment by the state;
or subventions to domestic entrepreneurs, which may include tax holi-
days, low-interest loans or outright grants from state development
banks, or price subsidies.[27] The distribution of largesse to mobilized

and mobilizable societal groups—bonanza development can be a defensive strategy designed to head off autonomous popular mobilization—takes place through welfare programs, public works construction, and increased state employment, all paid for out of the state's share of the "bonanza"; and through higher wages and greater employment creation in the private sector, encouraged or ordered by official policy. Passing some of the benefits on to workers and middle-class staff, via higher pay and more job creation than justified by narrowly economic criteria, is a quid pro quo demanded of the private sector by the state in exchange for the subventions that it provides.

5. The state that undertakes bonanza development must evidently be "relatively autonomous" of particular and short-range bourgeois interests in the private sector.[28] There are probably several paths from which such a state may emerge; a comparison of the Peruvian, Zambian, and Nigerian cases suggests that the onset of bonanza development may precede as well as follow the appearance of the initial nuclei of the corporate manageriat and organized working class.

Bonanza development is a *political* concept. It reaches beyond the specification of a strategy of economic development to address two related issues: the social changes (with their political ramifications) wrought by the implementation of the strategy itself, and the political ends overtly served by capitalist development of natural resources. The concept of bonanza development supplements the idea of postimperialism by specifying a domestic socioeconomic and political dynamic that explains the appearance in the host country of a stable capitalist order with a potential for industrialization. First of all, bonanza development allows a dominant class to enjoy the fruits of an administratively strong and capable state without paying for them out of its own pockets in higher taxes on enterprise profits and personal income. Second, upward mobility opportunities are opened (either by industrialization, whose extent in the "third world" has been documented by Warren,[29] or by the government's use of the "bonanza" to expand bureaucratic employment) to ambitious local citizens—in their majority members of the middle class who, if angered by "blocked ascent," would be capable of mounting serious revolutionary threats to the status quo.[30] Furthermore, industrial growth enables the dominant class to seek legitimacy on the basis of its apparent developmentalism. When added to the ideological nationalism rendered feasible by the class's association with a stronger state, industrializing developmentalism has always been an efficacious device for legitimizing class domination.

Third, the availability of the "bonanza" renders unnecessary the initial acquisition of reinvestable surpluses from an intensified squeeze on largely agricultural producers—i.e., "primitive accumulation." Industrializing elites no longer need preoccupy themselves with the always difficult task of reorganizing agriculture in the face of peasant resistance as a prerequisite to capitalist development. One result is to award the industrializers greater freedom in choosing class allies. They can avoid a head-on confrontation with landed elites; or, alternatively, they can support land reform with much less concern for its effect on agricultural productivity. They are also in a position to coopt the organized working class with promises of material gains, at lesser cost to their own ability to accumulate capital. The possibility of such gains, meanwhile, encourages "economistic" tendencies within working-class organizations.

It might be added that bonanza development stabilizes capitalism as a system by making comparatively less attractive to *state* elites in newly developing countries the main historical alternative strategy of rapid industrial development: "socialist mercantilism," as practiced in the USSR under Stalin.[31] Aspects of the bonanza development model may also appeal to state-socialist elites who want to accelerate the pace of economic development without a repetition of Stalinism's excesses.[32]

The Peruvian Version of Bonanza Development

Present-day Peru is a classic instance of bonanza development. Metals, ores, and petroleum, about 90 percent of whose production is exported, account for the lion's share of primary-product export value (Table 4.1). Mineral exports (including petroleum) increased their share of total export value by almost 40 percent from 1960 to 1980; note also the correspondingly dramatic decline in the export salience of agricultural commodities and fishmeal. The capitalist mode of production is universal in mining, and technologies in the paramount *gran minería* (large-scale mining subsector) are advanced and capital-intensive (with one qualification, to be taken up later on). Important foreign investments remain in the sector despite expropriations, the constitution of new state enterprises, and the establishment of a state mineral export sales monopoly (since abolished) during the 1968–80 period of military rule. Data do not exist that would enable us to compute the aggregate contribution of the minerals industries to state finances, but it must be very great. Mining firms are the country's biggest corporate taxpayers, and their employees, whose remunerations at all job levels are far above the national average, pay much more than the average in income and indirect taxes. The state channels a variety of

Table 4.1   Contributions to Peruvian Export Value by Commodity
(columns A, percent of local value; columns B, percent of value
excluding petroleum and derivatives)

	1960		1970	
	A	B	A	B
Coffee	4.3	4.5	3.7	4.7
Copper	21.9	22.8	17.6	22.5
Cotton	16.9	17.7	2.0	2.6
Fishmeal	12.0	12.5	4.7	6.0
Iron ore	7.6	7.9	2.5	3.2
Lead	5.0	5.2	2.7	3.5
Petroleum	4.1		21.9	
Silver	5.6	5.8	14.8	19.0
Sugar	11.0	11.5	0.3	0.4
Zinc	3.9	4.0	5.0	6.4
Other[a]	7.7	8.1	24.8	31.7
Total	100.0	100.0	100.0	100.0

SOURCE: Elaborated by the author from data provided by the National Mining Society
and the Central Reserve Bank of Peru.

NOTES: [a] Mostly manufactured products.

direct and indirect benefits to politically mobilized societal groups.
Post-1968 policies of industrial promotion resulted in an 11.4 percent
mean annual increase in industrial output between 1969 and 1975, versus a 1960–69 average of 9.7 percent starting from a far lower base.[33]

Table 4.2 shows that the shift to bonanza development has coin-
cided with a diversification of Peru's export trade outlets, especially in
other non-Western regions. The penetration of foreign capital into
critical areas of the economy is said to weaken the institutional base of
the domestic bourgeoisie, thereby inhibiting its development as an in-
dependently entrepreneurial class.[34] However, the evidence from
Peruvian mining does not support that claim. Within the *mediana minería* (medium-scale mining subsector), only 15 of 71 firms are controlled by foreign interests. Among the domestic firms are seven large
corporations and corporate groups each of which is fully rationalized
and professionally managed, controls assets valued in millions of dollars, and employs over a thousand persons. Three of these display the
wide diffusion (by local standards) of shareholding and the separation
of formal ownership from actual control that are typical of the "mature" business corporation.[35] At least one has enough of an international reputation that it can maintain a sizable line of credit with a major
U.S. bank. The mediana minería produces over half of the national

Table 4.2   Peruvian Export Trade by Destination
(percent of total value except as noted)

Country (or Region)	1962	1977
United States	34.9	30.6
Canada	0.4	0.7
Latin America	10.0	16.0
United Kingdom	9.7	3.8
EEC (excluding United Kingdom)[a]	31.6	16.2
Japan	6.5	12.0
OPEC nations	0.0 [b]	0.0 [b]
Soviet bloc	0.4	9.9
Total	100.0	100.0
Total trade value ($ millions)	539.4	1665.8

SOURCES: Elaborated by the author from data compiled by the International Monetary Fund and the Central Reserve Bank of Peru.

NOTES: [a] Denmark and Ireland added to 1962 datum for sake of consistent comparison.

   [b] Less than 0.1%

output of all nonferrous metals other than copper—three fourths, in the case of silver. Its most rapid growth has come since 1950, which is also the period of the most rapid growth of foreign investment.

As important as the mediana minería is, it no longer marks the outer bound of the native mining bourgeoisie. The addition to the gran minería of a wholly new parastatal firm in 1970, along with the nationalization of two formerly foreign companies in 1973–74, have given that class element other, larger bastions of economic support.

The Historical Origins of Peruvian Bonanza Development

Reliance on intensive exploitation of mineral resources for state revenues and for coopting politically active subordinate groups can be traced back in time to the nineteenth-century "age of guano."[36] The political use of "bonanza" revenues was the capstone of the economic policy pursued until 1968 by the ruling "oligarchy"—a policy otherwise typified by laissez-faire.[37]

Metals replaced fertilizers as the principal "bonanza" resource after 1901, with the arrival of the Cerro de Pasco Corporation. Headquartered in New York, it was formed for the express purpose of exploiting Peru's rich, extensive copper deposits; its welcome was assured in advance by a favorable revision of the Peruvian Mining

Code.[38] By 1914, Cerro was the largest business enterprise on Peruvian soil (a status it would keep for many years; at its demise in 1973, it was still Peru's largest private employer) and a major purveyor of copper to the industries of the United States and Europe. Before the close of the next decade, it was also producing appreciable quantities of lead, zinc, silver, and minor metals. It built smelters and refineries in the Andean town of La Oroya, on the rail line to the port of Callao. It purchased several haciendas whose owners had sued it for damages caused by smelter fumes, thereby becoming Peru's largest landowner. As such it was a de facto ally of the oligarchy; it promptly formalized the alliance by joining the National Agrarian Society, a principal institutional embodiment of oligarchic power. This close association with the politically dominant elite of the time ensured that Cerro's influence over all matters of mining policy would be preponderant; every significant piece of mining legislation from 1901 through the 1950s was adopted subject to the company's "advice and consent," and frequently at its instigation.

The term "segmentary incorporation" has been coined to describe the process of political development in oligarchic Peru.[39] Segmentary incorporation was a second line of defense for oligarchic power, resorted to when coercion alone could no longer bridle subordinate groups with growing aspirations. Since any real popular challenge to the system depended above all on the unity of diverse subordinate groups, the oligarchic counterstrategy was to divide—by selectively admitting the best organized and most cohesive of them to a measure of economic privilege and limited political participation—and conquer. Cooptation of middle-class groups took the form of expanded state employment, legal protection of white-collar employee rights, and social insurance programs. In time, organized working-class and urban underclass elements were coopted through public works programs and the gradual extension of legal protections and insurance programs. The availability of the "bonanza" made all this possible: it financed the cooptative benefits extended directly by the state, and it permitted the government to compensate private employers for the benefits demanded of them in lower taxes than they would have otherwise had to pay. Meanwhile, repressive force continued to be used against less cohesive, less well organized popular groups that did not yet pose a comparable threat.

The problem with segmentary incorporation was that economic development itself, no matter how retarded by laissez-faire, gradually brought into existence ever more actual or potential popular mobilization, thus, ever more actual or potential demands on the system. Consequently, the "bonanza" had to be enlarged periodically in order to forestall systemic crisis.

An incipient crisis point was reached in the late 1940s,[40] lending urgency to a drive for "bonanza" expansion through additional foreign investment in mining. In order to attract it, in 1950 a new Mining Code was enacted; a revision of a draft prepared by Robert Koenig, Cerro's chief executive, it duplicated in Peruvian law most of the relevant provisions of the U.S. Code, including the taxation of net income rather than export value and the provision of generous deductions for depreciation and depletion. It also contained special incentives for investment in open-pit mining. In response, the Southern Peru Copper Corporation was formed by American Smelting and Refining (Asarco) to exploit the Toquepala copper deposit in the southern Andes. Constituted as a joint venture with three other transnational parents, including Cerro,[41] and having secured its incentives with a development contract entered into with the Peruvian state under the 1950 Code, the new company brought the Toquepala mine and its smelter into production in 1960. The mine was an instant financial success[42] and caused Southern to surpass Cerro as the largest firm in the gran minería by all criteria save total employment. Another new entrant was the Marcona Mining Company, which in 1952 began the large-scale exploitation of Peruvian iron ore; it was a joint venture of the Utah Construction Company and Cyprus Mines. Both Southern and Marcona used state-of-the-art production technologies, mining many times the volume of material that Cerro did with less than a third as many workers. Both interacted less with the domestic economy, except for their tax payments, than did Cerro. But their presence made possible the "populistic" policies of expanded state benefits and public works construction that were adopted by the authoritarian regime of Gen. Manuel Odría (1948–56).

Given the open character of pre-1968 economic policy, however, the "bonanza" operated only in the political plane. Bereft of official promotion and kept subservient to the oligarchic interest in agriculture, industrialization advanced but slowly and with heavy penetration by transnational manufacturing firms. The formation of a domestic industrial bourgeoisie was correspondingly held back, and that class remained under the domination of oligarchic money capital.

But there was a significant exception: the managerially oriented mining bourgeoisie. Its class formation was propelled forward by the 1950 Mining Code, whose taxation clauses facilitated corporate planning and helped make corporate growth independent of oligarchic investment capital. Bourgeois class formation in the mediana minería was also spurred by Cerro. When its declining mine output ceased to match its smelter and refinery capacity, it made up the deficit with ore purchases from independent medium firms. Those purchases accelerated after 1950, since Cerro management saw bigger profits from investments in smelting and refining than from new mines. At about the same time, Cerro started to indigenize its managerial staff in order to reduce the expense of hiring expatriates. Hoping to enlarge the pool of local mining professionals, it made financial contributions to the National Engineering University (UNI), offered summer jobs to students, and established scholarships for engineering study abroad. In short order it became the premier on-the-job training ground for Peruvian mining professionals. It also contributed loan and equity "seed money" to the foundation of several locally owned medium firms, provided technical aid, and even sold difficult-to-obtain spare parts and equipment from its stocks.[43] It was instrumental in reorganizing and refinancing the industry's trade association, the National Mining Society. The Society became more than just a political lobby; in keeping with the generally corporatist tradition of Peruvian politics,[44] it enjoyed formal representation within many state institutions.

The Military Regime's Bonanza Development Strategies: Content and Context

The military government of 1968–80 brought bonanza development to full fruition by adding the elements that had been missing under oligarchic rule: prioritization of industrial development, and an economically active state whose resources would be used to foster development. The nationalization of the banking system and establishment of the Corporación Financiera de Desarrollo (COFIDE), a state development bank, gave the government the means for accumulating capital and directing it toward industrialization projects. Restrictions were placed on the activities of transnational corporations in order to prevent industrial promotion from redounding disproportionately to their advantage. Higher education was reformed so as to stress teaching and research in areas of immediate social utility: the natural and social sciences, engineering, and management. A reform of the state administration improved policy coordination and laid the groundwork for full-scale economic planning, which was begun in 1971.

The generals acted as if they understood from the start the political value of a bonanza development strategy. They wanted their "revolution" to be a neat surgical excision of oligarchic power (i.e., an organizational revolution that would not uncap socially revolutionary pressures from below), which required that segmentary incorporation be continued and extended. In particular, it would have to reach more members of the working class and urban underclass, and a start would have to be made toward incorporating the peasantry.[45] To do all this at once meant that the "bonanza" had to be enlarged as never before.

That the regime's mining policies would be broadly developmentalist and *dirigiste* was assured by the presence of Gen. Jorge Fernández Maldonado at the helm of the new Ministry of Energy and Mines; the general, a devotee of Social Christian and *dependencista* ideology,[46] was at this time a close confidante of the president, Gen. Juan Velasco Alvarado (1968–75)—whose own political views, to the degree that they had coherence, were still farther to the left.

But within the guidelines laid down from above, policy was shaped in the main by a cadre of technocrats, with whom Fernández Maldonado enjoyed a close and mutually respectful relationship. Most had come to state service from the ranks of the private manageriat. They were motivated by professional stewardship, the opportunity to use their expertise on behalf of the nation; by the regime's administrative reform, which had vastly improved the conditions, status, and remunerations of state employment; and by the fact that, as the Peruvian political tradition does not share the North American concern with conflict of interest, they could retain their holdings in, and even their salaries from, private mining enterprises. Not surprisingly and with no noteworthy exceptions, the policy options that attracted them reflected the interests of domestic private capital in the industry. But their approach was novel in perceiving a need for the state to cease being *el gran ausente* ("the great absentee") of the minería, to become instead an active planner and investor, and to combine incentives with disciplinary sanctions against foreign-owned firms that failed to contribute adequately to bonanza development.

Nationalization in natural resources was never a prime policy objective. It was seen as unduly costly. Bonanza development demanded accelerated foreign investment, and prospective investors would be scared off if existing resource firms were expropriated without compensation; but the payment of compensation would require an outflow of capital that would buy not one ton's worth of increased production. Also, the technocrats were not persuaded that resource nationalization elsewhere (they had studied closely the examples of Chile and the African copper producers) had done much either to increase output or to reduce dependence. Tighter state regulation and oversight of corporate operations, they felt, could accomplish as much or more and do so less expensively.

This approach found favor, of course, with the private-sector mine owners and managers. As contributors to the "bonanza," they would rise in public esteem by being directly associated with the new nationalist-developmentalist orientation of official policy; they were assured that the state would not become a mining monopolist at their expense; and they would not be cut off by an antagonized international mining establishment from participation in the world industry's markets and technical forums. They did not oppose stricter state oversight, as might have been anticipated; they saw it as tending to "sanitize" the industry politically. That is to say, it spiked the guns of radical nationalists who had been accusing the industry of various abuses,[47] and, by guaranteeing that laws and contracts would henceforth be written *ab initio* with the maximization of Peruvian interests in mind, placed relations with foreign capital on a more equitable—and, thereby, more stable—basis.

The Military Regime and Transnational Mining Capital

The pragmatic, nonideological orientation of sectorial policy did not rule out nationalization altogether but reserved it as the ultimate sanction to be applied against companies that would not abide by the government's authoritative definition of "good corporate citizenship." Cerro and Marcona ended by being nationalized—the first because it was institutionally incapable of performing in the new role laid out for it, the second as a result of political infighting within high military councils.[48] Southern Peru Copper, which did act to increase the Peruvian mining "bonanza," was allowed to remain under exclusively private, and foreign, ownership, although it had to surrender certain traditional prerogatives.

Cerro, though a transnational firm in the technical sense, was neither a core member of the world copper oligopoly nor a vertically integrated producer of nonferrous metal products in the usual meaning of the phrase.[49] All of its working mines but one, and all of its processing facilities, were in Peru. Indeed, until the early 1950s all of its operations except for top management were located in Peru. Thereafter it used its Peruvian profits to acquire an assortment of U.S. subsidiaries; but as a conglomerate it was poorly integrated and not very profitable. By the late 1960s, returns on invested capital were too low to generate the cash flow needed for further acquisitions; the company then attempted, without success, to arrange a "friendly" merger with a larger, cash-rich partner.

The company's Peruvian operations had become technologically obsolete. Most mining was of the underground variety, was resistant to mechanization, and necessitated a sizable workforce. Not only was this workforce very expensive to maintain after the mines were unionized in the 1940s, it was also ill-disciplined. For Cerro's workers distrusted and resented their employer, whose past practices, in the memory of many still alive, included low wages (in some instances, debt peonage), coercive supervision, unhealthful working conditions, abysmally inadequate camps, and militant anti-unionism; while this "social debt" had ceased to mount up at the same rate as in the early days, neither had it been repaid.[50] Profit rates were marginal—the bulk of Peruvian returns came from Cerro's minority holding in the very profitable Southern—and the firm's overall financial position did not permit the huge investments in new technologies needed to augment them.

As was previously observed, the company had based its survival in the country on its ability to curry political favor with the oligarchy and the government of the day. However, the military regime's land reform[51]—the Cerro haciendas were its first target—and the general eclipse of oligarchic power closed off Cerro's traditional channels of influence. Whatever else it might do, the military regime would not risk its nationalist *bona fides* by seeming to award preferential policy access to the representatives of foreign capital. From 1968 on, Cerro's ability to do business in Peru became conditioned, as with all other foreign mining enterprises, on its economic contribution. In view of what has already been said regarding the company's history and institutional limitations, it should come as no surprise that it failed the test.

By proceeding methodically and nonideologically, government officials were able to establish a solid legal basis for a punitive expropriation,[52] to choose the most convenient moment to implement the expropriation, and to cut Cerro off from its putative allies in international mining and financial circles and in the U.S. government.[53] Cerro's Peruvian minero-metallurgical complex was transferred to state ownership on January 1, 1974. For an out-of-pocket cost of $28.5 million, the state obtained title to assets worth $175 million on books,[54] without upsetting its ongoing relationship with other mining firms or with the international financial establishment—which had already become a principal underwriter of Peruvian development. No extranational entity opposed the settlement, and the Nixon administration gave it a formal stamp of approval.

In light of the military regime's concern with the size of the "bonanza," it can be argued that Cerro might have escaped nationalization, in spite of its limitations and deficiencies, had state technocrats believed that foreign managerial expertise were necessary to operate its installations. They did not so believe, due to their confidence in their own capabilities—acquired, in many instances, with Cerro's help. Was their confidence misplaced? Table 4.3 summarizes the financial performance of Cerro and its parastatal successor, Centromin-Peru, over the 30-year period from 1950 to 1980; the performance of the latter compares very favorably, the more so considering that between 1975 and 1977, parastatal management had to contend with severely depressed world metals prices. Production data, such as volume of ore mined and quantity of metal extracted, confirm that the parastatal entity operates more efficiently than did its private predecessor. What is more, Centromin has embarked on an ambitious program of capital improvements, which include infrastructure investments intended to erase the "social debt." It has been able to finance this program with loans, at commercial rates equivalent to what the transnationals must pay, from a group of metropolitan banks; they, it would seem, have confidence in Centromin's all-Peruvian management team.

Southern's situation was quite different from Cerro's. Its majority parent, Asarco, *was* a central oligopolist in the world nonferrous metals industry, and Peruvian mining was a vital part of its global strategy of oligopolistic competition for market share. The Toquepala mine was but one of three associated orebodies, all of which the company held

Table 4.3 Financial Performance of Cerro de Pasco Corporation, 1960–73, and Centromin-Peru, 1974–80
(millions of U.S. dollars; profit on sales in percent)

Year	Total Sales	Total Earnings	Net Profit	Profit on Sales
1950–54	46.6		6.1	11.1
1955–59	59.8		4.3	7.2
1960–64	78.4		5.5	7.0
1965–68	135.4		8.0	5.9
1969	162.8	56.8	10.2	6.3
1970	165.7	41.7	4.4	2.6
1971	133.9	18.6	-3.8	-2.8
1972	149.0	44.5	7.9	5.3
1973	264.6	86.6	20.7	7.8
1974	315.9	120.0	32.6	10.3
1975	271.7	36.1	5.6	2.0
1976	303.4	71.9	11.1	3.7
1977	328.0	39.3	21.4	6.5
1978	304.9	63.1	36.8	12.1
1979	566.1	185.7	81.3	14.4
1980	724.9	139.3	69.0	9.5

SOURCE: Elaborated by the author from data published in the firm's annual reports.
Original data in *soles*, converted to dollars at the average exchange rate for the year(s).

NOTE: Tabulated data for 1950–68 are annual averages over the time periods indicated.

under concession. Asarco planned on the eventual development of all three, but sequentially. That is, the stream of profits from Toquepala would finance the construction of the second mine, Cuajone, and their combined cash flows would pay for the third, Quellaveco. Toquepala's infrastructure had been designed and built for easy expansion, with this plan in mind. Consequently, at stake for Asarco was not only its Peruvian operations but its entire corporate strategy.

The Cuajone mine was built under the terms of a development contract approved in late 1969. Originally estimated at $355 million, the project's cost at completion in 1976 exceeded $700 million. It was financed by a veritable *Who's Who* of international banking: 34.3 percent from a consortium of U.S., Canadian, European, and Japanese banks, led by Chase Manhattan; 10.2 percent from the U.S. Export-Import Bank; 1.4 percent from the International Finance Corporation (IFC), an arm of the World Bank; 6.8 percent from other international banks (for working capital); and 16.1 percent in credits and loans from equipment suppliers and copper purchasers. Billiton N.V., a Royal Dutch/Shell metals subsidiary, became a joint venturer in the project by contributing 3.7 percent of the cost in the form of an equity investment, and Southern's owners added 5.5 percent in new equity capital. The remaining 22 percent—the only part that did not represent an inflow of new capital—was drawn from Southern's corporate reserves, which, by law, had to be reinvested in Peru. All loans except those for working capital were secured by the advance commitment of two-thirds of Cuajone's annual output to copper buyers spread among the countries whose banks participated,[55] for a contractual term of fifteen years.

Cuajone's financing arrangements have set up a network of powerful international interests with a stake in the project—an excellent "insurance policy" against any future move toward nationalization.[56] But insurance against adverse host-government action is one thing, enforced policy compliance quite another: despite its impatience with Peruvian bargaining tactics, this international constellation of interests never once succeeded in forcing the Peruvians to back down from a policy position that mattered deeply to them.[57] Rather than increasing its dependence, Cuajone has helped Peru by stabilizing its balance of payments and allowing it a bit of breathing room as it struggles to resolve the problem of its crushing foreign debt burden.

The Peruvian authorities, by dint of hard and clever bargaining, gained considerable "bonanza" benefits from Cuajone and achieved political objectives of stellar importance to them. In general, they came away from their discussions with Southern and Asarco having attained more of their ends than did the companies:

1. Taxation was higher, and other incentives fewer, than for Toquepala. Moreover, the privileges received by Southern were
less than the maximum allowed by law. This enabled the regime
to validate the charge of *entrequismo* that it had levelled against
its predecessors while protecting it from a similar accusation.

2. The government wanted a refinery included in the project in
order to capture additional local value added and to act as a
check on the company's pricing arrangements.[58] When Southern adamantly refused, government authorities secretly ar-
ranged to obtain financing and equipment for a state-owned refinery from Japan. They then used their political leverage to
force Southern to patronize it, at considerable cost to the company's marketing flexibility. Refining charges assessed to
Southern's account have been higher than those charged by
metropolitan refineries, even though actual processing costs
are lower; the difference represents a forced transfer payment
from the company to the Peruvian state.

3. Southern had to accept a so-called "Calvo clause"[59] in its contract, subjecting it to the sole jurisdiction of the Peruvian courts
and renouncing all right of appeal through diplomatic channels
or to international arbitration.

4. The government withdrew the Quellaveco concession. Since it
is inconceivable that Quellaveco could be developed save as an
integral part of the Southern complex, it will probably be constituted one day as a joint venture, with state participation of 25
percent or more secured solely by the return of concessionary
rights (as the current Mining Code provides). Hence, without
disturbing its existing relationship with Southern or spending a
single *sol*, the state should ultimately gain direct participation in
the only remaining fully private enterprise in the gran minería.

5. Against Southern-Asarco opposition, but with the support of
the international banks, the government elbowed its way into
the long-term copper sales agreements. In so doing it
strengthened its control over export sales, received a small commission the earning of which cost it nothing, and guaranteed itself the availability of feedstocks for its new refinery (at government insistence, clauses were written into the sales contracts to
require local refining of much of the metal). And without disturbing existing market relationships, the government saw to it
that the disposition of Cuajone copper would further its objective of market diversification.

6. The government vetoed the proposed equity participation of
the IFC when the latter tried to compel the abrogation of the

"Calvo clause" and sought to alter other provisions of the Cuajone agreements. It succeeded in this defiance of one of the central institutions of international capitalism.

The attainment by the Peruvian government of its principal bargaining aims, even against much powerful opposition, was due primarily to the knowledge and expertise of its negotiators and their staffs. These technocrats, with their extensive managerial experience in the private sector, were well versed in the international copper business. Moreover, the improved oversight capabilities of the state administration made it possible for them to form a clear picture of Southern's financial condition and concerns. The information proved to be an invaluable bargaining asset. Since the government side did not need to move the discussions off the economic plane, it did not have to resort to ideological arguments (which would have been shot down as "unrealistic"), or to the risky strategy of taking extreme positions in hopes of being able to split the differences. In financial matters, such as the rates of taxation to be applied, mining ministry officials used the data at their disposal to compute for themselves what state exactions would still leave the company with a fair rate of profit; their proposals were then placed on the table on a take-it-or-leave-it basis.

This record confirms an important point made by Stepan.[60] Transnational investments may indeed weaken the *short-run* control capabilities of the host state. However, the sensation of its own debility poses a challenge to which the host government may rise. The outcome in the long run may be an overall strengthening of the host state and a net improvement of its control capabilities—a dialectic that the dependency paradigm tends to overlook.[61]

The Political Meaning of Transnational Corporate Behavior

Cerro's owners, in seeking to keep control of their installations, and Southern's, in planning and executing their Cuajone project, had to adapt themselves as best they could to a far more aggressively nationalist political environment than they had ever before encountered in Peru. The first, as we saw, failed miserably; the second succeeded. In fact, Southern's parent firms had so much faith in the outcome that they committed to Cuajone almost $68 million of new corporate funds (i.e., discretionary funds that were not legally obligated to be spent in Peru), plus over $500 million of borrowed capital whose repayment they alone were responsible for. (They had attempted to get the government to act as a guarantor, but their efforts were rejected out of hand.) Southern's parents evidently saw no fundamental contradiction between Peruvian nationalism and their global interests.

Southern's behavior was wholly in keeping with Sklar's concept of a corporate doctrine of domicile. This self-imposed ideological standard does not require corporate altruism, of which Southern displayed none. It demands only that if a host country is willing to accept foreign resource investment at all—*implying that its government will, at a minimum, allow the local subsidiary a reasonable chance to earn profits*—the subsidiary should respect and voluntarily obey the government's policy decisions in regard to local issues that the latter deems important.[62] Ideology makes such a doctrine possible: as good capitalists, transnational managers ideologically divide the political and the economic into separate spheres of action; this mental operation enables them to leave to government the control of such political matters as affect governing elites' ability to secure their legitimacy in power. Good business sense makes the doctrine viable: there is a payoff in government's reciprocal tolerance of the business activity and its profit opportunities, which reduces political risk.

Two questions arise, however. How can the concept of the doctrine of domicile be reconciled with Cerro's manifestly "bad citizenship"? Second, how was Cerro's behavior perceived and reacted to by the Peruvian mining bourgeoisie (which had at stake a set of historically positive associations and concrete business interests)?

The answer to the first question turns on the observation that the market situation and institutional characteristics of a mining company like Cerro are so different from those of the technologically advanced, centrally oligopolistic transnationals as to warrant a separate classification. Cerro can be labelled a "colonial company," the phrase connoting that this kind of foreign-owned resource firm arose during the colonialist phase of international capitalism when cheap labor made even labor-intensive "third world" mining operations attractive.[63] Since they exploited local resources, both human and material, but contributed no more to local development than they could get away with, colonial companies needed to rely on political means to secure their privileges. There was no problem, naturally, if they were based in a true colony. If not, they could accomplish their ends by allying themselves with domestic compradors, the alliances resting on the political value to comprador dominance of the "bonanza" and supplemented as needed with more direct, personal favors.

Thanks to the unionization of labor, the exhaustion of the richest ores, and technological obsolescence, colonial companies that have not successfully "transnationalized" themselves are no longer profitable. As a result, they are unable to marshal great amounts of outside capital for new mining ventures. Their management methods are, today, well within the capabilities of host-country professionals, and they have long since indigenized their managerial staffs except at the very top. Thus, they have ceased to command those bonanza development assets that only foreign capital can provide. At the same time, the presence of a cadre of domestic manager-technologists in the host country signals that older, comprador ruling elites have vanished from the seats of power—or, at the least, that power is rapidly slipping from their grasp. In consequence, political alliances built up by these companies in earlier times avail little today. In an era when foreign capital survives on the basis of its indispensability to development strategies pursued by nationalistic leadership groups, colonial companies are doomed.[64]

Such considerations point to the likelihood that the private Peruvian mining bourgeoisie would have acquiesced in the nationalization of Cerro, and that is indeed what happened. Although many of the members of this class element owed their careers and personal wealth to Cerro's presence, they understood that the company had in great measure created its own economic and political problems; they had no desire to be held politically guilty by association in the minds of anti-Cerro nationalists within the government; they had expected far more for themselves from Cerro after the promulgation of the 1950 Mining Code and had been disappointed[65]; and, most of all, they drew a distinction between Cerro as a going enterprise, which was important to them, and as a foreign-owned and -managed enterprise, which was much less so—since they knew that Peruvians were equal to the task of running it. They therefore stood completely aside from the issue of Cerro's future, so long as they were convinced, as they were, that the method of expropriation would not cause conflict with other extranational interests of concern to them (viz., market access and the ability to borrow abroad). It is noteworthy that the National Mining Society took no stand on the expropriation other than to applaud it mildly after the fact, even though Cerro was a founding member and major duespayer. In business, as in politics, past favors never suffice to secure current loyalties; rather, interests are determinant.

The attitude of the mining bourgeoisie in respect to Southern is clearer. This enterprise operates in a completely different economic realm from that of Peruvian mining businesses, which are not yet in a condition to consider operations on its scale. On the other hand, domestic mining capital benefits from the "bonanza" and from anything that increases the salience of the industry in the national economy or generates international financial and consumer interest in Peru as a provider of metals. Thus, the only concerns of local mine operators vis-à-vis Cuajone were that the "bonanza" benefits to Peru be great, that the new contract be written such that later controversy over its terms (which might lessen the prestige of the entire industry) be avoided, and that Southern not receive privileges inordinately greater than theirs. The arrangements reached with the company satisfied them on all counts.

The Military Regime and Domestic Mining Capital

The seven years of Velasco's presidency represent a radical phase of the Peruvian "revolution," marked by an effort on the part of the military regime to destroy the remnants of oligarchic power. Private businesses, some of them Peruvian, were expropriated; the state's role in the economy was vastly enlarged and strengthened; controversial enterprise reforms—mandatory profit sharing, comanagement, "social property"—were introduced.[66] A sector of the local industrial bourgeoisie reacted by mounting vociferous, ideological attacks against the regime for having violated "the sanctity of private property," and by embarking on a virtual "investment strike."[67] At least one analyst regards these events as proof that the Peruvian state had become almost totally autonomous from domestic class forces.[68]

It is therefore noteworthy that relations between the government and the mining bourgeoisie never deteriorated to a comparable extent. The National Mining Society studiously refrained from ideological combat and limited itself to interest representation, a function in which it was quite successful whenever the interests at issue were those of the domestic industry. The reasons for this reserve become clear upon examining the effects of the regime's bonanza development policies on the interests of the mining bourgeoisie. They were overwhelmingly positive.

The government established *ex novo* a parastatal mining enterprise, MineroPeru. Rather than impinging on the interests of domestic private capital in the sector, its mission consisted in the development of areas of the minería that the latter was unable to exploit. It built and now operates refineries for both copper and zinc. Its several large mining concessions were idle ones that were seized from their former, exclusively foreign, owners when they would not agree to develop them actively. It is a firmly capitalist organization, and its management has been drawn from the private sector.

MineroPeru's first mining project, Cerro Verde, has pioneered a radically new hydrometallurgical technology that had never before been used on such a large scale or for the reduction of copper.[69] This important technological advance has added to both the mining bourgeoisie's sense of self-importance and its claim of equality with the international bourgeoisie of the industry. What is more, technological "fallout" from the project promises to be highly useful in the purification of the complex polymetallic ores that are the main product of the domestic mediana minería.

In seeking to enlarge the mining "bonanza," the military regime did not overlook the domestic industry. It was favored by taxation whose burden fell lightly on locally owned firms but much more heavily on foreign-owned ones. The lending authority of the state mining bank, the Banco Minero, was expanded, and the bank was authorized for the first time to extend loans for new project development as well as for bailing out companies in distress.[70] COFIDE made direct capital investments in mining ventures controlled by private Peruvian capital. Before they were applied to the mining sector, the enterprise reforms were modified so that Southern would effectively subsidize profit-sharing in the mediana minería; the modifications also had the effect of greatly delaying the approach of real workers' comanagement. A new state research institute was set up to develop mining and metallurgical technologies, which are offered to the mediana minería at no cost as soon as they are proven.

Reform of the state administration eliminated the formal, corporatist representation that property owners' associations, such as the National Mining Society, used to enjoy. However, that form of representation has simply been replaced by an equally effective (and equally corporatist in practice) informal working relationship between the state and the private sector, based on interests held in common. The National Mining Society is still consulted routinely whenever mining policy or legislation is under discussion. It also works closely with state officials in the gathering and analysis of the economic data on which the government's planning depends. The private sector knows that it need not fear enhanced government oversight of its operations when that oversight relies on data developed by the private sector itself. The cooperative nature of the relationship is attested to by the fact that all of the parastatal mining enterprises have become full voting members of the Mining Society.

Under the military regime, local mining capital was strengthened and consolidated. The seven large, Peruvian-owned corporate groups that were mentioned previously grew enormously during the period of military rule. Between 1967 and 1975, their combined shares of the domestic industry's gross production value, net fixed assets, and paid-up capital increased, respectively, from 46 to 66 percent; from 17 to 66 percent; and from 43 to 66 percent. This growth was almost completely self-financed out of retained corporate reserves. Self-financing, which implies that profits are not distributed as dividends, testifies to the subsidiary position of rentier capital (most of it provided by oligarchic remnants) in the industry. It also bears witness to the fact that in most years, these local enterprises are very profitable; in fact, their earnings performance is fully on a par with, and occasionally exceeds, that of the several foreign-owned medium firms. Throughout the 1968–80 period, in no case did formerly Peruvian mining assets fall under foreign control, but in a number of cases the opposite occurred.

Secure in its managerial control of modern corporate enterprises, in no way subservient to outside money capital, and able to hold its own against foreign competition, the mining-bourgeois class element is well placed to be part of the politically and ideologically leading stratum of the national bourgeoisie. It owes this status to a policy of development that dissected the export sector of the economy into its agroindustrial and mining components, divorced them, and enlisted the latter into a new pro-development coalition with a revitalized capitalist state.

The Military Regime, Bonanza Development, and the
Subordinate Classes

Insofar as they promoted corporate rationalization, managerialism, industrial growth, and the technical reorientation of higher education, the regime's policies of bonanza development fortified the middle class by aggrandizing it in size, salience, and economic rewards,[71] and by opening new avenues for some of its members to ascend into the bourgeoisie proper. The availability of more opportunities for upward mobility, along with the transformation of the bourgeoisie into a class led by manager-technocrats whose power is firmly based on education and expertise, wed the middle class more solidly than ever to the dominant capitalist class. Thus, the latter's exercise of moral and ideological leadership—in Gramsci's terms, its hegemony[72]—was reinforced.

This strengthening of the bourgeoisie and middle class did not come at the expense of working-class living standards. Whereas military industrialization strategies elsewhere have entailed an upward shift of the income distribution in order to enlarge the domestic market for consumer durables,[73] the Peruvian military's bonanza development strategy sought to coopt organized workers with offers of large wage increases. Organized labor in the mines, and especially in the foreign-owned gran minería, was highly effective in winning government support both for its wage demands in the aggregate and for a distribution of raises that improved class solidarity by erasing invidious distinctions that had previously existed among various subgroups of workers. More than that, the regime, hoping to rupture what it mistakenly believed to be strong ties between the labor unions and some political parties of the old order, encouraged the formation of autonomous labor centrals. (Unlike Brazil and Argentina, Peru lacked a tradition of state-controlled unionism, and the regime never felt secure enough to attempt the establishment of such a system.) The unforeseen outcome was the emergence of a stronger labor movement that is less subject than before to manipulation by political elites and more responsive to its members' concerns. Working-class organizational capabilities have also been enhanced by the general expansion of the mining industry that bonanza development has brought about. The more that mining companies are enlarged, rationalized, and "technified," the more the working class approximates to a cohesive, class-conscious, "true" proletariat; the farther removed it becomes from from the anarchic, violence-prone protoproletariat of Cerro's early years[74]; and the more its members acquire technical skills that insulate them somewhat from the downward pressure on wages otherwise exerted by the presence of a large, unskilled "industrial reserve army."

Behind the radical rhetoric of its leaders, however, the working class of the mines is "economistic" in its political behavior. That is, its members show little real concern with either the seizure of state power or the reform of hierarchical structures of social control within corporate enterprise.[75] Working-class formation under bonanza development, therefore, is not of a sort that would place obstacles in the path of bourgeois hegemony—*provided* that the bourgeoisie goes on accommodating as best it can these "economistic" demands.[76] It may be suggested that the working class's improved organizational effectiveness, though falling well short of what would be needed to institute socialism, bodes well for the preservation and extension of democratic institutions within capitalism; for this effectiveness was not achieved by subjecting the members of the class to the hierarchical control of some self-appointed "vanguard." In any event, workers ought not to be blamed—as they are by those radical populists who employ the deprecatory phrase, "labor aristocracy"—for giving primary attention to the goals whose pursuit engenders the least elite resistance.

It is in regard to the peasantry that, in some ways, the effects of bonanza development are most interesting. Without the mining "bonanza," of course, the land reform implemented after 1969 would have been unthinkable: the "bonanza" marginalized landowner interests, eroded the power of the oligarchy, and permitted otherwise "productionist" army officers to contemplate a thoroughgoing agrarian transformation despite the likelihood of a short-term disruption of output.[77] The extensive literature on the Peruvian *reforma agraria* makes plain that, except for an abortive attempt to impose corporatist controls through SINAMOS (the "National Social Mobilization Support System," now defunct), and except on the coastal estates (where capitalist relations of production had been implanted years ago), the reform did not materially advance the capitalization of agriculture and did not impose a new system of social control on a recalcitrant peasantry.[78] Particularly since 1975, the attitude of the military regime and its civilian successor toward the peasantry can best be described as "benign neglect."

In its conception and execution, then, land reform was a political device for destroying oligarchic power and for extending cooptation to the peasantry for the first time.[79] A policy of "benign neglect" is easy to comprehend when it is remembered that the peasantry is in numerical decline (agriculturalists of all sorts now number less than forty percent of the economically active population), and that peasant culture is held in low esteem even by the "cholified" (urban and Westernized) working class and underclass. "Benign neglect" will probably result in the strengthening of a petty-bourgeois smallholder agriculture, the proletarianization of some poorer peasants, and a continuing exodus from the countryside. In the interim it satisfies the age-old peasant desire to be left alone. If the train of populist, peasant-based "socialist" revolution ever came down the Peruvian track, it has passed without stopping. The military's land reform, made possible by bonanza development, assures that there will be no second section to the "populist express."[80]

Bonanza Development, New-Bourgeois Class Formation, and the Nature of Domination in Peru

Class formation relates to the capacity for collective action on the part of structured social groups. An analytical perspective that concerns itself with class formation, as does the one advanced in this chapter, is consequently interested less in determinants of class that merely define a position in a socioeconomic structure than in those that create interests which are amenable to pursuit through collective political action. Furthermore, it regards political power and social control as the fundamental interests of every class, for they are the means by which other privileges and benefits are secured.

We ought not to reify classes; they are analytical constructs, and their only "real" existence is that of the men and women whom the analyst consigns to them. Yet, they are relevant categories for political analysis—because their members tend to form social bonds that incorporate and illuminate their common interests. With the help of such bonds, they unite and pool resources for political action in pursuit of these interests. A dominant class is one whose members are in a position to buttress and enlarge their base of power by reorganizing structures of social and political authority to accord with their needs. Class consolidation of this sort often takes place in the shelter of authoritarianism. But a dominant class truly "arrives" only when it has become hegemonic in the Gramscian sense: when, through a combination of ideological projection and accommodation to minimal subordinate-class material demands and modes of organization, its leading members feel sufficiently secure in their power to dispense with the protection of authoritarian rule.[81]

On the Class Character of Peru's New Bourgeoisie

Nascent bourgeois groups in newly developing countries generally adopt the latest organizational forms, modes of action, and ideologies that capitalism has to offer; they do not try to reinstitute the market capitalism of their forebears in Western Europe and North America.[82] Capitalist development in today's "third world" is usually an adaptation of the late, or "organizational," capitalism that evolved in the West in the postwar era. Chief among the borrowed late-capitalist institutions are the corporate form of business organization, welfare-statism, and government planning of the macroeconomy. Except in avowedly state-socialist systems (and even there, history may hold surprises in store), industrialization leads to the economic supremacy of the corporate form—and, thereby, to the rise of a new-bourgeois class element based in the control of corporate enterprise. This new bourgeoisie is a sub-class of managerial professionals with organizational and technical expertise. It is typified by a distinctive "managerial ideology" that stresses meritocracy (technocratic elitism) in a context of professional values of stewardship and service.[83] One anticipates that the "managerial ideology" will prove more useful for promoting class hegemony than traditional liberal, individualist values, for they have been undermined by both the rise of corporate oligopoly and the revelation that the market is a system of power. In Latin America, moreover, liberal individualism has had to coexist uneasily with a political culture containing many illiberal elements.[84]

The new bourgeoisies of the "third world" are not out to reconstruct society from basement to attic. It therefore seems pointless and ahistorical to stigmatize them as deficient—or "dependent"—for failing to do what they are in any event disinclined to do. Their members, staid corporate professionals rather than idiosyncratic individualists, are not Lockean democrats and do not view state power as a threat to their freedoms, although they may very much want to reorganize it and use it for new ends. To the degree that those ends are affected by the social-private contradiction of capitalism,[85] new-bourgeois class action tries to resolve the contradiction by "technifying" (depoliticizing) the making of authoritative decisions for the collectivity. The clash of interests in the political arena is distrusted; the methodology of administration is favored.

In Peru, the new bourgeoisie is nationalist and developmentalist. Its members have not forgotten how colonialism reserved social and economic privilege to foreigners and their comprador allies in the oligarchy. Their raison d'être, they believe, is industrial growth—especially when, as is true of bonanza development, it is defined as a job for managerial experts. Not coincidentally, industrial development adds to the class's numbers, prestige, and rewards. Yet the norms that underpin the new bourgeoisie are the most universalistic, the least culturally particularistic, of any; hence, it is the most internationally minded of all present-day classes. This is not as contradictory as it seems. By hosting and participating in international economic, scientific, and engineering forums, and by continuing to act as a junior partner in an international market system, the Peruvian new bourgeoisie can advance a claim to equality with the international bourgeoisie of the metropoli, even though its ambition is still far from being realized. What better way to promote that ambition, to incorporate it into the class's national practice, than to press for a controlling role in a process of industrialization?

Transnational Resource Corporations and
Local Class Formation

The resource export "bonanza" was tapped first by ruling elites who understood its political value, even though they were uninterested in industrial development. They opened Peru to transnational resource corporations, which then played a pivotal role in the formation of the country's new bourgeoisie. Its formation, in turn, made bonanza development possible. This sequence of events underscores the fact that local subsidiaries of transnational firms are effective conduits for transmitting the late-capitalist ethos and organizational forms that they embody into host societies. The process of diffusion is not, however, something that the transnationals can simply impose: there is no teaching without willing students. It goes on because domestic socioeconomic groups want it to, for their own reasons. Their interest is proportional to their dependence on corporate institutions for their class position and privileges.

Transnational resource corporations facilitated new-bourgeois class formation in Peru by:

1. Making feasible a strategy of development in which the "bonanza" was coupled to a drive for industrialization—a strategy that attracted important bourgeois elements and the military, separated the interests of the corporate bourgeoisie from those of the oligarchy, and created thereby a new coalition whose concern with industrialization was not compromised by dependence on labor-intensive agriculture;

2. Providing "seed money" and business opportunities that promoted the growth of domestic corporate enterprise;

3. Backing the National Mining Society and helping it to become a more effective institutional representative of mining-bourgeois interests[86];

4. Directly and indirectly encouraging the Peruvian educational system's new emphasis on scientific and technical fields, which ensures the continual renovation of the new bourgeoisie;

5. Creating staff employment opportunities that indoctrinated local citizens in the methods and values of transnational management—an indoctrination that they retained when they transferred to the staffs of domestic private or parastatal firms or to the state administration, or when they went into business for themselves.

A sixth contribution of transnational enterprises was perhaps the most important of all: their mere presence set in motion a redefinition of interests that promoted class consolidation. State elites, who needed both a better working knowledge of the transnationals' modus operandi and better marketing intelligence in order to maximize Peru's share of the "bonanza," recruited into their ranks manager-technocrats from the private sector who possessed the requisite expertise. By this means, and by their establishment of parastatal corporations under solidly new-bourgeois managerial control, they advanced the embourgeoisment of the state. Domestic industrialists, meanwhile, finding themselves in need of an ally to protect them against the transnationals' monopolistic tendencies, began to seek out the protection that only an economically active state could offer. Their need was great enough to erode any residual ideological sympathy that they might have harbored for the oligarchic practice of laissez-faire.

New-Bourgeois Class Consolidation

In Peru, as elsewhere, the ascent of the new bourgeoisie takes the form of an organizational revolution, a restructuring of the *institutions* of power and control that stops short of changing their *class content*. An organizational revolution may entail the displacement of an old dominant class stratum. Alternatively, an old dominant stratum of moneyed elites may simply be overwhelmed and absorbed. The Peruvian new bourgeoisie has incorporated oligarchic money capital into its enterprises. However, money capital is subservient to the managerial "knowledge capital" that controls corporate hierarchies. Since by 1968 the oligarchic aspects of Peruvian capitalism were rapidly decaying of their own accord, the full emergence of the new bourgeoisie required no more than a reorganization of state authority to institutionalize its dominance. The military, which shared core interests and had ideological affinities with the new bourgeoisie but which in addition had the advantage of a presence within the state apparatus, was the logical group to lead that reorganization of authority. It did so as the ally of the rising dominant class, not as some "autonomous" entity standing outside the interplay of class forces.

Although Peru's epoch of bonanza development is surely over,[87] the new system of domination shows signs of being able to outlive it. In the two general elections and two municipal elections since the end of military rule in 1980, the public has demonstrated its belief in the present political order and its rejection of non-constitutional revolutionary alternatives. The new bourgeoisie was prominent among the social forces that began pressing in the late 1970s for the reinstitution of civilian governance; in the 1985 general election it offered important financial support to the campaign of the reformist alternative represented by the APRA party and its successful candidate, Alan García Pérez.[88] It would therefore appear that the new-bourgeois ideology of managerialism, nationalism-developmentalism, and the ideal of "equality of opportunity" (the last operationalized as meritocracy and as a real increase in upward mobility chances) is efficacious in securing the hegemony of the dominant class, even in the present period of great economic stress. The recent political behavior of the new bourgeoisie suggests a self-confident dominant class, capable of dispensing with authoritarian props.

While these are progressive developments, dedicated democrats would do well to regard them with an element of reserve. In the economic realm the dominant class faces the difficult task of continuing the country's economic development without the aid of an export "bonanza"; this will require the deepening of social reforms, the reactivation of agriculture, and the restructuring of the industrial economy to make it less dependent on imported inputs and more capable of competing internationally through exports of manufactured goods. In the political realm the chief uncertainty is that the new bourgeoisie's idea of democracy is not popular participation but "democratic elitism," in which participatory forms serve mainly for legitimation while real authority is exercised by technocratic elites. Even that interest is instrumental rather than moral.[89] The new bourgeoisie supports democracy only insofar as it is useful—a more efficient and less costly means of maintaining control than political repression.

Nevertheless, this study has shown that the Peruvian new bourgeoisie has undergone a process of class consolidation from which it has emerged as a leading element of a local dominant class. Thus, despite its manifest economic weakness, Peru cannot be described as a "dependent" country or a "neocolony" in any political sense. The proof of that thesis lies in the new bourgeoisie's successful use of state power for its own chief purposes: controlling relations with foreign investors so that these promote industrial development without preempting present or foreseeable future business opportunities that the class hopes to take advantage of; and assisting the class to secure its hegemony and maintain its social control.

Remaining to be investigated is the question of whether the form of class domination that has evolved in Peru is a general product of bonanza development; or whether, on the contrary, it should be attributed to the singular features of bonanza development in this one country. It also remains to be seen how, if at all, the Peruvian form of class domination differs from those produced by other strategies of development practiced in the "third world." An accumulation of additional case studies should enable us to approach the answers. But in the interim the following proposition may be advanced with reasonable confidence: The appearance in even a few newly developing countries of a form of *local* class domination that is potentially hegemonic and that does not require the protection of authoritarian governance is a thorough refutation of certain radical dependency theories of class— namely, those theories which are grounded in assumptions regarding systemic "laws" of international capitalism, and those which derive political dependency solely from the fact of economic exploitation.

Notes

Funding for the field research portion of this study was provided by a Fulbright-Hayes Dissertation Research Abroad Fellowship awarded by the U.S. Department of Health, Education, and Welfare, Office of Education.

1. Richard L. Sklar, *Corporate Power in an African State* (Berkeley and Los Angeles: University of California Press, 1975), p. 175.

2. See Fernando Henrique Cardoso, "The Consumption of Dependency Theory in the United States," *Latin American Research Review* 12, 3 (1977):7–24; also Gabriel Palma, "Dependency: A Formal Theory of Underdevelopment or a Methodology for the Analysis of Concrete Situations of Underdevelopment?" *World Development* 6, 7–8 (1978):881–924.

3. The literature on dependency is vast; to do justice to it would require a far lengthier bibliography than can be reproduced here. Thus, with apologies for incompleteness: Dependency ideas are reviewed historically by Joseph A. Kahl, *Modernization, Exploitation, and Dependency in Latin America* (New Brunswick, NJ: Transaction, 1976); and by Palma, "Dependency" (which is especially useful for its treatment of the relationship between dependency and Marxism). The highest development of the dependency approach, it is often said, is found in Fernando Henrique Cardoso, "Dependency and Development in Latin America," *New Left Review*, 74 (1972):83–95; also Cardoso and Enzo Faletto, *Dependency and Development in Latin America*, trans. Marjory Mattingly Urquidi (Berkeley and Los Angeles: University of California Press, 1979), esp. the authors' preface to the English language edition, pp. vii–xxv. Critical reviews of the literature include James A. Caporaso, "Dependence, Dependency, and Power in the Global System: A Structural Analysis," *International Organization* 32, 1 (1978):13–43; Caporaso and Behrouz Zare, "An Interpretation and Evaluation of Dependency Theory," in Heraldo Muñoz (ed.), *From Dependency to Development* (Boulder, CO: Westview Press, 1981), pp. 43–56; Tony Smith, "The Underdevelopment of Development Literature: The Case of Dependency Theory," *World Politics* 31, 2 (1979):247–288; Philip J. O'Brien, "A Critique of Latin American Theories of Dependency," in Ivar Oxaal, Tony Barnett, and David Booth (eds.), *Beyond the Sociology of Development* (London: Routledge & Kegan Paul, 1975), pp. 7–27; and Anthony Brewer, *Marxist Theories of Imperialism* (London: Routledge & Kegan Paul, 1980), pp. 158–257, 274–294. Colin Henfrey, "Dependency, Modes of Production, and the Class Analysis of Latin America," *Latin American Perspectives* 8, 3–4 (1981):17–54, argues that the dependency approach has thus far lacked a suitable class analysis; see also Manuel Castells, "Class, State and Dependency in Latin America: Some Theoretical Guidelines," paper presented at the Joint Meeting of the African Studies Association and the Latin American Studies Association, Houston, November 1977 (mimeographed).

4. As does, e.g., Theotonio Dos Santos, "The Structure of Dependence," *American Economic Review* 60, 2 (1970):231–236; for him, dependency is "a situation in which the economy of certain countries is conditioned by the development and expansion of another economy to which the former is subjected" (p. 231). Cardoso and Faletto, *Dependency and Development*, claim to have eschewed that kind of approach. But for them, too, dependency derives from an abstract

structural feature of international capitalism: the imputed need of newly developing countries, due to their lack of capital goods production and technological capabilities, to articulate their economies with the international system in order "to complete the cycle of capital reproduction" (see pp. xx–xxii).

5. Class analysis, unlike elite analysis, deals in a systematic way with the explication of political change as an outcome of relations of power and conflict in society. See James A. Bill and Robert L. Hardgrave, Jr., *Comparative Politics: The Quest for Theory* (Columbus, OH: Merrill, 1973), pp. 195–199; also Richard L. Sklar, "On the Concept of Power in Political Economy," in Dalmas H. Nelson and Richard L. Sklar (eds.), *Toward a Humanistic Science of Politics: Essays in Honor of Francis Dunham Wormuth* (Lanham, MD: University Press of America, 1983), pp. 179–206.

6. Antonio Gramsci, *Selections from the Prison Notebooks* (New York: International Publishers, 1971), pp. 55–60 and passim; Joseph V. Femia, "The Gramsci Phenomenon: Some Reflections," *Political Studies* 27, 3 (1979):472–483; and Walter L. Adamson, *Hegemony and Revolution: Antonio Gramsci's Political and Cultural Theory* (Berkeley and Los Angeles: University of California Press, 1980), pp. 170–179 and passim.

7. On this point see Eugene F. Sofer, "Recent Trends in Latin American Labor Historiography," *Latin American Research Review* 15, 1 (1980):167–176; also Henfrey, "Dependency, Modes of Production."

8. André Gunder Frank, "The Development of Underdevelopment," *Monthly Review* 18, 4 (1966):17–31; *Capitalism and Underdevelopment in Latin America: Historical Studies of Chile and Brazil,* rev. ed. (New York: Monthly Review Press, 1969); and *Lumpenbourgeoisie: Lumpendevelopment: Dependence, Class, and Politics in Latin America,* trans. Marion Davis Berdecio (New York: Monthly Review Press, 1973).

9. Fernando Henrique Cardoso, "Associated-Dependent Development: Theoretical and Practical Implications," in Alfred Stepan (ed.), *Authoritarian Brazil* (New Haven: Yale University Press, 1973), pp. 142–176.

10. Dos Santos, "The Structure of Dependence."

11. Osvaldo Sunkel, "Transnational Capitalism and National Disintegration in Latin America," *Social and Economic Studies* 22, 1 (1973):132–176.

12. Guillermo A. O'Donnell, *Modernization and Bureaucratic-Authoritarianism: Studies in South American Politics* (Berkeley: Institute of International Studies, University of California, 1973); "Reflections on the Patterns of Change in the Bureaucratic-Authoritarian State," *Latin American Research Review* 13, 1 (1978):3–38; and "Tensions in the Bureaucratic-Authoritarian State and the Question of Democracy," in David Collier (ed.), *The New Authoritarianism in Latin America* (Princeton: Princeton University Press, 1979), pp. 285–318.

13. V.I. Lenin, *Imperialism, the Highest Stage of Capitalism* (New York: International Publishers, 1933); and Paul A. Baran, *The Political Economy of Growth* (New York: Monthly Review, 1957), esp. pp. 178–200. Among the recent writings in the same vein are Heraldo Muñoz, "The Strategic Dependency of the Centers and the Importance of the Latin American Periphery," in Muñoz (ed.), *From Dependency to Development* (fn. 3), pp. 59–92; many of the contributions to

Anne Seidman (ed.), *Natural Resources and National Welfare: The Case of Copper* (New York: Praeger, 1975); Norman Girvan, "Multinational Corporations and Dependent Underdevelopment in Mineral-Exporting Economies," *Social and Economic Studies* 19, 4 (1970):490–526; and on Peru, Claes Brundenius, "The Anatomy of Imperialism: The Case of Multinational Mining Corporations in Peru," *Journal of Peace Research* 9, 3 (1972):189–206.

14. See, for example, Julio Cotler, "State and Regime: Comparative Notes on the Southern Cone and the 'Enclave' Societies," in Collier (ed.), *New Authoritarianism* (fn. 12), pp. 255–282).

15. The term "new bourgeoisie" has been used in Latin American studies with reference to entrepreneurial groups that arose in the 1930s on the basis of import-substitution industrialization and that later suffered a "hegemonic crisis"; see José Nun, *Latin America: The Hegemonic Crisis and the Military Coup* (Berkeley: Institute of International Studies, University of California, 1973). In my usage, however, the term always refers to a class stratum whose power stems ultimately from specialized knowledge gained through education and proximately from control of the economic hierarchies embodied in modern business corporations. It excludes "middle management" and other middle-class professionals, who lack the power "to formulate and implement strategies for solving problems and achieving goals" at the level of the whole society.

16. David G. Becker, *The New Bourgeoisie and the Limits of Dependency* (Princeton: Princeton University Press, 1983); and "Modern Mine Labour and Politics in Peru since 1968," *Boletín de Estudios Latinoamericanos y del Caribe*, 32 (1982):35–60. There is no implication in the foregoing that capitalist development in Peru or elsewhere is equitable or just. Capitalism can survive and has, without the protection of coercive force, even though it is neither. I am, however, calling into question the populist belief that socioeconomic evils would disappear were "foreign domination" to be broken.

17. On the former see Sayre P. Schatz, *Nigerian Capitalism* (Berkeley and Los Angeles: University of California Press, 1977); on the latter, Sklar, *Corporate Power*.

18. Sklar, "Postimperialism" (ch. 2, this volume); and "Socialism at Bay: Class Domination in Africa," paper presented at the Joint Meeting of the African Studies Association and the Latin American Studies Association, Houston, November 1977 (mimeographed).

19. Becker, *New Bourgeoisie*, p. 13, emphasis in original.

20. "Colonialism," the domination of one people or nation by another, adequately describes both the bulk of official U.S. action in Latin America since 1898 and the activities of certain U.S. business firms, especially in the prewar period and in the agricultural sectors of the Central American economies. This is so whether or not direct political control was established. I want to avoid the use of "neocolonialism" to distinguish these activities from the formal colonial domination practiced by other powers—partly because the difference is not greatly significant, partly because the latter term has been appropriated as a quasi-synonym for dependency.

21. Consider, e.g., the heavy foreign shareholding in such "U.S." resource firms as AMAX, Asarco, and Newmont Mining, the first two of which

list their shares on both the New York and London exchanges; the ambiguous nationality of Kennecott Copper, now owned by British Petroleum through Standard Oil of Ohio; and the several important African, Asian, and Australian joint mining ventures that have brought together American, European, and Japanese partners. The international nonferrous metals industries are examined in Becker, *New Bourgeoisie,* pp. 72–92.

22. Raymond F. Mikesell, *The World Copper Industry* (Baltimore: Johns Hopkins University Press, 1975), pp. 271–281 and passim; Mikesell, "Mining Agreements and Conflict Resolution," in Sandro Sideri and Sheridan Johns (eds.), *Mining for Development in the Third World* (New York: Pergamon, 1980), pp. 198–209; Marian Radetzki, "LDC Policies Towards Foreign Mineral Investors," in Sideri and Johns (eds.), pp. 283–296; and Stephen Zorn, "Recent Trends in LDC Mining Agreements," in Sideri and Johns (eds.), pp. 210–228.

23. Sklar, *Corporate Power,* pp. 182–188 and passim. Sklar goes further still, contending that the doctrine of domicile counsels the subsidiary's compliance even in matters of regional foreign policy that run counter to the policies of other states in whose countries the corporation does business; subsidiaries in each of those other countries, meanwhile, defer to the policy preferences of *their* host government.

24. The case of petroleum needs no comment. In the case of nonferrous metals, Peruvian terms of trade vary irregularly with world prices; data adduced by E.V.K. FitzGerald, *The State and Economic Development: Peru since 1968* (Cambridge: Cambridge University Press, 1976), p. 14, show an improvement in Peruvian terms of trade between 1960 and 1972. (Admittedly, its terms of trade have since become highly adverse, but there is no reason to assume that the current depression of world nonferrous metal prices will be permanent.) On the theory of declining terms of trade in the "third world," see Raúl Prebisch, *Towards a Dynamic Development Policy for Latin America* (New York: United Nations, 1963).

25. Bonanza development's nonreliance on low-cost, coerced labor raises serious questions about Immanuel Wallerstein's analytical framework, in which the prevalence of coerced labor in key economic sectors is a major criterion of "peripheral" status in the "world-system." See Wallerstein, *The Modern World-System* (New York: Academic Press, 1974); and "The Rise and Future Demise of the World Capitalist System: Concepts for Comparative Analysis," *Comparative Studies in Society and History* 16, 4 (1974):387–415. See also the critiques offered by Ernesto Laclau, "Feudalism and Capitalism in Latin America," *New Left Review,* 67 (1971):19–38; and by Robert Brenner, "The Origins of Capitalist Development: A Critique of Neo-Smithian Marxism," *New Left Review,* 104 (1977):25–92.

26. Foreign investment in minerals extraction need not have originated with the adoption of a strategy of bonanza development by the host government. In many cases such investments were first made during an earlier colonial epoch, without reference to the desires of the host. But once national independence has been attained and bonanza development instituted, existing foreign investment comes to serve new purposes and interests. Old institutional relationships between it and the host country are then modified accordingly.

27. See Osvaldo Sunkel, "National Development Policy and External Dependence in Latin America," *Journal of Development Studies* 6, 1 (1969):23–48, esp. p. 30.

28. On the Marxian concept of "relative autonomy," see Ralph Miliband, *The State in Capitalist Society* (New York: Basic books, 1969), esp. pp. 68–118; and David A. Gold, Clarence Y.H. Lo, and Erik Olin Wright, "Recent Developments in Marxist Theories of the Capitalist State," *Monthly Review* 27, 5 (1975):29–43, and 27, 6 (1975):36–51.

29. Bill Warren, "Imperialism and Capitalist Industrialization," *New Left Review*, 81 (1973):3–44.

30. Alvin W. Gouldner, *The Future of Intellectuals and the Rise of the New Class* (New York: Seabury Press, 1979).

31. Richard L. Sklar, "Lectures on Socialism and Development," unpublished draft, n.d. (mimeographed).

32. This may be true of post-Maoist China; it remains to be seen whether bonanza development can be adapted to socialist ends, or whether it invariably sets the nation selecting it onto the capitalist road.

33. My computation, from data in John W. Wilkie and Peter Reich (eds.), *Statistical Abstract of Latin America Vol. 20* (Los Angeles: UCLA Latin American Center, 1980), p. 219. For a general discussion of the Peruvian economy since the onset of industrialization, see E.V.K. FitzGerald, *The State and Economic Development*; and his *The Political Economy of Peru, 1956–78* (Cambridge: Cambridge University Press, 1979).

34. See, e.g., Osvaldo Sunkel, "Big Business and 'Dependencia': A Latin American View," *Foreign Affairs* 50, 3 (1972):517–531.

35. Adolf A. Berle, Jr. and Gardiner C. Means, *The Modern Corporation and Private Property* (New York: Macmillan, 1932).

36. Shane Hunt, "Growth and Guano in the Nineteenth Century in Peru," working paper, Woodrow Wilson School of Public and International Affairs, Princeton University, 1973 (mimeographed); Heraclio Bonilla, *Guano y burguesía en el Perú* (Lima: Instituto de Estudios Peruanos, 1974); Julio Cotler, *Clases, Estado y nación en el Perú* (Lima: Instituto de Estudios Peruanos, 1978), pp. 85–114.

37. Peru's *oligarquía* was a closed elite comprised of three somewhat distinct class elements: owners of coastal plantations, who were agroindustrial, export-oriented capitalists; *hacendados* of the interior highlands, whose economic behavior was not unlike that of a precapitalist landed class; and a Lima "plutocracy," whose considerable wealth derived mostly from rentier investment. See François Bourricaud, *Poder y sociedad en el Perú contemporáneo* (Buenos Aires: Editorial Sur, 1967), esp. pp. 194–203; also Magali Sarfatti Larson and Adele Eisen Bergen, *Social Stratification in Peru* (Berkeley: Institute of International Studies, University of California, 1969).

38. The 1901 Code extended financial incentives (including a fifteen-year tax holiday) and reformed concession tenure to accord better with the interests of capital. Previously, underground minerals were the property of the state, in the Spanish tradition, although private individuals could obtain grants of concessionary rights. Concession tenure was contingent on regular royalty payments to the state and could be revoked at any time. The 1901 Code ap-

proached privatization by providing for concessions to be held in perpetuity, subject only to payment of a small annual ground rent. See W.F.C. Purser, *Metal-Mining in Peru, Past and Present* (New York: Praeger, 1971), pp. 54–55; also Mario Samamé Boggio, *Minería peruana: biografía y estrategia de una actividad decisiva*, 2d ed., 2 vols. (Lima: Editorial Gráfica Labor, 1974), 1:202–203.

39. Julio Cotler, "The Mechanics of Internal Domination and Social Change in Peru," in David Chaplin (ed.), *Peruvian Nationalism* (New Brunswick NJ: Transaction, 1976), pp. 35–71 (esp. pp. 55–57).

40. See, e.g., James L. Payne, *Labor and Politics in Peru* (New Haven: Yale University Press, 1965), pp. 48–50.

41. Southern's ownership is today distributed as follows: Asarco, 52.3 percent; the Marmon Group of Chicago, which in 1975 bought what was left of Cerro, 21 percent; Newmont Mining, 10.4 percent; and the Phelps-Dodge Corporation, 16.3 percent. Billiton N.V. of the Netherlands, a subsidiary of Royal Dutch/Shell, owns 11.5 percent of Southern's newest mine. The story of Southern's origins is an intriguing tale of corporate maneuver; see Becker, *New Bourgeoisie*, pp. 36–38.

42. Raymond F. Mikesell, *Foreign Investment in Copper Mining: Case Studies of Mines in Peru and Papua New Guinea* (Baltimore: Johns Hopkins University Press, 1975), pp. 48–51.

43. Several writers have interpreted these business connections as meaning that the Peruvian medium firms were "directly or indirectly" controlled by Cerro; see Henrique Espinosa Uriarte and José Osorio, "Dependencia y poder económico: caso minería y pesquería," in Espinosa Uriarte et al., *Dependencia económica y tecnológica: caso peruano* (Lima: Centro de Investigaciones Sociales, Universidad Nacional Federico Villarreal, 1971), pp. 69–230; and Brundenius, "Anatomy of Imperialism." In Becker, *New Bourgeoisie*, pp. 174–175, I have criticized their conclusions on the ground that their concept of control is fatally flawed.

44. Alfred Stepan, *The State and Society: Peru in Comparative Perspective* (Princeton: Princeton University Press, 1978), pp. 3–45.

45. Luigi R. Einaudi and Alfred C. Stepan III, *Latin American Institutional Development: Changing Military Perspectives in Brazil and Peru* (Santa Monica, CA: RAND Corporation, 1971), R-586-DOS, esp. pp. 16–31; Einaudi, "Revolution from Within? Military Rule in Peru since 1968," in Chaplin (ed.), *Peruvian Nationalism* (fn. 39), pp. 401–427; George Philip, "The Soldier as Radical: The Peruvian Military Government, 1968–1975," *Journal of Latin American Studies* 8, 1 (1976):29–51; Liisa North and Tanya Korovkin, *The Peruvian Revolution and the Officers in Power, 1967–1976* (Montréal: Centre for Developing-Area Studies, McGill University, 1981). The attempt to integrate the long-neglected peasantry into the economic and political life of the nation, from which it had been rigidly excluded during the entire period of oligarchic domination, is the sort of action that justifies the use of the term "organizational revolution" to describe the character of the military regime.

46. His political sympathies had been formed in the classrooms of CAEM, the Center for Higher Military Studies. On its key role in the ideological formation of Peruvian officers and in the "revolution" of 1968, see Einaudi and Stepan,

Latin American Institutional Development; and Víctor Villanueva, *El CAEM y la Revolución de la Fuerza Armada* (Lima: Instituto de Estudios Peruanos, 1972).

47. Brundenius, "Anatomy of Imperialism," repeats most of these charges; see also José C. Bossio Rotundo, "Cambios en la política minero-metalúrgica," in Ernst-J. Kerbusch (ed.), *Cambios estructurales en el Perú* (Lima: Instituto Latinoamericano de Investigaciones Sociales, 1976), pp. 121–144, esp. p. 126.

48. According to the best available accounts, in 1974 some hard-line, Rightist army generals had gained the ear of the ailing Velasco and sought to consolidate their power by easing out the "progressives" such as Fernández Maldonado. Knowing that he had firmly opposed the nationalization of Marcona, they waited until he was on an extended tour abroad to urge that action on the president. Their aim was twofold: to tap radical nationalist support for their own rise to power, and to weaken Fernández Maldonado's position by loosening his hold over mining policy and confronting him with the choice of either repudiating his own policy or opposing the president. Upon his return to Peru he went along with the decision in public, albeit with a notable lack of enthusiasm. He later retaliated by lending his support to Velasco's ouster in 1975; however, within a year the new president, Gen. Morales Bermúdez, had forced him into retirement. Because its expropriation was so exceptional, the Marcona case will not be discussed further.

49. The company had wire, cable, and brass manufacturing subsidiaries in the United States. But there was no match between output of one stage of production and the input requirements of the next; the U.S. subsidiaries customarily purchased raw copper on the open market, while copper and other nonferrous metals produced in Peru were sold mostly to unaffiliated buyers in Europe. Cerro's share of the European market for these metals was less than five percent in every year between 1960 and 1970.

50. On Cerro's sorry record in the area of labor relations, see Heraclio Bonilla, *El minero de los Andes: una aproximación a su estudio* (Lima: Instituto de Estudios Peruanos, 1974); Alberto Flores Galindo, *Los mineros de la Cerro de Pasco, 1900–1930 (un intento de caracterización social)* (Lima: Departamento Académico de Ciencias Sociales, Pontificia Universidad Católica del Perú, 1974); and Dirk Kruijt and Menno Vellinga, *Labor Relations and Multinational Corporations: The Cerro de Pasco Corporation in Peru (1902–1974)* (Assen, Neth.: Van Gorcum, 1979), pp. 58–98.

51. Susan C. Bourque and David Scott Palmer, "Transforming the Rural Sector: Government Policy and Peasant Response," in Abraham F. Lowenthal (ed.), *The Peruvian Experiment* (Princeton: Princeton University Press, 1975), pp. 197–219; and Colin Harding, "Land Reform and Social Conflict in Peru," in Lowenthal (ed.), pp. 220–253.

52. That is, one in which the company incurred fines and liabilities sufficient to offset most of what it would otherwise be owed by way of compensation.

53. For further detail, see Becker, *New Bourgeoisie*, pp. 148–155.

54. Cerro made a cash profit on the transaction, thanks to writeoffs on its U.S. income taxes. But any claim that it benefited from the nationalization cannot be sustained. The truncated Cerro Corporation could not fight off an "un-

friendly" takeover by the Marmon Group. The first act of the new owners was to oust the entire Cerro management team, which was rightly held responsible for massive errors of judgment leading up to the expropriation fiasco.

55. Except for the United States. American banks' investments, in Eurodollars, were made solely for the interest income.

56. See Theodore H. Moran, "Transnational Strategies of Protection and Defense by Multinational Corporations: Spreading the Risk and Raising the Cost for Nationalization in Natural Resources," *International Organization* 27, 2 (1973):273–287. What Moran shows, however, is not that this "insurance" can prevent nationalization but, rather, that it can compel the payment of compensation.

57. Rumors of external pressure are bruited by Paul Sigmund, *Multinationals in Latin America* (Madison,WI: University of Wisconsin Press, 1980), p. 200; and by FitzGerald, *Political Economy of Peru*, p. 111; cf. Becker, *New Bourgeoisie*, pp. 112–122, where an analysis of hitherto secret files of the Ministry of Energy and Mines shows that these rumors are without foundation.

58. Prices are based on open-market quotations, but they apply only to refined metals. When the product is unrefined metallic copper, the buyer deducts a refining charge from the open-market price. These charges, however, are arrived at by private negotiation. Thus, unless the government has an independent means of verifying whether reported refining charges are fair and justified by processing costs, there is always the possibility that the producer might manipulate them in order to shift profits out of the country.

59. Sigmund, *Multinationals*, pp. 22–23.

60. Stepan, *State and Society*, pp. 230–289.

61. Also see Sayre P. Schatz's parallel discussion of bargaining dynamics, especially his concept of "self-fulfilling aspiration growth," in ch. 5 of this volume.

62. The acid test of the doctrine, one that Sklar applies in *Corporate Power,* is whether the subsidiary complies in matters of regional foreign policy that run counter to the policies of other states in which the corporation has operations (fn. 23). No such test was possible in the Peruvian case, since Peru is not currently embroiled in a political conflict with another state in which Southern's parents have major investments. However, Sigmund, *Multinationals in Latin America,* notes (pp. 7–23 and passim) that U.S. foreign economic policy has consistently fought the idea embodied in the Calvo Doctrine, that foreign investment should be governed solely by the laws and customs of the host state. Southern's acceptance of a "Calvo clause" in its Cuajone contract thus supports a Peruvian foreign policy objective that contradicts an objective of the company's home government. On the other hand, Asarco, as a company with major smelting and refining operations in the United States, was among the copper producers that recently (1983–84) petitioned the U.S. International Trade Commission for tariff protection against imported copper—a petition that, if it had been approved, would have struck hard at a fundamental Peruvian economic interest. But there is no contradiction here. For in the ITC action, Asarco was also acting in accordance with the doctrine of domicile: as a "good corporate citizen" of the United States, it has a duty to concern itself (insofar as

profitability allows) with the job security and welfare of its U.S. employees.

63. The appellation "colonial company" is particularly justified in Cerro's case by its status as an *hacendado*. I suggest that colonial companies are the real objects of Baran's bitter criticism of foreign resource firms in the "third world"; see Baran, *Political Economy of Growth,* pp. 197–198.

64. It does not follow that technological prowess and solid finances are always sufficient to protect a transnational mining firm against expropriation; obviously, the Chilean example—see Theodore H. Moran, *Multinational Corporations and the Politics of Dependence* (Princeton: Princeton University Press, 1974)—proves otherwise. Still, nationalization occurred in Chile for the same reason argued here: the subsidiaries were no longer able to supply the host country with indispensable bonanza development benefits that it could not provide for itself. The lesson seems to be that, at a suitably advanced stage, direct transnational participation in bonanza development is self-extinguishing; it is plain that the "bonanza" cannot be enlarged forever, and that in technologically stable industries like mining, foreign managements will not always have something to teach to local citizens. Nonetheless, the bonanza development phase of capitalist development in the "third world" will remain relevant for years to come. Of the newly developing countries that appear to be following bonanza development strategies, only Mexico, which combines a high level of industrialization with a strong indigenous tradition in natural resources exploitation, seems to be approaching the point of self-extinguishment.

65. Peruvian mine owners had wanted Cerro to build a zinc refinery that might eventually purchase zinc ores—a principal product of the mediana minería—from them. It did so, but its planning was very conservative; even with later expansions, the facility was never able to absorb the output of Cerro's own mines. The long-standing desire for a domestic zinc refinery is documented by Samamé Boggio, *Minería peruana,* pp. 437–473.

66. These and other reforms are discussed by Peter T. Knight, "New Forms of Economic Organization in Peru: Toward Workers' Self-Management," in Lowenthal (ed.), *The Peruvian Experiment* (fn. 51), pp. 350–401; David W. Pearson, "The Comunidad Industrial: Peru's Experiment in Worker Management," *Inter-American Economic Affairs* 27, 1 (1973):15–29; and Evelyne Huber Stephens, *The Politics of Workers' Participation* (New York: Academic Press, 1980).

67. Henry Pease García, *El ocaso del poder oligárquico* (Lima: DESCO, 1977), pp. 71–122. The evidence suggests that the bourgeois protestors were overwhelmingly small manufacturers, whose businesses were personally owned and whose operations were geared to the domestic market.

68. Thomas Bamat, "Relative State Autonomy and Capitalism in Brazil and Peru," *The Insurgent Sociologist* 7, 2 (1977):74–84. But Bamat maintains that this autonomy served only to make the state still more dependent on foreign capital.

69. This achievement was wholly Peruvian. Foreign technology is present only in some purchased equipment, which was bought piecemeal and integrated into the system by Peruvian engineers.

70. Only domestic firms may draw on the resources of the Banco Minero. Until this extension of its functions, the bank was limited to making small loans for working capital.

71. FitzGerald, *Political Economy of Peru*, pp. 140–141, shows that during these years Peru's income distribution shifted in favor of the middle deciles—something not seen in any of the other major countries of the region. My data (Becker, *New Bourgeoisie*, p. 243) indicate that middle-class employment in the mining sector approximately doubled between 1970 and 1978.

72. See fn. 6.

73. The argument has been made most tellingly in the case of Brazil; see Thomas E. Skidmore, "Politics and Economic Policy Making in Authoritarian Brazil, 1937–71," in Stepan (ed.), *Authoritarian Brazil* (fn. 9), pp. 3–46.

74. Kruijt and Vellinga, *Labor Relations and Multinational Corporations*, pp. 58–66, 164–199.

75. David G. Becker, "The Workers of the Modern Mines in Southern Peru: Socio-Economic Change and Trade-Union Militancy in the Rise of a Labor Elite," in Thomas Greaves and William Culver (eds.), *Miners and Mining in the Americas* (Manchester, Eng.: University of Manchester Press, 1986), pp. 226–256.

76. Workers' purchasing power has recently fallen drastically, the combined result of low world metals prices and a very high rate of domestic inflation. In my view, however, the system of domination should be able to contain workers' complaints so long as the mining companies' balance sheets do not show grand profits, and so long as their difficulties can plausibly be attributed to external conditions beyond the control of the companies or of any Peruvian government. "Containment," in this sense, means forestalling a direct proletarian challenge to the existing socioeconomic and political order; it does not mean that there will be no labor unrest, or that strikes will be unmarred by violent incidents.

77. In fact, per capita food production has fallen well below the already marginally adequate levels of the mid-1960s.

78. Cynthia McClintock, *Peasant Cooperatives and Political Change in Peru* (Princeton: Princeton University Press, 1981); and Adolfo Figueroa, *Capitalist Development and the Peasant Economy in Peru* (Cambridge: Cambridge University Press, 1984).

79. The reform was also intended to spur industrialization by enabling the peasantry at large to enter the money economy and, thereby, to become potential consumers of locally manufactured goods.

80. Among those left behind on the platform are the radical populists of the Sendero Luminoso movement, who, though capable of spilling enough blood and destroying enough property to make a still-fragile order tremble, cannot hope to bring it down.

81. See Sklar, "Socialism at Bay." Unlike a ruling caste or a closed, oligarchic elite, a large and diverse dominant class such as the bourgeoisie needs a political form that can reconcile (or mediate among) its members' various parochial interests, so that the long-range interest of the class as a whole

emerges. Every authoritarianism has a built-in tendency toward partiality that can endanger class cohesiveness and obscure this long-range interest.

82. Alexander Gerschenkron, *Economic Backwardness in Historical Perspective* (Cambridge: Belknap Press, Harvard University Press, 1962).

83. Magali Sarfatti Larson, *The Rise of Professionalism* (Berkeley and Los Angeles: University of California Press, 1977), pp. 220–232; and Koula Mellos, "Developments in Advanced Capitalist Ideology," *Canadian Journal of Political Science* 11, 4 (1978):829–860 (see esp. pp. 837–838, 844ff). On "managerial ideology" in Peru, see Alberto García de Romana, "Comportamiento gremial y político de los empresarios industriales, 1968–73," Taller de Estudios Urbano-Industriales, Pontificia Universidad Católica del Perú, 1975 (mimeographed).

84. Howard J. Wiarda, "Toward a Framework for the Study of Political Change in the Iberic-Latin Tradition: The Corporative Model," *World Politics* 25, 2 (1973):206–235.

85. See Sayre P. Schatz's discussion in ch. 7 of this volume.

86. Which, as is shown by its failure to involve itself on the side of the transnationals in their disputes with the government, did not make it subservient to its foreign patrons.

87. International metal and petroleum prices have fallen so low that hard-currency earnings from export sales of these products no longer suffice to meet the country's import demand; no price upturn is likely any time soon, nor is there on the horizon a new resource export "bonanza" that might make up the deficit.

88. Suffrage in Peru is universal and mandatory for all those over eighteen years of age, including illiterates. Consequently, the outcomes of the elections since 1980—in all of which the total of blank and spoiled ballots has been quite small despite a rather complicated voting procedure—must be taken as reflecting real popular preferences. The general election of 1985 not only resulted in a thoroughgoing change from Fernando Belaúnde's neoliberalism to García's nationalist reformism; it also marked the first time since 1912 that one freely elected national government succeeded another.

89. On the nature of the modern bourgeois interest in political democracy, see Bob Jessop, "Capitalism and Democracy: The Best Possible Political Shell?" in Gary Littlejohn et al. (eds.), *Power and the State* (New York: St. Martin's, 1978), pp. 10–51.

CHAPTER FIVE

Assertive Pragmatism and the Multinational Enterprise

SAYRE P. SCHATZ

Given the sheer volume of writing on multinational enterprises (MNEs), the wide range of opinion on most facets of the subject, and the passion with which contending positions are asserted, one feels a need for a guide through the embattled, and changing, terrain. This chapter proposes a simple conceptual framework, focusing on the impact of MNEs on developing host countries; it submits a brief for one of the approaches delineated in that framework; and it suggests that a process of convergence toward such an approach is under way.

Despite the considerable oversimplification involved, it is useful to distinguish three main approaches to MNEs. Of course, any taxonomy of an extensive and often highly sophisticated literature, even a more highly differentiated one than that presented here, inevitably involves oversimplification: there is considerable diversity within each of the three categories; moreover, the classification is not exhaustive because some writings do not fit well into any of the categories. Still, we can usefully distinguish the acceptance, rejection, and pragmatic approaches to MNEs. This paper will present only a single prototypical position for each approach, not suggesting that it is fully representative of all who may follow that approach.[1]

The three approaches lie along a continuum, without clear-cut demarcations between them. The *acceptance approach* conceives of MNE expansion as economically rational, with benefits considerably outweighing costs for the host as well as the home country; considers host-government pressures on MNEs generally harmful on balance; and thus advocates a minimal or restricted role for government. Towards the left end of the continuum, the *rejection approach* sees MNE activities as essentially baleful, with harm to host countries overshadowing bene-

This article originally appeared in *World Development* 9, 1 (1981):93–105. Reprinted with permission.

fits. Rejectors believe that host-government efforts to tip the balance toward the beneficial either cannot succeed or entail costs (in terms of expending scarce government capabilities) that exceed the benefits. They therefore propose that government should either reject MNEs entirely or allow them a marginal role, one in which they accord with and accommodate to host-country policies (which should be directed toward fundamental restructuring of the nation's economy). Between these two is the *pragmatic approach,* which views MNE operations as mixed in effect; which believes that feasible government pressures on the MNEs can produce a worthwhile improvement in the benefit-cost mix; and which therefore advocates intelligent bargaining by host countries. A particular form of pragmatism, which we call assertive pragmatism, will be specified in this paper.

1. The Acceptance Approach

A considerable spectrum of writers follows the acceptance approach, ranging from strong partisans who can see, hear, or speak no evil of MNEs[2] to social scientists of the highest caliber and sophistication. The approach has been persuasively articulated by Raymond Vernon, conceivably the world's leading authority on MNEs, and because of his pre-eminent status, the prototypical acceptance position presented here is based upon Vernon's argument, although other writers are also referred to. Vernon's position can be presented in the form of six propositions[3]:

1. The pervasive frictions between the world's nation-states and the MNEs are based upon a fundamental conflict between economics and politics.[4] Technological progress and the economic processes that flow therefrom produce enormous economic benefits. However, these processes also heighten world economic interdependence, thereby reducing national autonomy. This occurs just when national governments, committed to promoting welfare and development in an historically new way, fiercely desire to *increase* their autonomy and sense of control. Governments thus experience the fundamental economic-political conflict as an excruciating ambivalence: a simultaneous heightening of both their desire for the economic benefits of interdependence and their aversion to its political constraints.

2. The MNE is a major manifestation and embodiment of the economic forces promoting global economic integration and human welfare. World-scale specialization promoted by MNE expansion raises the gross world product and allows higher living standards for all. The giant enterprises have the resources required for costly research and development activities and can spread the costs over their worldwide

operations. They can finance huge productive investments that would otherwise be neglected. They increase employment and income in the host countries, raise the levels of worker skills and managerial and entrepreneurial capability, create linkage effects, and promote economic development in many other ways.

3. In contrast, the political forces of nationalism are impeditive and costly. Host-country governments may make demands that impede or prevent useful investment. Within the host-government bureaucracy, unreasoning hostility toward foreign investors may slow down the many processes relating to MNE operations and thereby raise costs. Governments may impose unreasonable and even conflicting requirements. For example, Mexico has required foreign-owned automobile producers not only to produce components domestically, but also to export them to other markets.[5] If such requirements were generalized they would be impossible for the MNEs to meet.

4. Most political criticisms of MNEs, particularly those emanating from developing countries, are emotional and irrational. They arise from frustrations that are not validly attributable to MNEs, and "the imperviousness of the debate to facts" arises from the impotent anger generated by these frustrations. The MNEs have the misfortune to serve as "unwitting and unwilling lightning rods" for this anger.[6] Consider the following analyses by Vernon of antagonism toward MNEs.

Heightened world interdependence, which is caused primarily by improvements in travel and communications and merely epitomized by the MNE, *could* be accompanied by a "sense of equality and mutuality," but because of "the internal capabilities and self-perceptions of the leadership" it is likely to be experienced as "a sense of inferiority and dependency," particularly in developing countries.[7]

All the ills accompanying industrialization tend to be blamed on the MNE. In less developed countries especially, the MNE "has come to be seen as the embodiment of almost anything disconcerting about modern industrial society," but this is irrational. "Hegemony, corruption, inequity, pollution, and indifference to consumer interest were endemic in mankind's history long before the multinational enterprise existed."[8]

In the industrialized societies also, the charges made against MNEs tend primarily to be manifestations of "the real uneasiness of our times." The fundamental cause of these complaints is a "pervasive mood of alienation" (caused by factors that are variously identified by different social scientists).[9]

5. This is not to say that there are no real conflicts between governments and MNEs. There are many: governments want the capacity to control capital movements but MNEs are capable of avoiding controls;

governments want foreign exchange stability but the MNEs "have the potential for contributing substantially to the instability of currencies"; governments want the power to tax as they wish, but "the consequences of unilateral [tax] action by any major country can be quite substantial"; in general, "[t]he capacity of any government to undertake a specified task in support of a public policy . . . has been reduced."[10]

Government's desire for firmer powers is understandable, but even on most of these real issues the criticisms of multinationals are misguided. The various governments are often pursuing conflicting national interests in a zero-sum game; the gain of one country is offset by the loss of another. Such interactions, furthermore, threaten the spread of beggar-thy-neighbor policies which would sharply diminish the welfare of all.[11]

6. Finally, as a practical matter, government action specifically aimed at MNEs should be quite limited.[12] This follows partially from a pessimistic view of the realities of state intervention. Some public measures would clearly be worth undertaking if it were possible to implement them. For example, because of the multinationality of MNEs, government action even on affairs normally considered domestic might have international repercussions; on such matters it would be worthwhile to secure international agreement aimed at avoiding unilateral actions inadvertently harmful to other states, and at achieving multilateral actions where coordination is desirable. However, given the domestic sensitivity of the issues, which are subject to fierce political struggles within each country, useful international agreement has been virtually unobtainable. In point of fact, the measures which are actually being implemented tend to do more harm than good. Thus what *should* be and *can* be done is minimal and what *is* being done tends to be harmful.[13]

---

2. The Rejection Approach

The rejection approach is based typically on Marxian theory or on quasi-Marxian dependence theory,[14] although the Rejectors include other writers as well.[15] The formulation presented in the next paragraph is my own but is based on Marxian theory.[16]

The tensions associated with the spread of MNEs can be seen in this formulation as manifestations on a global scale of the basic Marxian contradiction of capitalism: between the social or interdependent nature of the productive system itself and the private nature and purpose of the control of that system.[17] (Production involves a highly interdependent meshing of a country's many different productive undertakings; it is carried on by a complex *system* of thoroughly interrelated enterprises. But the productive operations are *governed* by separate companies, seeking their own individual, not necessarily coordinated and often conflicting, profit-related goals.) This *social-private contradiction* results in poorly coordinated decisions, coordination being achieved only through the *ex post* action of the market ("anarchy of production"), and in decisions based on the criterion of private gain that are often in conflict with the criterion of the public good (e.g., divergences between private profitability and social benefit). The growth of the MNEs represents an extension of the basic Marxist contradiction in a wider arena. The interdependence of the productive system becomes more fully international[18] while the means and purpose of control remain relatively narrow.[19] Thus the MNE is just one more instrument, though a relatively new and important one, of an exploitative, anachronistic economic system.

The social-private contradiction inherent in MNE expansion produces or at least reinforces and extends a characteristic structuring of the world economy: one that may be called hierarchical-geographical as well as imperialistic.[20] The growth of MNEs tends to "produce a hierarchical division of labor between geographical regions. . . . [It tends to] centralize high-level decision-making occupations in a few key cities in the advanced countries, surrounded by a number of regional subcapitals, and confine the rest of the world to lower levels of activity and income. . . . [T]he existing pattern of inequality and dependency . . . [is] perpetuated. . . . [T]he basic relationship between different countries . . . [is] one of superior and subordinate."[21] This hierarchical division of the world arises from the private, profit-oriented character of the MNEs and not from the basic nature of the productive forces. "It must be stressed that the dependency relationship . . . should not be attributed to technology. The new technology . . . implies greater interdependence but not necessarily a hierarchical structure."[22] Under a different form of control, an entirely different, more rational, more humane world economic structure could emerge.[23]

The rejection approach focuses on the harmful effects for the developing countries of MNE expansion: imperialism and dependence, exploitative transfer pricing, the formation or reinforcement of a baleful set of class relations, an outflow of dividends, interest, royalties, and fees exceeding the inflow of capital, which is viewed as a drainage of capital, and many other negative consequences.[24] Conversely, the approach gives short shrift to host-country benefits generated by the MNEs. Such benefits are seen as accruing primarily to a narrow ruling class or set of elites, including perhaps a small "labor aristocracy" employed by the MNEs, with little or nothing trickling down to the mass of the population.[25]

Thus, the only appropriate and ethical[26] stance is either to reject the MNEs more or less entirely or to allow them a marginal role, completely subordinate to the government economic development orientation,[27] while government devotes its limited capabilities to the fundamental task of reconstructing the nation's political economy, probably on a socialist basis.[28]

3. The Pragmatic Approach

(a) Assertive Pragmatism Delineated

Lying between the acceptance and rejection approaches, the pragmatic approach declares the mixed nature of the MNE impact on developing host countries, and in direct contrast with the other approaches' rejections of active government involvement with MNEs, the pragmatic approach favors active host-government bargaining with and regulation of MNEs in order to improve the cost-benefit mix. This approach is in consonance with the strategy employed by most developing countries and with the thought of many social scientists,[29] and represents, I suggest, a position towards which Acceptors and Rejectors are tending to converge (more on this later). This article distinguishes between the pragmatic approach in its most general form and a particular expression of the approach which may be called *assertive pragmatism*. The rationales for both general and assertive pragmatism presented here are the writer's own and would surely not be acceptable to all other pragmatists. For expositional convenience, however, we will speak of *the* pragmatic or *the* assertive pragmatic approach.

Our rationale for pragmatism in general is based upon a social science *uncertainty principle* which simply states that social science is capable of providing only uncertain answers at best. The important issues, particularly in developing countries, are engulfed by uncertainty. Existing theory is inadequate and the real-world situation is immersed in all manner of unknowns.[30]

Uncertainty engulfs attempts at overall appraisal of any major development. Evaluating the costs and benefits of any historical process requires an assessment of the alternatives foregone, and such counterfactual hypotheses are unavoidably highly speculative. Implicit differences in conceptions of the alternatives foregone largely account for the seemingly evidence-resistant nature of many of the grand arguments over the impact of the MNEs. Given these implicit differences, the antagonists commonly talk past one another. Even specifying the actual process is a formidable undertaking. One is hard put simply to identify the vast multiplicity of important economic, political, sociological, and other effects of any major development, let alone to measure them.

It follows from the uncertainty principle that it is more concretely useful to eschew grand historical appraisals in favor of narrower evaluative tasks. The focus most congenial to the pragmatic approach is on the inquiry: in the existing real-world situation, by what means can welfare—of some particular group or class, or of some country or group of countries or of the world—be enhanced. This paper's focus is on the welfare of the "third world" peoples.

It also follows that one should be skeptical of putative, large, long-term gains from a proposed set of measures. The Pragmatist places less credence in such predicted benefits, i.e., attaches a greater discount for risk, than the more convinced analysts who pay little heed to the possibility that they may be wrong, and he or she gives greater weight than they do to definite immediate benefits. The Pragmatist also tends to place a higher premium on measures which are reversible and a greater discount on policies which entail substantial social pain.

The approach is not necessarily conservative. Proposals promising definite, near-term benefits are often opposed because of fears of indirect, long-term harm. The Pragmatist, with her or his greater skepticism about roundabout, long-term effects, is more likely to favor such proposals than the Acceptor who deplores unwarranted interference with the market mechanism or the Rejector who fears diversion of popular energies from the basic task of fundamental social restructuring. Nor is the approach linked only to minor changes. While it does tend to favor piecemeal decisions, allowing evidence and experience to accumulate before proceeding further, even profound social changes can be achieved on a step-by-step basis.[31]

Turning specifically to assertive pragmatism, our rationale is based also on a second conception—an extension of the already discussed Marxian concept of the social-private conflict. This extension departs from the original Marxian vision; even if one considers the Marxian concept a highly useful insight, one need not believe that Marx's horizon was unlimited. Marx did not foresee the unfolding of that conflict.

It can be argued that capitalism's viability has been extended in the face of the social-private conflict by the superimposition of a degree of social management upon the private control of the productive system. This social management took the form of state intervention to deal with system-threatening problems; the state undertook economy-stabilizing fiscal and monetary policy, more effective regulation of the banks, unemployment insurance, social security, and all the other functions that characterize the modern mixed economic system. The social stewardship of the socially interdependent productive system curbed the most ominous domestic malfunctions of the capitalist economies.

We have already suggested that the expansion of the MNEs can be seen within the Marxist paradigm as an extension of the social-private conflict on a global scale. Productive interdependence becomes more thoroughly international, but the means of state control remain national. Once again the means of control are more parochial than the productive system they attempt to harness.

This extension of the Marxian conception depicts a problem but it also directs attention to a possible means of coping with the problem. It suggests the possibility of developing still broader means of control, i.e., some form of governmental action of transnational scope.

Intellectual symmetry suggests parallelism: just as national manifestations of the social-private conflict are dealt with on a national governmental level, so the global manifestations should be handled on a world governmental level. But such an orientation would be visionary. It is more realistic to discuss moves toward more cosmopolitan means of control through increasing the effectiveness and scope of international agencies and international agreements, and more important, through the implementation by individual governments of complementary policies.[32]

Our extension of the Marxian social-private contradiction implies that the web of interdependence in the national and international political economy is loosely enough interwoven so that separate elements can be altered in a way that would improve the functioning of the system. In contrast, systemic interrelations are considered (perhaps implicitly) much more tightly interwoven by Acceptors and Rejectors. For the Acceptor, government interference with the market mechanism is likely to have broad consequences of a negative character that will outweigh apparent improvements. For the Rejector, the system will compensate to preserve the privileges of the ruling class, so that improvement can only be minimal at best while energies are diverted from replacing the system itself. Related to the pragmatic conceptions of loosely woven interdependence and improvability is the associated judgment that despite all their shortcomings governments can be a vehicle for achieving potential improvements.

Assertive pragmatism—with its skepticism about soul-satisfying ideological scenarios, its preference for more certain short-run benefits and distrust of putative long-run benefits, its predisposition toward active use of government—is essentially a mindset, a predisposition on how to proceed. Assertive Pragmatists may differ in many ways: in their degree of assertiveness (for a particular level of bargaining strength), in their preferences for capitalism or socialism, in their conceptions of the balance of benefits and dysbenefits generated by MNE activities, etc. Similarly, assertive pragmatic stances may be adopted by countries with different class structures, different bargaining positions, and other major differences. The approach adumbrates a general position, but it nevertheless leaves wide scope for disagreement, doubt, and indecision.[33]

Let us wind up our definition of assertive pragmatism by returning briefly to Rejector criticisms: that the Pragmatist, even if assertive, is willing to settle for relatively small gains; that the benefits that occupy the Pragmatist accrue primarily to a narrow ruling class or set of elites; and that the harm done by MNEs—in aggravating dependence, forming and solidifying exploitative class relations, directing economic growth along capitalist rather than socialist lines—is monumental.

The Assertive Pragmatist does not dismiss Rejector criticisms of the MNE lightly and agrees that a serious case can be made that the impact of the MNE may on balance be injurious. Nevertheless, the Pragmatist (or this one at any rate) justifies his or her position by pointing out that the benefits that do "trickle down" are often too lightly dismissed[34]—such dismissal is only for the affluent[35]—and by reiterating both his uncertainty-based skepticism about trading off these benefits for speculative benefits of a broader nature and also his observation that the capitalist state *has* proved capable of ameliorating fundamental problems.[36] The Pragmatist considers the rejection approach doctrinaire.[37] He also finds that the rejection approach exhibits a curious ahistorical strand that contrasts sharply with the broadly historical character of Marxist and dependence theory. The major problems of any period are typically characterized as inherent in capitalism and ineradicable except through socialism. If in fact the problem is alleviated, attention is then refocused single-mindedly on the new problems that inevitably emerge out of the modified conditions. The improvements are ignored; the error in calling the previous problem immutable is forgotten; and the new problems are again considered ineradicable.

For example, Marxists maintained that foreign investment ineluctably thrust the less developed economies into a primary producing role in the world division of labor. When in fact the MNEs began investing in the industrial subsidiaries in poor countries, neither the industrial progress made nor the error in the previous pronouncements were seriously noted. Instead attention shifted to the problems generated by these subsidiaries—enterprises which used inappropriate technology and employed a small labor aristocracy to produce inappropriate products for a small elite, thereby increasing unemployment, restricting local demand and thus local production, preventing the emergence of a local capital goods industry producing simpler capital goods, aggravating technological dependence, generating excessive payments to the MNEs, etc. Thus, say some Marxists, industrial growth under MNE auspices "may properly be characterized as 'perverse growth'; that is, growth which undermines, rather than enhances, the potentialities of the economy for long-term growth."[38]

(b) Assertive Pragmatism Implemented

Many international organizations and programs for dealing with MNEs exist or have been proposed. The United Nations has set up a Center on Transnational Corporations. Other UN bodies, such as UNIDO, FAO, UNCTAD, and others try to assist the developing countries in their relations with the MNEs. International agreements or codes helpful to less developed countries on patents and on the transfer of technology are negotiated. There are proposals for a GATT type of agreement on MNEs. Broad groupings such as the Group of 77 and narrower ones such as the Andean Pact have concerned themselves with MNE-developing country relations, and many other varied schemes for international cooperation have been proposed.[39]

These international bodies and programs provide media for exchange of views and knowledge, for systematic collection and dissemination of information, for undertaking studies, for coordination of policies and reduction of competition between host countries, and for the establishment of informal contacts likely to facilitate cooperation between governments. International organizations might also assist developing nations in negotiations or other dealings with MNEs by providing foreign expertise and training for indigenous personnel.

More important than international bodies and programs, however, are the actions of the individual host countries.

Not long ago, the less developed countries had little confidence in their ability to assert themselves in the international economy. As a former Nigerian minister of economic development lamented, Nigerians must accept "that we shall continue to be under the control of the imperialists and capitalists who have taken the lead in this world in economic development."[40] To a substantial extent, the sense of weakness expressed in this statement was justified.

For one thing, there are significant internal differences within most of the developing countries concerning MNEs. The dominant classes have been in a position to benefit substantially from them, through positions, directorships, bribes, business linkages, and in other ways. The potential personal gains influence their perceptions of the national interest, often to the detriment of the majority. The "labor aristocracy," with good jobs in the large foreign firms, also has a direct stake in the MNEs. Even public interest-motivated government agencies might be partisans of an MNE. For example, the Western Nigeria Development Corporation successfully opposed the establishment of a competing cement company in Western Nigeria in order to protect the monopolistic profitability of the existing multinational subsidiary in which it had a 39 percent holding.[41]

Furthermore, the MNEs constitute formidable bargaining adversaries. Even in extractive industries, where the developing countries are relatively strong in negotiations, MNE negotiating strength generally has been impressive.[42] This is particularly true in the least developed countries, where MNE control of essential technology and market access may be firmer than elsewhere.[43]

In manufacturing for export, "third world" bargaining power with the MNEs is especially weak. The MNEs have firm control of the relevant technologies and of most marketing outlets, particularly if the developing nation is producing a component of some kind. Moreover, the MNEs have the political clout necessary to combat high developed-country trade barriers against manufactured imports from less developed countries. Competition to attract MNE export manufacturing subsidiaries further weakens the bargaining position of the developing countries.

When their leverage was slight, the developing countries naturally concluded poor bargains with the MNEs—a problem that was intensified by their very feelings of weakness, for outcome is partially a function of the assurance of the negotiators. Whatever the issue, whether a simple division of economic gain or a broad societal matter, the developing countries were able to capture only a small part of the distance between the minimums they would accept and the maximums the MNEs might concede.

In fact, developing countries have not infrequently incurred direct economic *losses* in their dealings with MNEs. A profitable foreign investment can quite easily reduce national income.[44] The likelihood of a net national loss rises if the host country offers investment incentives such as tariff protection (which imposes a transfer from domestic consumers to the foreign investors).[45] Further, when developing economy bargaining weakness was compounded by foreign swindling or sharp practices and/or by domestic political venality, many joint investment deals have been made which turned out to be complete fiascos for the host nations.[46] Moreover, some technological change, for example the introduction of labor-saving technology in a labor surplus economy, may also lower host-country welfare.[47] One major study found that almost 40 percent of the MNE manufacturing projects examined in developing economies had negative effects on host-country social income.[48]

If a developing country tried to make tough demands in the era of generally soft bargaining, they were usually unsuccessful. The MNEs could adopt an unyielding stance and if necessary could usually turn to other potential hosts, while the recalcitrants were likely to be left empty-handed.

Gradually, however, developing-country bargaining power has been strengthened, partially by the very process of MNE expansion that was encouraged by developing-country weakness. A variety of factors have been involved.

Once the capital has actually been sunk into a project, the negotiating potency of the host country is sharply increased, particularly if significant amounts of capital are involved. In successful ventures the very profitability of the enterprise makes the MNE more amenable to pressures. The MNE commitment to its overseas ventures also tends to be heightened by organizational changes institutionalizing this commitment and by increasing reliance on foreign markets. Growing familiarity in the host country with the operations of an established subsidiary tends to dispel the air of impenetrable mystery and expertise and increases host-country confidence. The proliferation of multinationals and increasing competition among them has been an important source of host-country stiffening, for these developments have made available multiple sources of capital, technology, other know-how, and even market access, including sources other than those provided by direct investment.[49] Local capability for carrying out operations that were once the exclusive purview of foreign investors has also increased.[50] Developing country ability to win better terms has also been enhanced by the various forms of international cooperation discussed earlier.

These elements of strength are reinforced by a process which we will call *self-fulfilling aspiration growth*. As already indicated, a feeling of bargaining weakness tends to exacerbate that weakness. But as the negotiating position of the developing countries improves they are encouraged to toughen their demands. At some point, a "critical mass" (or average level) of toughness[51] is reached, by which we mean a "mass" or level which institutes the spiral process of self-fulfilling aspiration growth.

The spiral works this way. The increasing demands and aspirations of the developing nations, emerging in a bargaining situation in which these nations have won relatively little, tend to be effective in winning better terms. Encouraged by this, their aspirations and negotiating demands rise. So long as the settlements actually reached fall far short of the maximums that the MNEs would be willing to concede, the heightening of aspirations and demands continues to be successful. A self-reinforcing spiral gets under way: rising aspirations bring about better terms which cause further heightening of aspirations and so on. This is the process of self-fulfilling aspiration growth.[52]

Possible gains are multidimensional, and countries with different goals will presumably seek somewhat different sets of gains. Those more favored by leftist countries, such as income equalization and significant reductions in unemployment, are probably more difficult to bargain for than the more commonly sought gains, such as increases in national income or in government revenue.

The spiral is not an endless one, of course. As the settlements between the developing countries and the MNEs move further from the developing countries' minimums toward the maximums the MNEs are willing to concede, MNE resistance increases and tends to slow down or halt the process. The developing countries find that wresting further concessions from the MNEs incurs increasing costs, particularly in the form of curtailing investment with its infusion of capital, technology, other know-how, and market access, so that after some point the marginal costs of further demands may exceed the marginal benefits.

Experience confirms that the developing countries have been benefiting from tougher bargaining with MNEs, as the thesis of self-fulfilling aspiration growth suggests.

Developing countries have been securing a more favorable distribution of direct economic gains. Many investments have yielded (and prospective investments have promised) considerable quasi-rent to the MNEs, i.e., a return beyond that needed to induce the investor to continue operations or to undertake further investment. It is clear in retrospect that there had been a substantial rent element in earnings related to minerals and petroleum, an element that the developing economies subsequently found that they could tap for themselves. And "there is growing evidence of the existence of 'quasi-rent' . . . in the earnings of transnational manufacturing enterprises in less developed countries as well."[53] The developing countries have been able to raise their share of such income through higher taxes, royalties, participation in ownership, and the like without serious consequences for themselves.

The developing nations have also pressured MNEs into actions which generate further domestic development. They have prodded domestic subsidiaries into creating local linkages. Although many such firms are disposed to secure from their own worldwide corporate family as many of their intermediate inputs as possible, under pressure they have "seemed to be accepting the desirability—or, at any rate, the inevitability—of maintaining close ties with the surrounding economies."[54]

The less developed nations have prevailed upon reluctant MNEs to establish domestically operations they would have preferred to carry out elsewhere.[55] They have also promoted deliberate adoption of appropriate technology.[56] They have sometimes spurred foreign investors into a continuing entrepreneurial role.[57] Under pressure many foreign-owned manufacturing subsidiaries "have moved on to other activities: from simple manufacturing processes toward complex ones; from easy marketing in the local economy to difficult marketing abroad."[58]

Developing countries have had relatively longstanding policies of accelerating indigenization of labor and management through informal insistence and formal government action. Indigenization of ownership, i.e., divestiture, has also been pushed, for example, in the Zambian copper mines (with neither of the two nationalized MNEs raising any objections in principle despite previous government denials of nationalization intent),[59] and in Nigeria through its Indigenization Decree.[60]

Local MNE subsidiaries have even been prevailed upon to support broad international political objectives of the host country, sometimes at considerable cost to the subsidiary. For example, Sklar relates how the Zambian copper mining subsidiaries of Anglo-American Corporation and AMAX "cooperated fully and loyally" in Zambia's costly efforts to free itself of logistical dependence upon white minority-ruled Rhodesia.[61]

The MNEs have generally accepted all the prodding and pressuring. They have come to expect continually escalating demands when they are successful,[62] and this is built into their initial investment calculations and decisions. In fact, in favorable circumstances, a "determined and stable public sector . . . can get foreign investors to accept 'unacceptable' conditions while obtaining a rising flow of" foreign investment.[63]

By now it is clear that developing countries have achieved absolute gains and that MNEs have continued to thrive in a milieu of government pressures on and bargaining with MNEs. This of course does not disprove the cases made by the Acceptors or Rejectors, but it has tended to persuade many to moderate their views. "There is no longer the sharp separation between those who think that what is good for General Motors is good for humanity and those who see in the multinational corporations the devil incorporated."[64] The basic orientations remain quite vigorous but there has been some degree of convergence toward the pragmatic approach. Many Acceptors have come to see possible "third world" gains in a somewhat wider range of host-government measures concerning MNEs, and many Rejectors have come to recognize a wider range of actual or potential host-country benefits from MNE activities. In the distribution of positions, the "standard deviation" around the pragmatic position in the center has decreased.

Notes

The author wishes to thank Professors K. Onwuka Dike and Martin J. Kilson of Harvard University, Gerald K. Helleiner of Toronto University, Jay Mandle of Temple University, and Richard L. Sklar of the University of California, Los Angeles, for their advice and stimulation. None, of course, can be held at all responsible for shortcomings.

1. There are, of course, other taxonomies. See, for example, the interesting sixfold classification proposed by Sanjaya Lall, "Less-Developed Countries and Private Foreign Investment: A Review Article," *World Development* 2, 4-5 (1974):43–48.

2. For example, a General Motors vice-president who discussed the United Nations objective of introducing "some form of accountability to the international community" solely in terms of harmonizing national laws so that MNEs could function with fewer impediments. United Nations, *Summary of the Hearings Before the Group of Eminent Persons to Study the Impact of Multinational Corporations on Development and on International Relations* (New York: United Nations, 1974), ST/ESA/15, p. 81.

3. We have distilled these six propositions from his latest book: Raymond Vernon, *Storm over the Multinationals: The Real Issues* (Cambridge: Harvard University Press, 1977). This book is intended to be the definitive survey of the role of MNEs, a presentation of "the real issues."

4. Johnson stated this point as follows: "In an important sense, the fundamental problem of the future is the conflict between the political forces of nationalism and the economic forces pressing for world economic integration. This conflict currently . . . is between the national government and the international corporation." Harry Johnson, *International Economic Questions Facing Britain, the United States and Canada in the Seventies* (London: British-North American Research Association, June 1970), p. 24; quoted by Robert Gilpin, *U.S. Power and the Multinational Corporation* (New York: Basic Books, 1975), p. 220.

5. Vernon, *Storm over the Multinationals,* pp. 212, 215.

6. Ibid., pp. 145, 152.

7. Raymond Vernon, "Storm over the Multinationals: Problems and Prospects," *Foreign Affairs* 55, 2 (1977):243–262; see p. 249. (This article is based on Vernon's book, cited in fn. 3.) Vernon also states that the MNEs have

aroused much "speculation and foreboding over their effects on the national economy . . . [and] much of it has been very wide of the mark." The sense of independence the developing countries are seeking is a "Holy Grail"; see his "Storm," pp. 245, 253; also his *Storm over the Multinationals,* pp. 204, 212.

8. Vernon, *Storm over the Multinationals,* pp. 14, 19.

9. Ibid., pp. 137–138. And (loc. cit.): "The multinational enterprise cannot escape the consequences of the pervasive unease in the industrialized world. It is a highly visible scapegoat."

10. Ibid., pp. 123, 125, 136.

11. C. Fred Bergsten, Thomas Horst, and Theodore H. Moran speak of "the threat of investment wars—primarily between home and host countries . . . because these countries increasingly seek to tilt the benefits of foreign direct investment in their national directions." See their *American Multinationals and American Interests* (Washington, DC: Brookings Institution, 1978), p. 487. Investment wars are "akin to the trade wars of a past generation" (p. 494).

12. Some of those grouped here among the Acceptors are labelled by Sanjaya Lall as neo-traditionalists who "believe in the good, old-fashioned virtues of early capitalism [but] are worried by the giantism and power of the present MNE." These tend to favor some intervention by host governments. Lall, "Less-Developed Countries and Private Foreign Investment," p. 44.

13. Vernon, *Storm over the Multinationals,* ch. 9. See also Bergsten at al., *American Multinationals,* pp. 493–495. According to Bergsten, the basic thrust of their policy recommendations "is to maximize global economic welfare by maximizing the scope for foreign direct investment to respond to market forces. This requires both widespread agreement that such rules are desirable and active intervention to thwart efforts by individual countries or groups to induce deviations from the norm, through either constraints or excessive inducements." They want an "open and effective international economic system." They are akin to Lall's neo-traditionalists, however, for they also favor policies "to deal with those cases where the social costs of unfettered corporate activity would simply be too high."

14. Lall refers to dependence theory which is "not quite Marxist" but not simply nationalistic. Lall, "Less-Developed Countries and Private Foreign Investment," p. 45.

15. Perhaps the most widely known work embodying the rejection approach is Richard J. Barnet and Ronald E. Müller, *Global Reach* (New York: Simon & Schuster, 1974), a book which is neither Marxist nor of the dependency school.

16. As the credo of a new Marxist journal states, there are "many Marxisms." *Marxist Perspectives* 1, 1 (1978):3.

17. In Marx's terms, the conflict between "the material forces of production in society" and "the existing relations of production . . . [i.e.,] the property relations." Marx sets forth this conflict in summing up the "general conclusion" he reached in his early study of political economy "which once reached, continued to serve as the leading thread in my studies." Karl Marx, *A Contribution to the Critique of Political Economy* (Chicago: Charles H. Kerr, 1904), pp. 11–12.

18. Of course, international economic interdependence existed before the spread of MNEs, but to a lesser degree.

19. An explicit reference to this social-private conflict is made by Hymer: "the MNE . . . demonstrates the social nature of production on a global scale" but it creates profound problems because "the MNE is still a private institution with a partial outlook." The era of the MNE "reveals once more the power of social cooperation . . . [but it] also shows the shortcomings of concentrating this power in private hands." Stephen Hymer, "The Multinational Corporation and the Law of Uneven Development," in Jagdish N. Bhagwati (ed.), *Economics and World Order from the 1970s to the 1990s* (New York: Macmillan, 1971), pp. 113–140 (see pp. 133–134). Further on Hymer in the next note.

20. This particular formulation is that of Hymer (fn. 19), one of the foremost theorists of the rejection approach. Hymer did some of the early significant work on MNEs when he was writing as a mainstream economist, but subsequently adopted a Marxist orientation. His hierarchical-geographical concept was, in our view, a significant development of Marxian thought about MNEs. Baran and Sweezy had emphasized the supranational aspects of MNEs; see Paul A. Baran and Paul M. Sweezy, "Notes on the Theory of Imperialism," *Monthly Review* 17, 10 (1966):15–33. Concerned with their own long-run interests and oblivious of nationality, making decisions on the basis of alternatives all over the world, the MNEs' impact on more developed or less developed countries, on home or host countries, was incidental: "the decisions and actions of the multinational companies are taken solely with a view to promoting the interests of the companies themselves and . . . whatever effects, beneficial or injurious, they may have on the various countries in which they operate are strictly incidental" (Baran and Sweezy, p. 29). The MNEs' common interests and objectives—and this is the basis of contemporary imperialism—lie in the preservation and extension of relatively unfettered capitalism. Hymer challenges the Baran-Sweezy notion of supranationality and restores a geographical base for Marxist imperialism theory by rendering the hierarchical, exploitative nature of MNE operations accordant with the North-South geographical division of the world.

21. Hymer, "The Multinational Corporation," p. 114; also pp. 124–125, 127.

22. Ibid., p. 126.

23. Ibid., pp. 126–127, 134–135.

24. These criticisms of MNE-generated benefits are discussed further at the end of Section 3(a).

25. A distinction might be made between the argument that the MNEs have a negative impact on development and the argument that whatever the proximate effect of MNEs they are harmful because they reinforce capitalism and obstruct the emergence of socialism.

26. The Rejectors, like many radicals, have a strong tendency to consider those who disagree with them as not only wrong but also morally tainted.

27. For example, Tanzania's "basic principle" with respect to foreign investment, says Neersø, "is that if foreign investors cannot adapt themselves to

the regulations considered necessary by Tanzania, she is better off without their investments." Peter Neersø, "Tanzania's Policies on Private Foreign Investment," in Carl Widstrand (ed.), *Multinational Firms in Africa* (New York: African Publishing, Holmes & Meier, 1975), p. 194.

28. "Multinational corporations and nations are . . . fundamentally and irrevocably opposed to each other. The logic of each, carried to its final conclusion, is to destroy the other. Or to put the point differently, the historic course of the global capitalist system is leading to one of two outcomes: world empire or world revolution." Paul M. Sweezy and Harry Magdoff, *The Dynamics of U.S. Capitalism* (New York: Monthly Review Press, 1972), p. 111. Hymer is equally sure that it is necessary "to go beyond the MNC" and to replace the capitalist system, but he is not at all sure what to replace it with ("The Multinational Corporation," pp. 131–135). He favors some vaguely defined kind of "alternative system of organization in the form of national planning," with emphasis on *local* "social and political control of economic decision making." (pp. 126–127).

29. For example, Díaz Alejandro, Helleiner, Lall, Penrose, and Streeten, all cited in this chapter. A development text with a pragmatic orientation is Michael P. Todaro, *Development in the Third World* (London: Longmans, 1977); see esp. pp. 326–332.

30. Streeten, who discusses many areas of uncertainty regarding MNEs, remarks: "A major difficulty in assessing [the effects of MNEs] . . . is that far from being able to quantify precisely these effects, we do not even know, in general, their direction." Paul Streeten, "The Multinational Enterprise and the Theory of Development Policy," *World Development* 1, 10 (1973):1–13 (quoted from p. 3).

31. One might maintain that the pragmatic approach puts ideology in its proper place. In the hurly-burly of the real world, "policy decisions are unavoidably influenced by ideology, more specifically by the prevailing policy predisposition and the desired politico-economic destination." In the presence of uncertainty, "decisions are inevitably influenced by the leadership's policy predispositions, based on a mélange of attitudes, emotions, and prior convictions. Decisions are also colored by the related matter of the desired politico-economic destinations of those with power, i.e., the kind of political economy they want to establish." While such reliance upon ideology is unavoidable for any decision-maker, the uncertain Pragmatist, skeptical of grand predictions, tends to keep ideological predispositions subservient to evidence and subject to review in light of experience. Sayre P. Schatz, *Nigerian Capitalism* (Berkeley and Los Angeles: University of California Press, 1977), pp. 282–283 (with apologies for quoting myself).

32. "Ultimately, the only proper response to an organization that takes a global view will be global control." In the meantime, however, "national governments will have to find ways." Streeten, "The Multinational Enterprise," p. 7. Vaitsos speaks of the need for "a certain degree of unity of action"; Constantine V. Vaitsos, "Power, Knowledge and Development Policy: Relations between Transnational Enterprises and Developing Countries," in Gerald K. Helleiner (ed.), *A World Divided* (Cambridge: Cambridge University Press, 1976), pp. 113–146 (quoted from p. 141).

33. For this reason, Carlos F. Díaz Alejandro recommends use of policy rules of thumb. Díaz Alejandro, "Direct Foreign Investment in Latin America," in Charles P. Kindleberger (ed.), *The International Corporation* (Cambridge: MIT Press, 1970), pp. 319–344 (esp. pp. 328, 342).

34. Hymer, for example, says: "At most, one-third of the population can be said to benefit in some sense." ("The Multinational Corporation," p. 131). However, this may amount to hundreds of millions of people. Moreover, Hymer dismisses even this gain by a relativity that grates in this era of emphasis on absolute poverty. The gain involves only "an illusion of upward mobility" because relative status remains unchanged. "In each period subordinates achieve (in part) the consumption standards of their superiors in a previous period and are thus torn in two directions: if they look backward . . . things *seem* [my emphasis] to be getting better; if they look upward they see that the relative position has not changed. They receive a consolation prize . . . softening the reality that in a competitive system, few succeed and many fail" (p. 125).

35. A recent study indicates that even in Brazil, where the income distribution effects of economic growth have been severely criticized, the absolutely poor made considerable gains, although those slightly higher on the economic ladder did not fare so well. Gary S. Fields, "Who Benefits from Economic Development? A Reexamination of Brazilian Growth in the 1960s," *American Economic Review* 67, 4 (1977):570–582.

36. "The relation between the MNE and these social objectives ['equality . . . jobs, livelihoods and generally meeting the needs of the masses of poor people'] will, to a large extent, depend upon the ability and willingness of the host government to pursue the 'right' policies." Streeten, "The Multinational Enterprise," p. 2. If, however, the host-country government does not carry out policies which capture MNE-generated benefits for its people, the Assertive Pragmatist stands with the Rejector in holding the MNE as well as the government responsible. The Pragmatist basically agrees with Baran's biting criticism of "the observation that what the government of a source country does with its receipts from foreign enterprise has after all nothing to do with the 'purely economic' appraisal of the foreign enterprise's contribution to . . . economic development. . . . This view affords a veritable textbook example of the inherent incapability of bourgeois economics to penetrate the subject matter of its investigation." The existence of foreign investment "and the existence of wasteful, corrupt, and reactionary comprador regimes . . . are not fortuitous coincidences but [are] . . . interconnected aspects of" one reality. Paul A. Baran, *The Political Economy of Growth* (New York: Monthly Review Press, 1957), pp. 217–218. Thus, Streeten asserts that if policies intended to capture MNE benefits for the host-country people "are absent or defective, or are themselves the result of the pressures of the MNE, the MNE may be judged by its impact on variables normally regarded as proper direct objectives of government policies." Streeten, "The Multinational Enterprise," p. 2.

37. Because of its tendency to be simplistic, the rejection approach is not embraced by all Marxists. Thus, in discussing oversimplifications regarding the impact of foreign investment on developing countries which "may easily lead to a false orthodoxy and have disastrous consequences in actual policy,"

the Hungarian Marxist economist Tamas Szentes takes essentially a pragmatic approach. He criticizes a "one-sided critique of colonialism. This version takes into account the fact of the exploited and disadvantageous position of the countries in question in the international capitalist division of labour, but it neglects the structural background of the latter as well as the shifts of power factors within it, and thus cavalierly suggests prompt and complete disengagement from the international capitalist system without considering the historical context, the conditions, and the costs of such a disengagement." Tamas Szentes, "Socioeconomic Effects of Two Patterns of Foreign Capital Investments, with Special Reference to East Africa," in Peter C.W. Gutkind and Immanuel Wallerstein (eds.), *The Political Economy of Contemporary Africa* (Beverly Hills CA: Sage, 1976), pp. 261–290 (quoted from pp. 261–262).

38. Giovanni Arrighi and John S. Saul, "Socialism and Economic Development in Tropical Africa," *Journal of Modern African Studies* 6, 2 (1968):141–169 (quoted from p. 150). The authors attribute the perverse development concept to Sachs in a 1966 paper. It is similar to Frank's concept of the underdevelopment of an economy. See, for example, André Gunder Frank, "The Development of Underdevelopment," *Monthly Review* 18, 4 (1966):17–31.

39. See, for example, United Nations, *Multinational Corporations in World Development* (New York: United Nations, 1973), ST/ECA/190/1, pp. 85–95.

40. Quoted in Schatz, *Nigerian Capitalism*, p. 261.

41. O.O. Soleye, "The Politico-Economic Position of Multinational Corporations: A Nigerian Example," in Widstrand (ed.), *Multinational Firms in Africa* (fn. 27), pp. 199–205.

42. Supply has often outstripped demand in the raw materials industries, and even the threat of surplus weakens the developing country bargaining position. In periods of surplus the MNEs tend to place primary reliance on "safe" sources in developed countries and in those developing countries which work out favorable supply agreements. Such agreements, by differentiating the interests of the developing countries, tend to weaken their bargaining power. For a succinct discussion of this and other sources of MNE bargaining strength in extractive industries, see Vernon, *Storm over the Multinationals*, pp. 256–258.

43. An abortive attempt by the government of Zambia to diversify foreign participation in copper mining provides an illustration. The government awarded prospecting licenses to a Japanese-American joint venture. However, the Japanese firm (Mitsui) soon lost interest, and the Americans concerned were "quick to speculate" that Mitsui had been dissuaded by the two MNCs already established in Zambian copper mining, Anglo-American Corporation and AMAX, which both had close connections with Mitsui elsewhere. Similarly, Zambian government attempts to integrate and rationalize parallel purchasing, marketing, and other operations of the Zambian subsidiaries of Anglo-American and AMAX were allegedly frustrated by the parent companies, despite Zambian government holdings of 51 percent in both subsidiaries. Each parent wanted its Zambian subsidiary to deal in so far as possible with other affiliates within its own corporate family. These examples are drawn from Richard L. Sklar, *Corporate Power in an African State* (Berkeley and Los Angeles:

University of California Press, 1975), pp. 72–73 and 187. This insightful and careful book is perhaps the best study so far published on multinational operations in Africa.

44. The direct increase in domestic output occasioned by the foreign investment may be small, particularly when many intermediate inputs are imported; this might be partially or more than fully offset by reductions in production by indigenous firms that lose customers or scarce inputs to the foreign investors. From any net increase in output that may remain, the foreign firm's profits and fees must then be subtracted to find the contribution to national product or national income. If profits and fees are high, this contribution might well be negative. Schatz, *Nigerian Capitalism*, p. 262. See also J. Ilett, "Inducements for Industrial Development: When Are They Worthwhile?" *Yorkshire Bulletin of Economic and Social Research* 19, 2 (1967):105.

45. Such revenues are lost if the activity would otherwise have been undertaken by a domestic, taxpaying firm.

46. See, for example, Sayre P. Schatz, "Crude Private Neo-Imperialism: A New Pattern in Africa," *Journal of Modern African Studies* 7, 4 (1969):677–688.

47. Gerald K. Helleiner, "International Technology Issues: Southern Needs and Northern Responses," in Jagdish N. Bhagwati (ed.), *The New International Economic Order* (Cambridge, MA: MIT Press, 1977), pp. 295–316 (see p. 303).

48. Paul P. Streeten and Sanjaya Lall, *Evaluation of Methods and Main Findings of UNCTAD Study of Private Overseas Investment in Selected Less Developed Countries* (New York: United Nations, 1973), TD/b/c.3/111. When one goes beyond relatively narrow economic measures, which are the focus of this paragraph, and considers political and social consequences, the costs and benefits of foreign investment are extremely difficult to estimate, but some critics of MNEs believe that the negative consequences are massive.

49. "The host country has a variety of choices. It can borrow the capital, hire managers, and acquire a licence; use domestic inputs for some components of the 'package'; or use consulting services, management contracts, importing houses or banks." Paul Streeten, "Multinationals Revisited," *Finance and Development* 16, 2 (1979):39–42 (quoted from p. 41). See also Gerald K. Helleiner, "Transnational Enterprises in the Manufacturing Sector of the Less Developed Countries," *World Development* 3, 9 (1975):641–650, esp. p. 645: "Technology may be supplied by a large foreign firm to less developed countries in a variety of ways. . . . [Besides providing it through a wholly-owned subsidiary or a joint venture, the firm may] license a firm in which it has no equity at all, or sell equipment, management or training programmes, or erect plant on a turn-key basis, all on a thoroughly arms'-length basis." Besides technology, other facets of the usual direct investment package may be provided in various ways.

50. Cohen concluded that local capabilities were sufficient to have carried out the direct foreign investments which he studied in Singapore, South Korea, and Taiwan, with positive national income effects at least as great as those yielded by foreign investment. Benjamin J. Cohen, *Multinational Firms and Asian Exports* (New Haven: Yale University Press, 1975), pp. 112–119; cited in

Gerald K. Helleiner, "Transnational Enterprise, Manufactured Exports and Employment in Less Developed Countries," *Economic and Political Weekly* 11, 5–7 (1976):289.

51. Achievement of this critical mass is facilitated by favorable circumstances, for example: economic prosperity in the home country (which probably increases the ability and willingness of the MNE to make concessions); balance-of-payments ease in the home country (which might encourage greater governmental cooperation with MNE concessions); the development of a world climate of opinion which is more supportive of poor country aspirations; a growing network of mutually encouraging and informative international interrelations among host nations.

52. Penrose believes that "less developed countries often have *more* scope to take independent and radical action with regard to multinational corporations than do governments of the larger industrialized countries. Retaliation is more difficult. . . . [Moreover] the less developed countries are often less inhibited by their own attitudes and by respect for the prevailing traditions and rules of international economic behavior, holding either that those traditions and rules were made in the interest of the industrial powers and have no moral claim to international acceptance, or that their own history justifies exceptions in their favour." Edith Penrose, "'Ownership and Control': Multinational Firms in Less Developed Countries," in Gerald K. Helleiner (ed.), *A World Divided*, pp. 147–174 (quoted from p. 151).

53. Helleiner, "Transnational Enterprise," p. 641, also p. 644.

54. Raymond Vernon, *Sovereignty at Bay* (New York: Basic Books, 1971), p. 54. The reference here is to foreign raw materials enterprises, but the process obtains more generally. See also Walter Chudson, "Africa," in H.R. Hahlo, J. Graham Smith, and Richard W. Wright (eds.), *Nationalism and the Multinational Enterprise* (Dobbs Ferry, NY: Oceana, 1973), pp. 136–161 (quoted from p. 148).

55. For example, when the Zambian government's desire to initiate local fabrication of its copper was opposed by the two multinational mining companies operating there, Zambia turned to an outside consortium of three American and Swedish firms. The government used this consortium "as a means of leverage to move the mining groups from an obstructive to an accommodative position," and after complicated negotiations a fabricating company was formed which was owned by all five companies and the Zambian Government. Sklar, *Corporate Power*, pp. 93–95.

56. For use in developing countries, for example, Philips NV of the Netherlands developed a small-scale production unit which was both low cost and more labor-intensive than its typical European unit. The Italian firm Oltramare designed specifically for use in Tanzania a highly successful mechanical cashew nut processing plant, which "radically improved the position of Tanzania in the [world] cashew nut market." Chudson, "Africa," pp. 152–153.

57. This has been one of the functions of Nigeria's Indigenization Decree, which mandated full or partial indigenous ownership in a wide range of economic activities. Through this decree, the "Government has . . . taken the first step not necessarily towards replacing multinationals but towards directing

them to areas where they are most needed. . . . Nigeria has been careful in taking over multinational corporations because it is believed that there is still room for the expertise and technology that they can provide." United Nations, *Hearings*, pp. 158–159. This writer observed a smaller-scale process of this nature in Tanzania in the late 1960s. With nationalization of existing operations, some Asian entrepreneurs who stayed on saw their future in terms of continually innovating new activities, profiting thereby, and again being nationalized at prices which included some reward for successful entrepreneurship.

58. Vernon, *Sovereignty at Bay*, p. 106.

59. Sklar, *Corporate Power*, pp. 34–42.

60. Schatz, *Nigerian Capitalism*, pp. 58–61; United Nations, *Hearings*, p. 162. Nicholas Balabkins, of Lehigh University, has a thorough study under way of Nigeria's indigenization of ownership.

The possibilities of indigenizing ownership are quite varied; for example, Yugoslavia retained full ownership of an MNE-established enterprise that was to produce parts and components for the MNE and used these parts as payments for production, training, and marketing assistance from the foreign firm. Chudson, "Africa," p. 150.

61. Sklar, *Corporate Power*, pp. 144–148. This is related to Sklar's highly interesting thesis of an MNE "doctrine of domicile," pp. 182–188.

62. "There may have been a time in international affairs when foreign producers of raw materials anticipated that a bargain with a government, once made, would not come unstuck. Today the opposite is generally assumed." Vernon, *Sovereignty at Bay*, pp. 178–179.

63. Díaz Alejandro, "Direct Foreign Investment," p. 324. In Tanzania, for example, despite nationalization (accompanied, to be sure, by adequate compensation), foreign companies continued to collaborate with government in joint ventures, management contracts, and in other ways. Neersø, "Tanzania's Policies," pp. 178–179.

64. Streeten, "Multinationals Revisited," p. 39.

Third World Indebted Industrialization: International Finance and State Capitalism in Mexico, Brazil, Algeria, and South Korea

JEFF FRIEDEN

The past few years have seen an upsurge of interest in the debt owed by the less developed countries (LDCs) to commercial banks. Yet most scholars, bankers, policy-makers, and journalists have focused on only one aspect of LDC debt, its implications for the international financial system. There has been little investigation of the impact of recent trends in "third world" borrowing on the borrowing LDCs themselves—quite unlike the post-World War II spread of multinational corporations into the LDCs, which provoked a substantial literature on the effects of foreign direct investment on developing countries. Yet LDC commercial bank debt is not simply an accumulation of numbers on bank balance sheets, a highly sophisticated form of electronic game; it represents the most rapid, most concentrated, most massive flow of investment capital to the "third world" in history.

As Table 6.1 shows in the case of Latin America, private financial institutions have displaced multinational corporations and official aid over the last fifteen years as the most important source of foreign capital available to "third world" countries. In the 1960s, in fact, foreign direct investment accounted for some 30 percent of the total flow of external financial resources to Latin America, while bank loans and bonds provided only 10 percent. In the 1970s banks and bondholders were responsible for 57 percent of this flow—up from an annual average of $214 million in the 1960s to $6.5 billion in the 1970s—while the multinationals' share had dropped to about 20 percent.

Multinational corporations brought modern industrial production to the "third world" and integrated it into the international capitalist system, but they also unleashed a torrent of nationalistic economic and

This paper originally appeared in *International Organization* 35, 3 (1981):407-431, copyright by the World Peace Foundation and Massachusetts Institute of Technology. Reprinted with permission.

Table 6.1 Net Inflow of External Resources to Latin America, 1961–1978
(annual averages in millions of current dollars; figures in parentheses are percentages[a])

	1961–1965		1966–1970		1971–1975		1976–1978	
Net Public Inflow	948.4	(59.8)	1,059.4	(40.4)	1,901.9	(25.3)	2,160.1	(12.1)
Net Private Inflow[b]	636.6	(40.2)	1,561.3	(59.6)	5,622.0	(74.7)	15,679.8	(87.9)
A. Suppliers	123.2	(7.8)	364.6	(13.9)	174.2	(2.3)	1,317.7	(7.4)
B. Banks & bonds	114.8	(7.2)	312.9	(11.9)	3,462.9	(46.0)	11,517.0	(64.6)
C. Direct investment	398.6	(25.1)	883.8	(33.7)	1,984.9	(26.4)	2,845.1	(15.9)
Total	1,585.0	(100.0)	2,620.7	(100.0)	7,523.9	(100.0)	17,839.9	(100.0)

SOURCE: Inter-American Development Bank, *Economic and Social Progress in Latin America: 1979 Report* (Washington, D.C.: IDB, 1980), p. 85.

NOTES: a Percentage totals may not add exactly to 100 percent due to rounding errors.
         b Does not include nationalization credits.

political forces within the most rapidly industrializing LDCs. Multinational corporations contributed to the training and mobilization of technicians, economists, and development planners, and called forth a political reaction that demanded and obtained a governmental commitment to concerted national economic development in these dozen or so LDCs. In the late 1960s governments in such widely varied countries as Algeria, Brazil, Mexico, and South Korea—in partnership with and financed by the international banks in a pattern of foreign *indirect* investment—began the systematic construction of integrated domestic economic structures. These nationalistic state-capitalist regimes have joined with the internationalist finance-capitalists of the Euromarkets: the banks provide the capital; the state provides the muscle and brains to force-march the countries involved into the industrialized world. This paper will examine the rise of bank debt-financed, government-led industrialization in the LDCs. It will analyze the interplay of international finance, the state sector, and industrial growth in the four countries mentioned above, and will attempt to point out the implications of the process for the LDCs and for the international capitalist system.

The Growth of LDC Commercial Bank Debt

In the past ten years the debt owed by the governments, government agencies, state-owned industries, and state-supported enterprises in the less developed countries has exploded. In 1970, according to the World Bank, the LDCs owed $63.9 billion to foreign creditors; by the end of 1978 they owed $313.5 billion.[1] With the general expansion of LDC external public debt[2] came a change in the composition of LDC borrowing: more and more loans came from private sources, especially from those banks active on the Eurocurrency market. While in 1970 $3.5 billion was committed to the LDCs by international financial markets (exclusive of suppliers' credits), 23 percent of total commitments, by 1978 $43.8 billion, 57 percent of the total, was so committed.[3] Even allowing for the galloping inflation of the 1970s, the LDCs' debt to bondholders and private financial institutions nearly tripled between 1970 and 1976.[4] The picture is quite clear: since the late 1960s LDCs have borrowed more heavily than ever before, and more of this borrowing has been done from private banks than anyone had imagined possible.

Some of the reasons for this enormous growth are clear, and have been amply treated by other authors.[5] Crucial, of course, was the internationalization of banking and the concurrent rise of the Euromarkets, a vast quantity of capital controlled by a handful of international banks.

Also important was the impressive economic growth of several LDCs in the 1960s, often fueled by foreign direct investment, which made them more attractive credit risks for the banks. The rapid increase in the price of oil late in 1973 gave a tremendous push to a process that was already in motion (see Table 6.2). On the one hand, Middle Eastern oil exporters deposited huge sums in the international banks—$49 billion between 1974 and 1976.[6] On the other hand, the oil price rise and the world recession raised the import bill of the LDCs at the same time as it reduced their exports to customers in the recession-ridden advanced capitalist countries.

Thus, while in 1973 the nonoil LDCs covered some 85 percent of their imports with exports, by 1975 exports paid for only 67 percent of imports.[7] It is well known that those LDCs with access to the international financial markets made up much of the difference by borrowing from the banks. Meanwhile, the 1974–1975 recession in the advanced capitalist countries reduced loan demand there. The international banks, faced with a mountain of OPEC deposits and dwindling corporate demand, began pursuing the more creditworthy LDCs (and even some entirely uncreditworthy ones) aggressively.

It is worthwhile here to make a few points about LDC borrowing from private financial markets. First, borrowing by less developed countries from private investors in the advanced capitalist countries is not new. Brazil floated its first "Eurobond" on the London market in 1824, and by 1960 Latin American governments owed some two billion dollars to foreign bondholders and financiers, an amount equal to about one-quarter of their debt to all creditors.[8] As can be seen in Table 6.2, private lenders (excluding suppliers) were owed $2.4 billion by the LDCs in 1960; this figure had more than doubled, to $5.3 billion, by 1965.[9] Borrowing by LDC governments from private lenders is not a new phenomenon, but its proportions since the late 1960s have been so large as to transform what was formerly a fairly insignificant provider of funds to a few favored borrowers into the single most important source of foreign investment capital available to dozens of LDCs.

Secondly, even today the vast majority of private lending to the LDCs is concentrated at both ends: some twenty-five to thirty international banks do the lion's share of the lending, and some fifteen countries do the lion's share of borrowing. Indeed, as Table 6.3 shows, five OPEC members (Venezuela, Algeria, Iran, Indonesia, and the United Arab Emirates) and ten other LDCs (Mexico, Brazil, South Korea, Argentina, the Philippines, Morocco, Chile, Taiwan, Malaysia, and Peru) accounted for some four-fifths of all the publicly announced Eurocurrency bank credits to LDCs between 1976 and 1979, even though they had less than one-quarter of the "third world's" population. In fact, in that four-year period, according to Morgan Guaranty

Table 6.2 Disbursed Debt of LDCs, Year End 1960–79: Owed to Private Lenders (Excluding Export Credits) and Owed to All Sources
(billions of dollars, except percent where noted)

Year	To Private Lenders	Annual Increase (%)	To All Sources	Annual Increase (%)
1960	2.4	—	17.9	—
1961	2.9	21	20.9	17
1962	3.5	21	24.0	15
1963	4.0	14	27.7	15
1964	4.7	18	32.4	17
1965	5.3	13	37.1	15
1966	6.1	15	42.2	14
1967	7.0	15	48.4	15
1968	8.1	16	55.8	15
1969	10.0	23	64.2	15
1970	12.6	26	74.7	15
1971	16.6	32	86.6	16
1972	22.1	33	98.2	13
1973	33.7	52	118.9	21
1974	44.6	32	145.6	22
1975	57.9	30	179.5	23
1976	76.0	31	216.8	21
1977	94.2	24	264.4	22
1978 (est.)	120.0	27	321.5	24
1979 (prelim.)	141.0	18	366.0	14

SOURCE: Development Assistance Committee, Organization for Economic Cooperation and Development, *Development Cooperation: 1977 Review* (Paris: OECD, 1977), p. 211; and *1979 Review* (Paris: OECD, 1979), p. 258.

Trust's authoritative *World Financial Markets*, five countries (Mexico, Brazil, Venezuela, South Korea, and Algeria) with one-tenth of the total population of the "third world" accounted for over half of all LDC Eurobank loans.

Thirdly, most commercial bank lending to the "third world" is in the form of loans made to or guaranteed by the public or state sector of the LDCs. A brief look at listings of Eurocurrency credits indicates who the major borrowers are: some 80 percent to 90 percent of these loans are to the public sector, with the remainder being guaranteed by the state. In the state sector major borrowers are, in varying proportions according to the country, the central government or central bank itself, state-owned industrial enterprises and public utilities, and national development banks. For example, in 1978 Mexican borrowers obtained some $6.5 billion in Eurocurrency credits and bonds. Of this amount

40 percent went to public development banks, 34 percent to state-owned utilities and industry, 12 percent to the central government, 11 percent to a number of private industrial companies, and 3 percent to a private bank. In all, some 86 percent of the borrowed funds went to public entities.[10] Thus, investment capital is usually administered or allocated by public officials in the borrowing country.

Finally, borrowing by the state sector reflects growing developmentalist and nationalist demands in the LDCs. In virtually all of the heavy-borrowing countries economic development is highly politicized, and public opinion demands both economic growth and a measure of economic autonomy. No matter what the ideological bent of the regime and no matter what its form, from the one-party states of Algeria and Mexico to the military junta of Brazil and the police states

Table 6.3   Eurocurrency Bank Credits to LDCs January 1976 Through December 1979

Country or Region	Amount ($ million)	As % of Subgroup	As % of All LDCs
All LDCs	118,125		100.0
Non-OPEC Countries	84,110	100.0	71.2
Mexico	19,895	23.7	16.8
Brazil	17,440	20.7	14.8
South Korea	7,312	8.7	6.2
Argentina	6,074	7.2	5.1
Philippines	5,725	6.8	4.8
Chile	2,639	3.1	2.2
Morocco	2,543	3.0	2.2
Malaysia	2,145	2.6	1.8
Taiwan	2,094	2.5	1.8
Peru	1,180	1.4	1.0
Other	17,066	20.3	14.4
OPEC Countries	34,011	100.0	28.8
Venezuela	11,420	33.6	9.7
Algeria	5,773	17.0	4.9
Iran	3,738	11.0	3.2
Indonesia	3,465	10.2	2.9
United Arab Emirates	2,268	6.7	1.9
Other	7,346	21.6	6.2

SOURCE: Morgan Guaranty Trust Company, *World Financial Markets*, December 1979, p. 10.

NOTE: Percentages may not total to 100 due to rounding.

of South Korea, Taiwan, and the Philippines, the government must satisfy these demands for rapid economic expansion. But the earlier reliance on multinational corporations is no longer sufficient to fund the development of an integrated national economy. On the one hand, foreign corporations are often unwilling to invest in key heavy industrial sectors, where capital requirements are high and rates of return low. On the other, there is generally a local consensus embracing technocrats, business executives, military officers, and labor that some industries are too politically sensitive or too important to national security to entrust to foreigners. Yet the only available alternative to foreign direct investment is foreign indirect investment, bank loans channeled through the public sector and used to establish or expand domestically controlled public or publicly supported enterprises. If in the past many LDC governments encouraged foreign corporate investment to build up a modern industrial sector, today more and more are themselves the major force in initiating, financing or intermediating the financing of, and often even managing productive investment in, modern industry. In the pursuit of local control over local investment, the state has taken over; yet, paradoxically, this state involvement in the economy has been based on borrowing from foreign banks. In short, the state sectors in the LDCs have in effect been mortgaged to the Eurobanks, and both the banks and their client states have staked their fortunes on rapid national economic development.

The Cases

A full appreciation of the background to and implications of LDC borrowing can only come from a detailed examination of the LDCs themselves. The great mystery of LDC debt, after all, is not why the banks lend; clearly they do it to make a profit, and the "supply side" of bank lending has been amply documented and dissected. The real questions that remain are why the LDCs borrow, where the money goes, and what the capital invested has created. My attempt to answer these questions led me to investigate four of the heaviest borrowers on the Euromarket. They are four widely varied cases: Mexico, Brazil, Algeria, and South Korea, by 1976 accounting for about half of all LDC debt to financial markets. Table 6.4 displays the growth of the public external debt of these four countries and of the LDCs as a whole.

In each case I shall summarize the general development strategies followed and the role of foreign borrowing in these strategies. Special attention will be paid to the interaction between the state sector, private foreign and domestic enterprises, foreign loans, and local national development strategies.

Table 6.4 Public External Debt (Including Undisbursed Portion), 1967–78: Mexico, Brazil, Algeria, South Korea, and All LDCs

	1967	1969	1971	1973	1975	1978
Mexico:						
All Lenders	2,675.5	3,443.7	4,206.5	7,249.3	13,547.7	27,021.5
Official sources	1,154.8	1,376.4	1,702.8	2,708.6	3,649.8	5,345.6
Suppliers & others	370.1	457.9	365.0	318.5	499.1	404.5
Financial markets	1,150.6	1,609.4	2,138.7	4,222.2	9,398.8	21,271.3
Brazil:						
All Lenders	3,434.4	4,085.9	6,295.4	9,176.7	14,707.8	31,757.7
Official sources	2,598.3	2,878.9	3,487.7	4,545.4	5,812.9	9,754.4
Suppliers & others	395.7	603.2	1,587.1	1,863.0	1,723.3	4,246.3
Financial markets	440.4	603.8	1,220.6	2,768.3	7,171.6	17,730.0
Algeria:						
All Lenders	n/a	n/a	2,241.2	4,916.4	9,590.8	19,113.5
Official sources	n/a	n/a	1,068.8	1,637.1	2,112.1	3,420.2
Suppliers & others	n/a	n/a	1,043.9	1,297.9	3,665.9	5,714.7
Financial markets	n/a	n/a	128.5	1,981.4	3,812.8	9,978.5
South Korea:						
All Lenders	1,199.2	2,226.4	3,243.8	4,940.0	7,173.9	18,146.3
Official sources	434.7	835.9	1,415.7	2,730.7	3,796.8	8,210.9
Suppliers & others	703.0	1,176.0	1,327.8	1,308.8	1,466.2	3,291.6
Financial markets	61.5	214.5	500.3	900.5	1,910.9	6,013.8
Total, All LDCs:						
All Lenders	45,069.5	56,934.5	76,158.5	109,763.0	167,446.8	310,598.0
Official sources	31,890.3	40,355.0	53,715.0	73,516.1	103,884.6	166,573.7
Suppliers & others	6,492.6	8,681.7	12,508.5	13,588.0	19,146.2	29,916.9
Financial markets	6,686.6	7,897.8	9,874.9	22,659.1	44,416.0	114,107.3

SOURCE: World Bank, *World Debt Tables: External Public Debt of LDCs* (Washington, D.C.:World Bank, 1975); and World Bank, *World Debt Tables: External Debt of Developing Countries* (Washington, D.C.: World Bank, 1979).

NOTE: Figures for 1967 and 1969 are for 79 developing countries, including Israel; figures for 1971–78 are for 88 developing countries, excluding Israel. (The exclusion of Israel, whose external public debt was $2.6 billion in 1970, accounts for some of the slowness in growth in total LDC debt to financial markets between 1969 and 1971.) Due to improved coverage after 1969, figures for all LDCs and for individual countries are not strictly comparable before and after that date. "Other private creditors" are included in financial markets until 1969, for they are primarily bondholders and other financial institutions; after 1969, when the World Bank changed its classification system, "other private," primarily nationalization compensation and unclassified debt, is included in suppliers' credits and is statistically insignificant.

Mexico. As in many less developed countries, the dynamics of economic development in Mexico have been détermined by two overriding facts: the legitimacy of the ruling elite has depended on rapid economic growth with a minimum of overt foreign involvement, yet there has been a chronic shortage of domestic investment capital to finance this growth. The legacy of the Revolution demanded Mexican control over the Mexican economy, and the regime of President Lázaro Cárdenas (1934–1940) spurred national economic development by nationalizing the petroleum industry and the railroads, and creating the Federal Electricity Commission and a series of national development banks of which *Nacional Financiera* (Nafinsa) was to become the most important.

It was the World War II-related isolation from traditional suppliers of manufactured goods that forced the Mexican state to play an active role in industrial development. Between 1941 and 1946 nearly 60 percent of all investment came from the public sector, and public-sector investment continued near this level after the war was over.[11] Most of this public investment was in infrastructure and such strategic heavy industries as steel, petroleum, and fertilizers, and it was coupled with a policy of high tariffs on imported consumer goods. The goal of the policy was to promote the domestic production of consumer necessities, and it was quite successful: while one-third of all non-durable consumer goods were imported in 1929, this was down to 7 percent by 1950, and the proportion of imports to total consumption of all manufactured goods (that is, including consumer durables and capital goods) dropped from 52 percent in 1929 to 31 percent in 1950.[12]

Yet this import-substituting industrial growth was achieved at great cost. Because Mexican capitalists were too few and Mexican taxpayers too poor to provide the large amounts of investment capital needed for industrial growth, and foreign investors were either preoccupied by the war or scared off by the nationalizations of the 1930s, the government was forced to fire up its printing presses to finance these enormous capital investments. Continual deficit financing of public-sector investments was highly inflationary: between 1948 and 1954 the wholesale price index rose 8.4 percent a year, well over four times the U.S. rate, and, given Mexico's economic weakness and close ties to the United States, this forced a series of devaluations that reduced the value of the peso from over twenty cents in 1948 to eight cents in 1954. By the mid-1950s the limits of what has been called "inflationary growth"[13] had been reached, and the government adopted the so-called "stabilizing growth" strategy in effect until 1970.

The two pillars of Mexico's "stabilizing growth," as an American observer has noted, were "a substantial and dynamic public sector . . . and an equally dynamic and very profitable private sector."[14] Indeed, government involvement in the economy grew steadily, especially in heavy industry and mining: government outlays went from 4.1 percent of Gross Domestic Product (GDP) in 1952 to over 13 percent in 1970.[15] Perhaps even more important was the government's financing of the private sector: in the 1950s and 1960s Nafinsa alone accounted for one-third to one-half of all loans to private industry.[16]

Government policy also encouraged private investment in manufacturing, especially by foreign corporations. The low levels of taxation and high level of effective protection of the domestic market for manufacturing—74 percent by 1960 as against 3.9 percent for agriculture—made it highly profitable for Mexican and foreign industrial corporations to expand local production, often as government-encouraged oligopolies.[17] Net foreign direct investment grew steadily from one billion pesos in 1954 to 2.7 billion pesos in 1965[18]; assets of U.S. corporations in Mexico quintupled in the 1960s, with most of this growth in manufacturing.[19]

Rapid industrialization, however, was not without problems. The country's balance of payments deficit grew rapidly as Mexican and foreign-owned corporations imported capital goods to run the new factories. A large portion of these imports had been financed by agricultural exports to the United States, but by the late 1960s rapid population growth and slow growth in the rural sector reduced the surplus available for export.[20] The simplest available alternative was to encourage more foreign investment. Yet rapid industrial growth had also strengthened the domestic industrialists, who began in the late 1950s to object to the competition that local subsidiaries of foreign corporations represented. Faced with a pressing need to attract foreign capital and powerful domestic demands to limit foreign investment, the government began to curb multinational corporations while attracting foreign investment in the form of bank loans and international bond issues.

It was during the administration of Gustavo Díaz Ordaz (1964–1970) that Mexico began to borrow from the banks in earnest. By 1966 the state was borrowing more from private sources than from official sources (AID, Eximbank, the World Bank group, the Inter-American Development Bank, etc.) and by 1967 the international banks alone were providing more than all official sources; between 1965 and 1970 public sources loaned $1.5 billion to Mexico, suppliers and others $675 million, and private financial institutions $2.3 billion.[21]

The subsequent administration of Luis Echeverría (1970–1976) inherited the problems of the thirty-year emphasis on import substitution: chronic balance of payments deficits, a distorted market and inefficient domestic industries, reliance on imports of capital equipment, and highly inequitable income distribution. In an attempt to satisfy increasing demands for social programs, government controls on foreign corporations, and state support for economic development, Echeverría embarked on a massive expansion of government involvement in the economy. Restraints on multinational corporations, stiffened in the early 1960s, were stiffened still further with the passage in 1973 of the Law to Promote Mexican Investment and Regulate Foreign Investment and the Law on Transfer of Technology. And, accelerating the process begun under Díaz Ordaz, the government financed its increased activities with foreign borrowing.

A coherent (if *ex post facto*) description of this strategy was given by the Mexican Ministry of Finance and Public Credit in July 1977:

> The policy of public indebtedness which has been followed by the Government of Mexico is based on the desire to expand productive activities, and on an effort to improve the standard of living of, and offer a more equitable life to a population growing at a considerable rate.
>
> As is the case in most developing countries, internal savings in Mexico are insufficient to meet the levels of investment required. Furthermore, our export-derived income does not cover the foreign currency requirements generated by our import needs. The complementary resources [i.e., from international financial markets] are required by our struggle to achieve a rate of capital formation that will enable us to attain a high rate of economic growth and a sustained increase in the levels of our exports.[22]

Between 1971 and 1976 Mexico's federal government budget deficit went from 4.8 billion pesos (1 percent of GDP) to 57.4 billion pesos (3.8 percent of GDP); public-sector investment, expressed in 1960 prices, more than doubled during that period while private investment increased only 16 percent.[23] The number of state-owned corporations jumped from 86 in 1970 to 740 in 1976; today the public enterprises dominate the oil, electricity, steel, petrochemicals, banking, transportation, and communications industries, and the public sector accounts for some 45 percent of GDP.[24] Although Echeverría's successor, José López Portillo, has undertaken to moderate both public expenditures and foreign borrowing, the economy remains heavily dependent on a state intervention that remains in turn heavily dependent on foreign borrowing. Thus in 1978 the fiscal deficit of the public sector was 162 billion pesos, of which 69.7 billion (43 percent) was financed by borrowing abroad; in the parastatal sector, which includes most of the public industrial enterprises, 86.6 percent of financing came from abroad. By the end of 1979 the Mexican government reported that its external debt was nearly $30 billion, the vast majority owed to private sources.[25]

By the end of Echeverría's administration international bankers had begun to worry about Mexico's creditworthiness, but these worries have dissolved as the state oil company, Pemex, has revealed and begun to exploit huge reserves of petroleum. Indeed, petroleum exports have gone from less than 5 percent of total exports in 1974 to nearly 45 percent in 1979.[26] Despite the oil bonanza, the government has continued Echeverría's attempts to increase the export of manufactured goods, most successfully in the machinery and transport equipment sectors where exports rose from $250 million in 1974 to $725 million in 1978.[27]

No discussion of the nexus between Mexican industrial growth, the state sector, and the international banks would be complete without a look at *Nacional Financiera*, or Nafinsa. Founded in 1934, Nafinsa is by now, in the words of its 1974 charter, "the most important investment bank in the country," with capital resources of 77.6 billion pesos (over $6 billion) in 1974.[28] As well as providing about one-third of all financing available to Mexican industry, it holds shares in ninety-eight enterprises in virtually every sector of the economy except agriculture. The sixty-seven industrial enterprises in which Nafinsa holds equity are concentrated in basic industry and include companies in steel, machinery, mining, fertilizers, pharmaceuticals, petrochemicals, pulp and paper, textiles, and food products.[29]

It is not surprising, given the Mexican government's liberal use of foreign borrowing to finance industrial development, that two-thirds of Nafinsa's financial resources come from abroad, the bulk from private banks. Indeed, at the end of 1975 Nafinsa was the most important public debtor, holding about one-third of Mexico's external public debt, a proportion that has since fallen as Pemex has borrowed ever more heavily.[30] The case of Nafinsa is perhaps the archetype of foreign indirect investment in Mexico: the international banks make loans to Nafinsa, Nafinsa uses the loans to finance productive investment deemed essential to Mexican industrial development, the borrower invests the funds, earns a profit, repays the loan to Nafinsa, and Nafinsa repays the banks.

The beauty of the arrangement is obvious: it provides the Mexican government with funds to be disbursed to capital-hungry Mexican industrialists, it allows the state to mold the economy, and it avoids the political difficulties caused by the multinational corporations. The international banks get their profits, the Mexican capitalists get their investment capital, and the Mexican government preserves domestic legitimacy by providing funds for economic growth and protection from foreign corporations.

Brazil.   In many ways the history of Brazil's industrial growth is very similar to that of Mexico's. As in Mexico, industrialization in Brazil began in the late 1930s and 1940s, and was based on import substitution and the creation of public corporations to provide basic inputs necessary for modern industry. In Brazil, the 1937–45 Estado Novo government of Getúlio Vargas oversaw the process: during World War II the national steel corporation was founded and construction begun on Latin America's first integrated steel mill, and government mining, automotive, and caustic soda corporations were formed. Extremely high tariff barriers were erected, and by 1949, 96.3 percent of all consumer nondurables were produced locally; by 1955 even consumer durables were 90 percent domestically manufactured.[31]

Government intervention continued during Vargas's second administration in the early 1950s. In 1953 and 1954 the public development bank Banco Nacional de Desenvolvimento Economico (BNDE) and the national petroleum monopoly Petrobrás were created, along with a series of regional development banks and power companies. State-supported industrial growth picked up steam under Kubitschek (1956-61), whose regime created a series of public enterprises in steel, electric power, and transportation. While in the early 1950s the public sector's share of gross fixed capital investment was 25 percent, Kubitschek's program of massive infrastructural construction increased this to 48 percent by 1960.[32] At the same time, foreign manufacturing corporations were encouraged to establish subsidiaries, and $100 million a year in foreign direct investment entered the country, an amount equal to 10 percent of total investment.[33] All the while, protectionism remained the rule; by 1966, before a liberalizing reform, effective protection of finished consumer goods averaged 190 percent.[34]

As in Mexico, the result of government intervention, high tariff protection, and encouragement to foreign investors was rapid industrial growth: between 1949 and 1961 manufacturing output more than tripled, growing from 22 percent of GDP to 34 percent.[35] Yet by the early 1960s import substitution was reaching its limits, as domestic producers supplied over 90 percent of all manufactured goods and even two-thirds of all capital goods by 1959.[36] In addition, rapid economic growth had been financed by huge government deficits in a process similar to Mexico's "inflationary growth" of the early 1950s. The result was rampant inflation, which could not be controlled by the populist Goulart government (1961–64). The economy stagnated from 1962 to 1968, and Brazil's economic problems contributed to the political turmoil of the early 1960s and to a right-wing reaction, which culminated in the military coup that overthrew Goulart in 1964.

The military government began almost immediately to orient the economy to the foreign sector. Coffee had always been the country's most important export, an important source of foreign exchange, while manufactured goods accounted for below 5 percent of total exports between 1946 and 1964.[37] In order to make Brazilian manufactures more competitive on the world market, in 1967 the military regime reduced the effective protection of manufactured goods to half its former level, and in 1968 began to subsidize manufactured exports at a rate equal to between 19 percent and 30 percent of their value.[38] Exports soared from $1.9 billion in 1968 to $2.7 billion in 1970 to $6.2 billion in 1973 and were $15.2 billion in 1979 of which industrial products constituted 56.2 percent.[39]

In addition to the promotion of manufacturing for export, two essential components of the government's industrialization strategy were the encouragement of foreign direct investment, which averaged over one billion dollars a year in the past decade, and the rapid growth of the public sector, financed in large part by borrowing abroad. Total foreign direct investment is now about $15 billion, and foreign-owned corporations dominate the transport equipment, pharmaceutical, rubber product, and machinery sectors. Nevertheless, the relative importance of foreign corporations in the Brazilian economy has declined as the role of the state has grown and, in the words of a leading business weekly, "the government has in recent years thrown an increasing number of restrictions around foreign investment."[40]

The Brazilian public sector is truly impressive. The twenty-five largest corporations in the country are state-owned (number 26 is Mercedes-Benz of Brazil), and public enterprises accounted for 78 percent of the assets of the country's two hundred largest companies in 1978, up from 64 percent in 1972. The corresponding share of foreign corporations dropped from 20 percent to 9 percent in this period, while that of domestic private firms dropped from 16 percent to 13 percent. Of the 6,430 nonfinancial corporations included in the authoritative annual compilation of Brazil's largest firms, the 382 public enterprises accounted for 51 percent of assets, foreign firms for 11 percent, and private domestic firms for 38 percent.[41]

The Brazilian government has also come to play the dominant role in domestic investment financing. In 1974 government sources, especially the Banco do Brasil and the BNDE, accounted for three-quarters of all investment capital provided to the private sector. In the words of Wilson Suzigan, a researcher at the government's Institute for Economic and Social Planning, "the State is directly or indirectly responsible for virtually all loans to the private sector for investment purposes."[42] All in all, the state now accounts for some 60 percent of all investment in the economy.[43]

As in the case of Mexico, this massive government intervention has depended in large part on loans from international banks. Borrowing on the Euromarkets has increased rapidly since 1969, both to finance major state-sector investments and to compensate for Brazil's post-oil-crisis balance of payments deficit. Since the late 1960s Brazil has alternated with Mexico as the most important LDC borrower on the Euromarket, with most of the loans going to Petrobrás, the public steel corporations, public utilities, and various development banks. In 1979 alone, Brazil raised some $5.8 billion in Eurocurrency bank loans and over $900 million in Eurobonds.[44]

The story of Brazil's public external debt, then, is first and foremost—as in Mexico—the story of a steadily growing state sector in need of ever-larger sums of investment capital. Because our next case is Algeria, a nation with a radical ruling group, it is important to emphasize that in Brazil and Mexico the establishment and growth of the state sector was not an ideological but a pragmatic phenomenon. As Suzigan wrote of the Brazilian state sector, "its expansion had a very atypical 'ideology,' that of priority to growth, developing those sectors which private initiative was unable or unwilling to develop."[45] The fact is simply that in Brazil and Mexico the political legitimacy of the regime had depended on the state's ensuring rapid economic growth. Since local entrepreneurs are unwilling or unable to raise the capital necessary to develop heavy industries, and many of these sectors are not profitable enough or too politically sensitive to be left to the multinationals, the government has been virtually forced to play a leading role in basic industrial development.[46] This role would be impossible without the huge sums provided by international financial markets.

Algeria.   In Algeria the process of industrial development carried out by the state with funds provided by international financiers is particularly clear. The Algerian state sector is all-encompassing, with domestic private enterprise permitted only in some portions of agriculture, trade, and light industry. The public corporations have borrowed extensively on the Euromarkets since 1970 to finance massive industrial investments. The nation's development strategy has been quite consistent since the mid-1960s, and it is based on the use of earnings from Algeria's petroleum and natural gas exports, supplemented by overseas borrowing, to build up modern hydrocarbons and basic industrial sectors. The goal is to create an integrated industrial system in order to guarantee economic independence.[47]

The revolutionary regime of Ben Bella, which took power in 1962, inherited an economy decimated by colonialism, eight years of revolutionary war, counterrevolutionary sabotage, and the exodus of virtually all trained personnel and capital. The first few years of independence were dedicated primarily to reconstruction and were characterized by intense political struggles. In 1965 Colonel Houari Boumedienne overthrew Ben Bella and it was not until 1969 that Boumedienne consolidated his rule by defeating both rebellious tribal leaders and ultraleftist trade unionists and students.

The state began almost immediately to concentrate the commanding heights of the economy in its hands. In 1966 and 1967 mining, insurance, the local distribution networks of British Petroleum, Esso, and Mobil, and former colonial landholdings were nationalized, and three national deposit banks were created. In 1968 most remaining foreign-owned businesses were nationalized, state monopolies were established in the steel, chemicals, and textile industries, and the state navigation company began a program of rapid expansion. In 1970 the local holdings of Shell, Phillips, and two other foreign oil companies were nationalized; and in 1971 the two remaining French producers (CFP and ERAP) were taken over by the state hydrocarbons enterprise, SONATRACH, along with the country's pipelines and natural gas deposits. The government now controls every significant sector of the economy—even the most productive agricultural lands are in the public or "self-managed" sectors. The private sector is still important, accounting for 50 percent of agricultural production, 60 percent of construction, 65 percent of textile production, and 80 percent of commerce.[48] Yet private business is almost exclusively to be found in farming, trade, and backward, labor-intensive light industries: with 40 percent of industrial-sector sales and 30 percent of industrial value-added in 1977, private business made less than 3 percent of the country's industrial investments and held less than 12 percent of industrial assets.[49]

Virtually all industrial and even much agricultural investment, then, is made either by the central government or by the state enterprises, and public investment has emphasized industry—particularly heavy industry.[50] In the 1967–1969 "pre-plan," which began industrial growth, 52 percent of government expenditures went to industry, of which 90 percent went to heavy industry, especially hydrocarbons and steel. But public investments began to soar with the first four-year plan (1970–1973), during which 27.9 billion dinars ($5.9 billion) were invested by the state, 44 percent in industry and 86 percent of this in heavy industry.[51] The second four-year plan (1974–1977) was even more ambitious, and total expenditures were over 126 billion dinars (about $31 billion); again, 52 percent of this went to industry, 88 percent of this to heavy industry.[52] Between 1970 and 1977, 270 new factories and 150 infrastructural projects were completed,[53] and GDP went from $8.0 billion in 1973 to $21.8 billion in 1978.[54] The hydrocarbons sector has predominated since the mid-1960s, and by 1977 it accounted for 29 percent of GDP. Meanwhile, industry and construction have grown rapidly; from below 15 percent of GDP in the early 1960s, they have been around 25 percent since 1970.[55] Manufacturing output, barely $500 million in 1967, was $2.2 billion in 1977, and this figure does not include hydrocarbons or construction. It is true that much of agriculture remains backward and much of industry inefficient, and that social welfare has been of lower priority than industrialization—which has led the post-Boumedienne government of Chadli Benjedid to place greater emphasis on agriculture and the production of consumer goods. Nevertheless it is beyond doubt that the Algerian economy sped towards industrial maturity in the 1970s.

This remarkable program of public investments and state-sector industrial growth was made possible primarily by Algeria's vast petroleum and natural gas reserves. Crude petroleum exports have been around fifty million tons a year for a decade, but the country's most important resource is natural gas, with the third largest estimated reserves in the world (three trillion cubic meters). Hydrocarbons account for over 90 percent of the country's exports, an estimated $10 billion in 1979.[56] Still, the government's ambitious development plans have led it to the Euromarkets, and the international banks have been more than willing to make huge loans to a country with great exportable reserves of oil and gas. The government, for its part, has demonstrated a willingness to pursue productive investment seriously: for several years gross fixed investment has been over 50 percent of GDP, a figure that is probably without parallel anywhere in the world.

Since 1970 Algeria has borrowed massively from the international banks. The country's debt owed to financial markets went from $129 million in 1971 to just short of $2 billion in 1973 (see Table 6.4), and borrowing has continued to climb. In 1978 and 1979 Algeria borrowed over five billion dollars in bank loans and bonds, and the current external public debt is about $19 billion. The most important Algerian borrower is SONATRACH, which needs enormous amounts of capital to finance the construction of new pipelines, refineries, and liquid natural gas plants. Other big borrowers are the national shipping company (CNAN), to expand the state's fleet; the national foreign commerce and consumer credit banks; and the state corporations in steel, hydraulic and construction material, electrical machinery, textiles, and chemical production.[57]

In many ways the partnership between Algeria's regime and the banks is ironic. The Algerian government is one of the more radical in the "third world." Foreign direct investment is prohibited, although the state corporations eagerly solicit participation by foreign investors in joint ventures. And while the regime is strongly anti-imperialist, and proclaims its chief domestic task to be the transition from the current state-capitalist system to socialism, it has recognized the utility of close economic relations with imperialist finance: as Boumedienne said in 1974, "The socialist countries have dealings with us on the basis of friendship. The capitalist countries have dealings with us on the basis of money."[58] The international bankers seem understanding, even appreciative: in the words of one candid banker, "We like Algeria because it's totalitarian and if the government says people will have to cut back consumption, they will."[59] The relationship, as in our previous examples, is symbiotic—although Algeria's hydrocarbons place it in a more favorable position than Brazil's. The banks make their profits on loans to the Algerian state sector and the regime relies on foreign financiers for about one-fifth of its investment capital.[60] Between the two they are industrializing Algeria.

South Korea.   Industrial growth in the Republic of Korea (South Korea) has been markedly different from that in our first three cases. In Korea, perhaps due to the need for a high level of ideological commitment to the letter if not the spirit of "free enterprise," governmen. intervention in the economy has been less direct than in Brazil, Mexico, or Algeria. Secondly, Korean industrialization has been characterized by a single-minded and all-encompassing focus on the manufacture of industrial products for export, and the desire for more balanced industrial development has been subordinate to the incessant drive to export. Finally, while foreign capital has been crucial to the South Korean economy since World War II, the form of this capital inflow has been unusual, with a low level of foreign direct investment until recently, and very high levels of foreign aid due to the country's strategic importance to the United States and Japan.

The industrial development policy, such as it was, of the Syngman Rhee government of the 1950s emphasized the substitution of nondurable consumer goods. Economic development as a whole was entirely dependent on foreign aid, which financed three-quarters of total investment between 1953 and 1963.[61] By the late 1950s the primitive import-substitution process had reached its limits, and economic stagnation set in. This, coupled with Rhee's legendary corruption and inefficiency, led to a student rebellion in May 1960, after which a civilian government came to power. Less than a year later Park Chung Hee led a military coup, and Park was officially "elected" president early in 1964. Throughout the 1960–1965 period, in the words of a Western economist, "the entire orientation of trade and exchange-rate policy shifted. The Korean economy was restructured toward export promotion and away from the earlier emphasis on import substitution."[62]

The 1964–1966 period saw a series of major changes in economic policy: an income tax reform raised government revenues, interest rates were hiked to raise domestic saving, and a series of export incentives and subsidies was introduced. At the same time the normalization of relations with Japan in 1965, the passage of a new Foreign Capital Inducement Law in 1966, and government encouragement of overseas borrowing brought hundreds of millions of dollars in previously unavailable private commercial loans into the country. Net indebtedness went from $301 million in 1965 to $2.57 billion in 1970, and by the late 1960s two-thirds of the loans were from private sources, primarily as suppliers' credits. It has been estimated that without this massive influx of foreign capital in the 1960s, Korean output in 1971 would have been smaller by one-third.[63]

As it was, streamlined domestic financial markets, state intervention, and foreign capital did the trick: Gross National Product (GNP, expressed in 1970 prices) grew from 1.5 trillion won in 1965 to 2.6 trillion won in 1970 to 4.1 trillion won in 1975. This growth was paced by manufacturing, which accounted for 40 percent of GNP growth while increasing its share of value added from 14 percent in 1965 to 32 percent in 1976.[64] Manufacturing growth in turn was due in large part to exports: the growth in exports was directly (i.e., without considering backward linkages or multiplier effects) responsible for 25 percent of manufacturing expansion.[65] Exports, indeed, grew from $39 million in 1961 to $175 million in 1965, then to $385 million in 1970, $5.08 billion in 1975, and some $15 billion in 1979. The composition of the country's exports also changed rapidly, from raw materials to light manufactures, and more recently towards heavy industrial products. In 1960 only 12.5 percent of exports were manufactured; by 1970 this proportion was up to 76 percent, and in 1978 they were 90 percent of all exports. In 1978 heavy industrial exports, insignificant before 1970, were 38.4 percent of all exports, and Korean firms sold 33,000 automobiles and $750 million worth of steel overseas in the year.[66] The government's huge Pohang Iron and Steel Company now has a capacity of 5.5 million tons, making the Korean steel industry the world's twelfth largest; the Hyundai conglomerate, which is number ninety-eight on the *Fortune* list of the world's five hundred largest non-American industrial corporations, operates the world's largest corporate shipyard in Ulsan and is building the world's largest integrated machinery plant in Changwon.[67]

Much of South Korea's industrial growth can be traced to the interaction of foreign capital inflows and government intervention, both direct and indirect. As we have noted, foreign direct investment was insignificant before 1965; by the end of 1978, as corporations took advantage of cheap labor, government incentives, and free-export zones, it was up to $940 million, and between 1970 and 1975 accounted for 17 percent of all manufacturing investment. Foreign corporate investments are primarily of Japanese origin and are concentrated in manufacturing, especially in chemicals, electronics, and textiles; by 1974 some 31 percent of manufactured exports were produced by subsidiaries of foreign firms.[68] Nevertheless, foreign loans are a much more important source of investment capital: while foreign direct investment between 1970 and 1975 was $700 million, net borrowing was $3.7 billion. Foreign loans have been concentrated in some of the same export-oriented manufacturing sectors as foreign direct investment, as well as in nonmetallic minerals, steel, transport equipment, and petroleum.[69] All in all, according to South Korea's Minister of Finance, foreign capital financed 40 percent of investment between 1962 and 1972.[70]

The South Korean state has played a major role in spurring industrial development. For one thing, the government has encouraged economic concentration in the interests of export-competing efficiency and has close ties with the huge conglomerates that do the bulk of South Korea's manufacturing and exporting: Hyundai, Samsung, Daewoo, and their like. The conglomerates and their affiliated trading companies are enticed and persecuted into continually increasing exports, and, in the words of one business magazine, their "intimacy with government policymakers . . . makes 'Japan, Inc.' seem like economic anarchy."[71] In the 1970s direct and indirect subsidies, and tax and tariff incentives to exporters, were equal to nearly one-quarter of the value of all exports, and the national medal of honor is awarded each year to the country's leading exporter.[72] But the state's role goes far beyond that of export incentives and encompasses the entire economy.

An exhaustive study of the Korean public sector in 1975 concluded that "public enterprises clearly constituted a leading sector during the period of rapid Korean growth," and also noted that:

> the Korean public enterprises sector . . . [is] surprisingly large, considering the government's capitalistic ideological orientation. The inertia of historical antecedent can explain only a fraction of the paradox. Much more can be explained in terms of President Park's devotion to economic growth and the role of public ownership and control in overcoming various forms of private market imperfection.[73]

The number of public enterprises grew rapidly in the late 1960s, from 59 in 1965 to 119 in 1969, while the value added of the parastatal sector (in 1970 prices) grew from 90.6 billion won in 1964 to 271.7 billion won in 1972, from 6.8 percent of GDP to 10 percent. The public sector as a whole accounted for about 18 percent of GDP by 1972. State involvement was concentrated in manufacturing, finance, transportation and communications, and utilities.[74] By 1972 Korea's public enterprises, both central government and parastatal, had 200,000 employees and an output of 870 billion won ($2.2 billion).[75] All told, the Korean public sector is responsible for between one-third and one-half of all investments in the economy.[76] Eurocurrency loans have been important in maintaining high levels of government investment, and among the public enterprises the utilities and the huge Pohang Iron and Steel Corporation have been major borrowers.

The Korean state's most important economic tool is in the realm of finance. Between 1963 and 1973 the government and its corporations accounted for around two-thirds of all financial intermediation.[77] There is an extensive network of specialized state banks, with almost half of all loans outstanding in 1976; the Korean Development Bank (KDB) alone provides half of all financing to the country's capital goods industries.[78] The specialized banks, especially the KDB and the Korean Exchange Bank, have borrowed extensively on the Euromarkets for relending to domestic business.

In order to expand production rapidly, the state has also actively encouraged private businesses to borrow heavily both at home and abroad. Indeed, Korea is unusual in that a good half of its external debt is owed by private firms; the public sector provides only a guarantee to the lender.[79] As a result, Korean companies are among the most highly leveraged in the world, with debt-to-equity ratios of 5:1 and 6:1 not uncommon.

In brief, in South Korea, as in Algeria, Brazil, and Mexico, the government has served as an intermediary between international financial markets and local productive investment. As one Korean official put it, "the emphasis on increases in production and export have [sic] placed almost all industries under the government's protection and support."[80] Whether its role has been to encourage foreign borrowing by private firms, to borrow abroad itself for relending at home, or to have public corporations borrow for capital investment, the South Korean state and its foreign financiers have played a crucial role in pushing the economy along the road of export-led industrialization at a dizzying pace.

Conclusions and Implications

The experiences of industrial growth in our four cases are quite varied. In Algeria and South Korea, the smallness of the local market led to a heavy emphasis on exports—of hydrocarbons in the one and manufactures in the other—to fuel industrialization. Brazil and Mexico, with larger domestic markets and more mature industrial structures, pursued more balanced paths, although both have rapidly increased exports in the process. Despite these differences a number of themes seem to be common to all four examples of indebted industrialization.

In all four cases industrial production has grown by any measure very rapidly. Output has expanded, the industrial structure has diversified, and modern production techniques have been mastered.[81]

Second, the relative importance of direct investment by multinational corporations in these economies is on the decline. Foreign direct investment provided a major impetus for industrial growth, and multinational corporations remain crucial in those very important sectors where they have access to otherwise unavailable capital, technology, expertise, and markets. Nevertheless, the process of industrialization, which foreign corporations did much to initiate, has increased both the desire for and the possibility of increased local private and public sector participation in industrial growth. Furthermore, there is increasing evidence that as local business executives and technocrats increase their economic and political strength they favor tighter controls over foreign corporations.[82]

Third, the place of multinational corporations as the main provider of foreign capital has been taken by the international banks. Each of the four countries is heavily dependent on foreign borrowing for its economic growth.

Fourth, the central roles of overseer of industrial growth and intermediary between foreign financiers and domestic productive investment have been played by the public sector. Under the pressure of local demands for national economic development the state, allied with foreign finance, has been the leading force in the economy.

In all cases the concurrent growth in industrial production and external indebtedness has led to very rapid increases in exports—in all but Algeria, of manufactured products, especially but not exclusively consumer goods.

The picture that emerges is clear. The dozen or so nations that have embarked to date on indebted industrialization have by so doing tied their fortunes more tightly than ever before to international trade, investment, and finance. Their state sectors have joined with the international financial empires to spur industrial growth and, in the process, increase their manufactured exports to the advanced capitalist countries. As these few select LDCs pile up industrial projects and bank debt, the relative importance of multinational corporations has been reduced, although they still play a significant role in these rapidly industrializing economies.

Indebted industrialization is a major component of the more general long-term transformation of the world's economy. More and more manufacturing production is taking place in the "third world," and much of this increased manufacturing capacity is made possible, directly or indirectly, by increased manufactured exports to the Organization for Economic Cooperation and Development (OECD) area. We may take as exemplary the ten non-OPEC LDCs that have borrowed most heavily (see Table 6.3); we find that their exports soared from $820 million in 1965 to $24.4 *billion* in 1977. In 1965 these ten countries accounted for 32 percent of all LDC manufactured exports; by 1975 they accounted for 67 percent.[83] By 1975 the "third world" was responsible for about one-fifth of all the manufactured imports of the advanced capitalist countries, and in certain sectors the proportion was much higher: LDCs accounted for over 80 percent of all U.S. imports of clothing, 61 percent of footwear, 43 percent of textiles, and 42 percent of electrical machinery. Over half of the entire western European market (i.e., imports plus domestic production) for men's shirts is supplied by LDCs; about half of all radios and black and white television sets purchased by U.S. consumers are manufactured in the "third world".[84]

In a general sense, OECD imports of manufactured products from the LDCs remain quite low, and nearly four-fifths of these imports are concentrated in just fifteen product lines—hardly a serious challenge to the industrial West.[85] Yet in a more immediate sense, the growth in LDC manufactured exports comes at a time of, and has contributed to, stagnation in some of the corresponding industrial sectors in the OECD countries: textiles, clothing, footwear, electrical machinery, and, increasingly, steel. The heavily indebted, rapidly industrializing LDCs cannot service their debt without selling their manufactured products in OECD markets, but the uncompetitive manufacturers of these products in the OECD countries themselves cannot survive without excluding LDC exports. One or the other must cede: either the uncompetitive OECD producers in these sectors must resign themselves to a slow decline as the locus of production shifts, or they must erect ever-higher protectionist barriers to save their domestic markets, a choice that will almost certainly bring about economic disaster for their LDC competitors. Given the rising strength of protectionism in the advanced capitalist countries the latter course of events might seem inevitable; yet we should not forget that indebted industrialization is a two-sided affair, involving both debtors and creditors. The international banks have as much of a stake in LDC access to OECD markets as the LDCs themselves, for without this access the banks' clients cannot service their debt. The same holds true for those multinational corporations that have become truly international and rely heavily on the free flow of capital and commodities.

This conflict will be a major issue in the international economic disputes of the 1980s. For if the 1970s saw an industrialization of many LDCs predicated on free access to Northern markets, this very process gave impetus to forces that are fighting to limit access. Manufacturers in threatened sectors—and their allies in the labor movement—may succeed in protecting their markets, but such success will call into question both continued economic growth in the LDCs and stability in international financial markets. Alternatively, the international financiers and corporations, allied with their LDC clients, may succeed in preserving LDC access to markets in the advanced capitalist countries, but this success—while it may bring about a significant reordering of international trade and production—will be achieved at the expense of many traditional OECD industries. In either case—or in the event of some form of compromise between, on the one hand, LDC elites and international financiers who have staked their fortunes on rapid "third world" industrialization and, on the other, threatened OECD manufacturers whose market shares and fortunes are equally at stake—the international economic and political system will have been transformed by the process of indebted industrialization.

Notes

The author would like to thank Robert Keohane, Charles Lipson, Lynn Mytelka, Glenda Rosenthal, John Ruggie, Joan Spero, Susan Strange, and two anonymous reviewers for their valuable comments and suggestions.

1. World Bank, *World Economic and Social Indicators 1980*. (Washington, DC: World Bank, 1980), p. 10.

2. External public debt will be defined here as debt owed to foreign creditors payable in foreign currency, with a maturity of over one year, by governments, government agencies, public entities, or private entities guaranteed for repayment by the government. Throughout this paper, the debt we are speaking of is of this kind—it does not include debts owed to domestic financial institutions (even when these are subsidiaries of foreign financial institutions), nor does it include debts owed by private sources not guaranteed by the government.

3. World Bank, *World Debt Tables 1979*, 2 vols. (Washington, DC: World Bank, 1979).

4. Reinhold Harringer, "The Development of International Debt," *Aussenwirtschaft* (March-June 1978):13.

5. Three recent collections of articles are extremely valuable: Jonathan David Aronson (ed.), *Debt and the Less Developed Countries* (Boulder, CO: Westview Press, 1979); Lawrence G. Franko and Marilyn Seiber (eds.), *Developing Country Debt* (New York: Pergamon, 1979); and Miguel Wionczek (ed.), *LDC External Debt and the World Economy* (Mexico City: El Colegio de México, 1978). *World Development* 7, 2 (1979), edited by Wionczek and devoted to "International Indebtedness and World Economic Stagnation," contains some of the articles in *LDC External Debt* as well as other studies. Other representative works include David C. Beek, "Commercial Bank Lending to the Developing Countries," *Federal Reserve Bank of New York Quarterly Review* 2, 2 (1977):1–8; Harold van B. Cleveland and W.H. Bruce Brittain, "Are the LDCs In over Their Heads?" *Foreign Affairs* 55, 4 (1977):732–750; Irving Friedman, *The Emerging Role of Private Banks in the Developing World* (New York: Citicorp, 1977); Karin Lissakers, *International Debt, the Banks and U.S. Foreign Policy*, staff report prepared for the Subcommittee on Foreign Economic Policy of the Committee on Foreign Relations, U.S. Senate (Washington, DC: U.S. Government Printing Office, 1977); Cheryl Payer, "Third World Debt Problems: The New Wave of Defaults," *Monthly Review* 28, 4 (1976):1–19; Howard Wachtel, *The New Gnomes: Multinational Banks in the Third World*, TNI Pamphlet no. 4 (Washington, DC: Transnational Institute, 1977); Paul Watson, *Debt and the Developing Countries: New Problems and New Actors*, Development Paper 26, NIEO Series (Washington, DC: Overseas Development Council, 1978).

6. Lissakers, *International Debt*, p. 36.

7. John Holsen and Jean Waelbroeck, "LDC Balance of Payments Policy and the International Monetary System," World Bank Staff Working Paper no. 226 (Washington, DC: World Bank, 1976), p. 10.

8. Inter-American Development Bank (IDB), *Economic and Social Progress in Latin America 1976 Report* (Washington, DC: IDB, 1977), pp. 432–433.

9. Figures on LDC debt are collected by a multitude of private and public entities. Because of differences in reporting practices and coverage, data from different sources are seldom comparable. For example, the fact that the Inter-American Development Bank reported Latin American debt to private financiers at $1.9 billion in 1960 and the OECD reported all LDC debt to private lenders at $2.4 billion does *not* mean that Latin America accounted for all but $500 million of the debt owed to private sources: the IDB's coverage is broader than that of the OECD.

10. Computed from data in the World Bank quarterly bulletin, *Borrowing in International Capital Markets*, for each quarter of 1978.

11. Timothy King, *Mexico: Industrialization and Trade Policies since 1940* (London: Oxford University Press, 1970), p. 48.

12. René Villarreal, "Del proyecto de crecimiento y sustitución de importaciones al de desarrollo y sustitución de exportaciones," *Comercio Exterior* 25, 3 (1975):315–323; see p. 317.

13. Leopoldo Solís, "Desarrollo económico mexicano," in Edmar Bacha et al., *Estrategias de desarrollo económico en algunos paises de América Latina* (Bogotá: Fundación para la Educación y el Desarrollo, 1974), pp. 18–19.

14. Robert E. Looney, *Mexico's Economy: A Policy Analysis with Forecasts to 1990* (Boulder, CO: Westview Press, 1978), p. 17.

15. Ibid., p. 43.

16. Rosa Oliva Villa M., *Nacional Financiera: banco de fomento del desarrollo económico de México* (México, D.F.: Nacional Financiera, 1976), p. 41.

17. Villarreal, "Del proyecto," p. 317.

18. King, *Mexico*, p. 63. Figures are in current pesos.

19. John Connor, *The Market Power of Multinationals* (New York: Praeger, 1977), pp. 68–69.

20. Grupo de Economía Mexicana-CIDE, "México: devaluación, petróleo y alternativas de desarrollo," *Economía de América Latina*, 2 (1979):171–187, esp. pp. 173–174.

21. Rosario Green, *El endeudamiento público externo de México 1940–1973* (Guanajuato: El Colegio de México, 1976), p. 154.

22. Ministry of Finance and Public Credit, "The First and Second Reports on the Public Debt Presented to the Congress of the Union," *Comercio Exterior de México* (English language edition) 24, 1 (1978):25.

23. Norris Clement and Louis Green, "The Political Economy of Devaluation in Mexico," *Inter-American Economic Affairs* 32, 3 (1978):47–75; see pp. 49–51.

24. See, for example, James L. Schlagheck, *The Political, Economic, and Labor Climate in Mexico* (Philadelphia: Industrial Research Unit, The Wharton School, 1977), pp. 32–34.

25. "Las relaciones económicas con el exterior en 1979," *Comercio Exterior* 30, 5 (1980):442–447, esp. p. 446.

26. Ibid., p. 443; Roberto Gutiérrez R., "La balanza petrolera de México, 1970–1982," *Comercio Exterior* 29, 8 (1979):839–850, esp. p. 841.

27. "El sector externo de México en 1978 y sus perspectivas," *Comercio Exterior* 29, 3 (1979):263–270; see p. 264.

28. Villa, *Nacional Financiera*, pp. 11, 96.

29. Ibid., pp. 65–70.

30. Ibid., p. 102.

31. Joel Bergsman, *Brazil: Industrialization and Trade Policies* (London: Oxford University Press, 1970), p. 92.

32. Peter Evans, *Dependent Development* (Princeton: Princeton University Press, 1979), p. 93.

33. Stefan Robock, *Brazil: A Study in Development Progress* (Lexington, MA: Lexington Books, 1975), p. 29.

34. Bergsman, *Brazil*, p. 51.

35. Ibid., p. 17.

36. Ibid., p. 92.

37. Ibid., p. 100.

38. José Augusto Savasini, *Export Promotion: The Case of Brazil* (New York: Praeger, 1978), p. 108.

39. João Paulo de Almeida Magalhães, *Modelo brasileiro de desenvolvimento* (Rio de Janeiro: Record, 1976), pp. 134–135; and *Business Latin America*, 23

April 1980, p. 136.

40. "Brazil's Political Change Is Nurturing Selectivity toward Foreign Investment," *Business Latin America*, 9 May 1979, p. 146; see also "Brazil Bans MNC Purchase of State Companies," *Business Latin America*, 5 September 1979, p. 287.

41. Visão, *Quem é Quem na economia brasileira*, 1973 and 1979 editions.

42. Wilson Suzigan, "As empresas do governo e o papel do Estado na economia brasileira," in Fernando Rezende et al., *Aspectos da participação do governo na economia* (Rio de Janeiro: IPEA/INPES, 1976), pp. 113–115. See also Sylvia Ann Hewlett, "The State and Brazilian Economic Development: The Contemporary Reality and Prospects for the Future," in William H. Overholt (ed.), *The Future of Brazil* (Boulder, CO: Westview Press, 1978), pp. 149–210.

43. "Focus on Brazil: Shifting Priorities Shape New Landscape," *Business Latin America*, 7 February 1979, p. 42.

44. Morgan Guaranty Trust, *World Financial Markets*, December 1979, pp. 16–17.

45. Suzigan, "As empresas do governo," p. 91.

46. For a succinct discussion of this point, see ibid., pp. 124–130.

47. For a good summary see Middle East Research and Information Project (MERIP), *State Capitalism in Algeria*, Report no. 35 (Washington, DC: MERIP, 1975); and Kader Ammour, Christian Leucate, and Jean-Jacques Moulin, *La Voie algérienne: Les Contradictions d'un développement national* (Paris: Maspero, 1974).

48. Nicole Grimaud, "Une Algérie en mutation a l'heure de la charte nationale," Maghreb-Machrek, 73 (1976):70–77.

49. "La Stratégie du developpement socialiste," *Révolution africaine*, 819 (1979):39–54, esp. p. 50.

50. "Algeria," in United Nations Economic Commission for Africa, *Survey of Economic and Social Conditions in Africa 1976–1977* (New York: United Nations, 1977), pp. 1–12.

51. "La Stratégie," p. 51; A. Farrah, "La Necessité de planification," *Révolution africaine*, 783 (1979):18–19.

52. "La Stratégie," pp. 50–51.

53. Howard Schissel, "After Industrialization More Cake for the Workers," *African Business*, March 1979, p. 24.

54. U.S. Industry and Trade Administration, *Foreign Economic Trends and Their Implications for the United States: Algeria* (Washington, DC: U.S. Department of Commerce, 1979), p. 2.

55. Ibid., p. 2; Nicole Grimaud, "Les Finances publiques de l'Algérie," *Maghreb-Machrek*, 56 (1973):30–37, esp. p. 31.

56. Susan Morgan, "Benjedid's New Broom Sweeps Away Old Priorities," *African Business*, June 1979, p. 26; "La Stratégie," p. 51; Howard Schissel, "Algeria Plans to Woo Consumers," *The Middle East*, October 1979, p. 93.

57. Margaret Greenhalgh, "Algerian Gas Wealth Impresses Western Bankers," *Middle East Economic Digest*, 23 February 1979, pp. 4–5; *Arab Banking: A Middle East Economic Digest Special Report*, May 1980, p. 86.

58. Quoted in MERIP, *State Capitalism in Algeria,* p. 8.

59. Quoted in "Algeria, the Country that Bankers Love to Hate," *Euromoney,* October 1977, p. 65.

60. *Algeria News Report,* 30 June 1978, pp. 4–5.

61. Charles Frank, Kwang Suk Kim, and Larry Westphal, *Foreign Trade Regimes and Economic Development: South Korea* (New York: Columbia University Press, 1975), p. 2.

62. Anne O. Krueger, *Studies in the Modernization of the Republic of Korea, 1945–1975* (Cambridge: Harvard University Press, 1979), p. 82.

63. Ibid., p. 145; and Frank, Kim, and Westphal, *Foreign Trade Regimes,* pp. 101–106.

64. Larry Westphal, "The Republic of Korea's Experience with Export-Led Industrial Development," *World Development* 6, 3 (1978):349–374.

65. Ibid., p. 374.

66. Ibid., p. 360; "Korea Export Target Means Additional Sales to the Local Market," *Business Asia,* 2 February 1979, pp. 33–34; "South Korea's Painful Road to Economic Maturity," *Financial Times World Business Weekly,* 15 October 1979, p. 22.

67. Harvey Shapiro, "Is South Korea's Economic Miracle in Trouble?" *Institutional Investor International Edition,* May 1979, p. 126.

68. Westphal, "Korea's Experience," p. 362; "Korean Opportunities: Prospects for Direct Investment," *Business Asia,* 9 February 1979, pp. 47–48; Sung-Hwan Jo, "The Impact of Multinational Firms on Employment and Income: The Case Study of South Korea," World Employment Programme Research Working Paper 12 (Geneva: International Labour Organisation, 1976), Table III-7.

69. Krueger, *Modernization of Korea,* pp. 145, 150–151.

70. Duck-woo Nam, "Mobilization of Domestic Resources," in *International Conference on Korean Futures* (Seoul: Asiatic Research Centre, Korea University, 1975), p. 263.

71. Shapiro, "Economic Miracle," p. 122.

72. Westphal, "Korea's Experience," p. 352.

73. Leroy P. Jones, *Public Enterprise and Economic Development: The Korean Case* (Seoul: Korea Development Institute, 1975), p. 202.

74. Ibid., pp. 73–79.

75. Ibid., p. 244.

76. Ibid., p. 85.

77. Ibid., p. 90.

78. "The Banking System Adapts to Korea's Particular Needs," *Euromoney,* April 1977 (supplement), pp. 22–25.

79. Krueger, *Modernization of Korea,* pp. 144–145.

80. O Won-chol, "Economic Development and Industrialization in Korea," in *International Conference on Korean Futures,* p. 289.

81. This rapid increase in LDC industrial production is of major significance for our theoretical understanding of economic development and underdevelopment. An example of attempts to come to grips with changing eco-

nomic conditions in the LDCs is the lively debate over the implications of LDC industrialization for Marxist theories of economic development. See, for example, Isaac Minian, "Rivalidad intercapitalista e industrialización en el subdesarrollo: notas para un estudio sobre la división internacional del trabajo," *Economía de América Latina*, 2 (1979):81–102; James F. Petras, "State Capitalism and the Third World," *Journal of Contemporary Asia* 6, 4 (1976):432–443; Richard L. Sklar, "Postimperialism," ch. 2 of this volume; and Bill Warren, "Imperialism and Capitalist Industrialization," *New Left Review*, 81 (1973):3–44.

82. See, for example, David A. Jodice, "Sources of Change in Third World Regimes for Foreign Direct Investment, 1968–1976," *International Organization* 34, 2 (1980):177–206. Independent corroboration of this increasing local business animosity to foreign corporations can be found in Jorge Dominguez, "National and Multinational Business and the State in Latin America," paper presented at the Annual Meeting of the American Political Science Association, Washington, D.C., September 1979. Dominguez, analyzing opinion polls of business in seven Latin American countries, found a drastic shift in the past decade away from the earlier local-capitalist openness to multinational corporations, towards what he calls a "national bourgeois" position advocating strict limits on foreign direct investment, including nationalizations. He concludes that "the long term trend across countries suggests a strong and persistent shift away from transnationalism and toward national bourgeois attitudes and behavior," and adds that "there may be a preference for foreign links through loans and licensing agreements rather than through direct investment" (p. 68).

83. Computed from Donald B. Keesing, "World Trade and Output of Manufactures: Structural Trends and Developing Countries' Exports," World Bank Staff Working Paper no. 316 (Washington, DC: World Bank, 1979), Annex B. In some cases figures used are for 1976. In the computation of all LDC manufactured exports, South Africa, Southern Europe, Hong Kong, and Singapore are not included.

84. Hollis B. Chenery and Donald B. Keesing, "The Changing Composition of Developing Country Exports," World Bank Staff Working Paper no. 314 (Washington, DC: World Bank, 1979), pp. 39–41.

85. Anthony Edwards, *The New Industrial Countries and Their Impact on Western Manufactures* (London: The Economist Intelligence Unit, 1979), p. 126.

CHAPTER SEVEN

Socializing Adaptation:
A Perspective on World Capitalism

SAYRE P. SCHATZ

This paper proposes a hypothesis on world capitalist development that is in apparent conflict with many current tendencies. The hypothesis is that capitalist societies manifest a particular pattern of responding to problems, which I call socializing adaptation, that this has been essentially a domestic process, but that—despite many significant movements in the opposite direction—a new global process of socializing adaptation is emerging.

1. Socializing Adaptation: National

My starting point is a Marxian concept—Marx's thesis on the basic source of capitalist economic problems. There is a fundamental incongruity (a "contradiction") between the social or interdependent nature of the productive system of a capitalist society and the private or fragmented nature of the decision-making system that directs the operations of the productive system.[1] The productive system itself is social. Production involves an intricate meshing of a nation's varied and dispersed economic undertakings; it is carried on by a complex network of interrelated enterprises. Not only do firms depend upon one another for supplies and for markets, but the inputs available to any given firm shape the nature of its productive processes, while conversely its input needs shape the productive processes of supplying firms. Furthermore, every firm is profoundly influenced by the economy-wide macroeconomic factors (such as the level of aggregate demand) which determine the health and vigor of the entire economy. The degree of interdependence in the productive network, moreover, tends continually to be enhanced by technological developments. On

This article first appeared in *World Development* 11, 1(1983):1–10. Reprinted with permission.

the other hand, decisions concerning production are made in an un-coordinated way, by individual companies relying on limited informa-tion and resources, seeking their own separate, often conflicting, profit-related goals.

This fundamental incongruity generates all manner of malfunc-tions, ranging from minor disorders to serious failings that threaten the viability of the capitalist system. Decisions which may be reasonable, taken individually and separately, and given the information and resources available and the interests served, often turn out in the aggregate to be socially irrational; they may cause substantial harm to the apparently rational decision-makers and to society as a whole. For example, investment decisions which in the aggregate fail to match sav-ings decisions cause a reduction in the level of economic activity, in-creased unemployment, heightened poverty, and a lower level of real income for almost all. Or, income-seeking decisions which add up to total claims on income exceeding the income available generate an in-flationary spiral. Or, production decisions based on the profitability criterion may damage the environment; more generally stated, in an unregulated market economy, externalities will be disregarded.[2]

Marxists long expected capitalism to collapse under the stress of the fundamental incongruity, but, particularly in the more developed economies, capitalism has flourished. This raises the question: can the failure of the Marxian prediction be attributed to simple faultiness in the fundamental incongruity concept itself, or is there some other ex-planation? I suggest the latter is the case.

Capitalism has endured because it has manifested a capability—which Marx did not foresee—to adapt when threatened by serious mal-functions in a way that alleviates and diminishes the fundamental in-congruity. With delays, spasmodically, and incompletely, capitalism has adapted its decision-making system.[3]

Of course, all viable societies adapt to threatening conditions. The capitalist process is, I suggest, a particular kind of adaptation: socializ-ing adaptation. This is characterized by three major properties.

First, it is socializing in the sense that it socializes or centralizes the governance of the productive system. As productive interdependence increases, the degree to which decision-making is coordinated also in-creases, though lagging behind. While in many respects the locus of economic decision-making remains unchanged, in other respects its base is broadened. Government takes actions which extend societal in-fluence or control over economic decisions.[4]

The economic problems of the Great Depression, for example, were dealt with by various forms of socializing adaptation. Compensa-tory fiscal policy and discretionary monetary policy constituted centralized decision-making concerning the level of aggregate demand—undertaken because individual decisions about the components of aggregate demand cause depressed levels of economic activity. Other forms of socializing adaptation included more extensive and effective regulation of the banks, provision of a welfare floor through such means as unemployment insurance and social security, labor legislation, farm legislation, and much more. These new forms of social management of the socially interdependent productive system curbed the most ominous domestic malfunctions of the capitalist economy.

A second property of socializing adaptation is that the changes tend toward the minimal, i.e., they tend to be little greater than necessary to deflect threats to the viability of the system. This moderation results from the underlying political processes.

Socializing adaptation proceeds through government responses to a great variety of conflicting pressures. Even highly authoritarian regimes are somewhat responsive, but capitalism is most likely to adapt constructively when it is democratic, and aggrieved groups can exert overt political pressure. Government reactions tend to be moderate. For one thing, the great diversity of the pressures is in itself somewhat immobilizing. More important, the interests favoring the status quo are strong. The owners and controllers of the existing economic entities tend to be effective in resisting government measures which encroach upon their autonomy, power, or income.

In such a setting, deliberate actions tend to be minimized if the natural functioning of the system and/or fortuitous events engender improvements in some problem area, but if problems deepen, government undertakes more substantial actions to defuse discontent. This is not a matter of a carefully calibrated state response nor of a neatly calculated decision by a tight ruling elite. It results from the give and take of many interests under the conditions of uncertainty about the effects of any proposed policy. The tendency, then, is for the state to do little more than it has to, and as a result capitalism tends to handle its problems no more than adequately.[5]

Third, socializing adaptation is an endless process; further doses are always needed.

The fundamental incongruity develops unremittingly. Productive interdependence continually heightens and, moreover, changes form. But effective coordination of the decision-making system, despite adaptive spurts, tends to lag behind. Thus capitalism keeps generating new malfunctions, and the alleviated disorders often emerge in new forms. Even the means of alleviating problems may give rise to new ones. For example, it can be argued that the policies that have successfully averted severe depressions and mass unemployment since the

Great Depression have attenuated the anti-inflationary forces in capitalist economies, have thereby nurtured stubborn and accelerating inflationary tendencies, and, to come full circle, have caused the increasing unemployment that results from fear of the inflationary consequences of expansionary fiscal and monetary policies.[6]

Thus, socializing adaptation is an ever-present manifestation of capitalism. Even in the early days of industrial capitalism, when the social order was threatened by widespread Luddite attacks on machinery and factories, by rampant crime, and by other expressions of misery and rage, government ameliorated some of the worst excesses of individual profit-oriented control of productive enterprises, e.g., by limiting working hours or barring employment of young children. Socializing adaptation has continued ever since.[7] It is manifested in the progressive increase in relative as well as absolute government expenditures in capitalist countries all over the world.[8]

2. Global Socializing Adaptation (GSA)

It is my thesis that the fundamental incongruity is operative on the global as well as the national level; that its most important manifestation is the complex of North-South problems which (despite impressive overall Southern economic growth since World War II) threatens the viability of world capitalism; and that (despite some contrary currents) a world pattern of socializing adaptation is developing.

In the world economy, the fundamental incongruity is manifesting itself to an ever-increasing degree. That modern production entails interdependence of productive processes over many parts of the earth is a commonplace. Such interdependence has been increasing gradually throughout the entire capitalist era and has accelerated since World War II. World trade, a good index of mutual dependence, has displayed this accelerating growth pattern. So has the spread of multinational corporations, with a particularly rapid postwar expansion. On the other hand, the various units of the world productive system continue to be governed on a relatively narrow basis for narrow ends. Each individual enterprise makes its own decisions based on its own information and resources and in pursuit of its own profit and growth. Even governmental policies (designed to exert social control) have been primarily national policies and thus have been more parochial than the world productive system they attempt to harness.

The fundamental incongruity, along with domestic development-retarding conditions, has been a basic cause of the development problems of the "third world."[9] Thus, when the major trading companies and shipping lines in the colonial 1950s encouraged importation of metropolitan manufactures and discouraged host-country industry, it was a manifestation of the fundamental incongruity. It is also such a manifestation when multinational corporations in the 1980s employ inappropriate technology[10] in the less developed countries (LDCs), or when they engage in transfer pricing[11] designed to avoid host-country taxes, or when, simply being prudent, they heighten exchange rate fluctuations or balance-of-payments pressures.[12] It is also such a manifestation when the more developed countries (MDCs) impede industrial development in the LDCs by imposing much higher effective rates of tariff protection on LDC manufactures than on their primary products. In sum, the fundamental incongruity is evinced whenever actions good for an individual company (or country) are, contrary to Adam Smith's invisible hand, harmful on balance to the world economy.

In the face of the "third world" awakening, which is one of the major social processes of the second half of the twentieth century, the North-South gap constitutes a comprehensive threat to "the collective Western economic and political system."[13] For one thing, turmoil in the "third world" directly endangers business interests in many ways: foreign investments might face physical damage, disruption of operations, forced divestiture of ownership at low prices, or outright expropriation; contracts might be abrogated; firms engaged in foreign operations might not be paid for their goods or services; funds might be frozen in foreign bank accounts or might be repatriable only at highly unfavorable exchange rates. Of broader concern, some of the LDCs might embark upon courses of action (such as effective cartelization in the manner of OPEC, or inward-looking development) that disrupt world trade or world investment patterns. Of still broader concern, some might defect (or attempt to defect) from capitalism altogether, or might use "nuclear blackmail" to force massive transfers of wealth to the LDCs, or might even undertake nuclear "wars of redistribution."[14]

The impact of Southern discontent has been enhanced by the formation of Southern coalitions. Knowing that some of the constraints on development lie in the areas of international trade and investment, and at the same time being glad to divert attention from domestic difficulties, Southern leaders have turned increasing attention to multilateral approaches, such as the United Nations Conferences on Trade and Development (UNCTAD) and proposals for a new international economic order. The power of the Southern groupings, while fluctuating, is increasing over the long run.[15]

The potency of "third world" challenges to the capitalist international economic order has also been greatly strengthened by the North's growing dependence upon the South. The classic theory of the economics of imperialism, with the major capitalist powers wanting dependencies as markets, sources of materials, and sources of investment opportunities, is a script that is, in a modified way, being more fully played out now than ever before. In the past, a standard and perhaps valid rebuttal to economic theories of imperialism has been that trade with and investment in the less developed areas was relatively unimportant for the MDCs. However, the facts have changed; the LDCs are becoming increasingly important to the advanced capitalist economies. This has caught the North unawares. In the words of the World Bank, "it is perhaps not yet fully understood how far . . . [interdependence in the world economy] has now come, nor how much further it will go even in the next decade."[16] The World Bank's analysis parallels the classic thesis on the economics of imperialism, although it subsumes it within a theory of interdependence. Bank data show that the LDCs "are increasingly important markets" for the exports of the advanced capitalist countries, that "increasing the supply of energy and food" is of vital importance to the MDCs, and that the poor countries "are an important element in the world capital markets and have helped to invest the vastly expanded supply of savings productively."[17] The growing dependence of the North upon the South provides a material base which powerfully reinforces Southern demands.[18]

The effectiveness of Southern challenges is further increased by other developments, such as decreased Northern ability to use the big stick or even clandestine intervention against recalcitrant LDCs and opposition within MDCs to abuse of big-nation power.

In response to the threats to its viability, the collective Western economic and political system is engaging to an increasing degree in socializing adaptation on a global scale. Since World War II, the advanced capitalist countries have been putting in place significant extensions of social control over the world economic order. More decisions are being made in a somewhat more collective fashion, and economic actions are becoming less predominantly based on the specific interests of individual countries or companies. Governments have collaborated or consulted. Multinational corporations have juggled the potentialities and interests of worldwide networks of subsidiaries. Business decisions have been influenced by national governments. International organizations, such as the World Bank, the International Monetary Fund, and others less potent, have helped to shape world economic affairs. The weighted average of all decision-making bearing on the world economy has been shifting somewhat from the atomistic toward the collective.

The decisions, moreover, are being influenced to a growing degree by more global concerns. The welfare of the poorer countries and possible threats to the capitalist economic order posed by North-South conflicts get greater attention.

Before sketching the hypothesized pattern of global socializing adaptation (GSA) more concretely, it may be worth making clear that the hypothesis is not a rhapsody. To be successful, socializing adaptation need not be generous or freely accorded or sufficient to meet minimal human needs. Changes can be grudging, mean-spirited, and stingy responses to problems that have become too painful to ignore. However, if they suffice to mollify dissatisfaction that jeopardizes the viability of the system, they constitute successful socializing adaptation. They might not improve conditions in the LDCs at all, but might merely alleviate a deterioration (which might even be attributable to other MDC policies). They are likely to be self-serving: "It has become increasingly clear that the only viable and lasting arrangements for preferential treatment are bound to be those that take account of the needs and interests of the developed countries as well as the LDCs."[19] Concessions may go only as far as the LDC strength appears to make necessary. The issue is not that such adjustments "would not overcome the impoverishment of the masses, backward agriculture, distorted industrial and economic structures subservient to the metropoles, illiteracy, inadequate education and health services, and all the other ills that beset these societies"[20]; the issue is whether the changes will suffice to sustain the viability of world capitalism.

The GSA process can (somewhat arbitrarily) be dated from World War II,[21] although it was preshadowed by the era of British international leadership before World War I, when international economic institutions were centered in Britain, which set the procedures and patterns. As the problems of the less developed areas posed no threats, however, there was no need for socializing adaptation.

After interwar disintegration of the Britain-centered pattern, the new Bretton Woods order with the United States as leader was established. Increasing collectivity was made possible in this order by technological factors (improved transport and communications), by political factors (the Bretton Woods and related agreements), and by organizational factors (the formation of the International Monetary Fund, the World Bank, the General Agreement on Tariffs and Trade, the United Nations, and related institutions). Increasing collectivity was also made desirable by the problems of the world's "economically backward" areas.[22] Given the backdrop of the Great Depression and wholesale postwar decolonization,[23] economic development assistance was widely seen as necessary. At first, the main collaborative efforts in development programs were between particular MDCs and their networks of former and emerging colonies and other client states, but increasing collaboration between the MDCs soon emerged, both directly and via the international organizations. MDC collaboration has been stimulated by the emergence of a more polycentric system within world capitalism as American economic, political, and military dominance has declined.

There have been numerous extensions of social control over the world order for the purpose of assisting LDCs, i.e., instances of GSA, usually in response to "third world" complaints about the workings of unfettered international capitalism. Consider, for example, the Northern-dominated International Monetary Fund, a businesslike and technical body concerned mainly with maintaining a smoothly functioning world monetary system. Even here there has been some small shift of power in favor of the less developed countries, and thus some small increase in the degree of socialization of the decision-making system. Nine LDCs were included in the IMF Committee of Reform of the International Monetary System (the "Committee of Twenty") established in 1972, an arrangement which carried over to its successor, the Interim Committee. This was more than token representation, for "the developing countries succeeded to a remarkable degree in leaving their imprint on the reports of these Committees."[24] LDC strength in the IMF has also been augmented slightly by an increase in the voting power of the OPEC countries. A partial shift of function is also under way, and the IMF has adopted several proposals "which . . . partially convert [it] into an aid-giving institution."[25]

The World Bank, unlike the IMF, was always aid-oriented. Its attention was originally directed toward the MDCs, and it was required to follow "sound banking practices." After the immediate postwar years, however, its attention progressively shifted to the LDCs, which are now its sole concern. The World Bank group has increasingly adapted its financing policies to the needs of the LDCs, and the funds available to it, which come primarily from the MDCs, have grown substantially.

The World Bank itself has become more and more flexible in its lending policies, financing many kinds of undertakings that were originally excluded by its adherence to conservative banking principles. Its lending terms have become increasingly concessional.[26] Moreover, the affiliated International Development Association was established in 1960 with even more flexible lending policies for the poorer LDCs and with highly concessional terms.[27] In addition, a Third Window has recently been established for countries with per capita incomes too high for access to IDA but which have difficulty in meeting the usual terms of the World Bank.[28]

There have been other forms of GSA. Official country-to-country aid has been important.[29] Although essentially bilateral, there has been some collaboration among the major aid-giving capitalist nations through the Organization for Economic Cooperation and Development's Development Assistance Committee, which was formed for the purpose of coordinating aid policies. United Nations development assistance, provided by a number of agencies, supplements national aid marginally.[30]

In international trade, the principle of differential treatment for LDCs had been definitely accepted and gradually extended. The principle was formally introduced into the GATT in 1957, when the "special needs" of LDCs were explicitly recognized. Following further agreements in 1961 and 1963, GATT's Part IV in 1965 stated: "The developed contracting parties do not expect reciprocity or commitments made by them in trade negotiations to reduce or remove tariffs and other barriers to the trade of less developed contracting parties." It added that "the less developed contracting parties should not be expected to make contributions which are inconsistent with their individual development, financial and trade needs, taking into consideration past trade developments." Part IV also committed the MDCs to facilitate market access and market stability for the exports of the LDCs. A generalized system of preferences (GSP) was introduced in 1970, permitting MDCs to grant unilateral tariff preferences on industrial exports of LDCs while maintaining normal rates on the same products from MDCs.

While movement has been slow, the trade-preference principle has in fact been implemented.[31] Estimates of its effect on LDCs vary considerably, but it appears to have had at least a modest impact.[32]

This pattern of concessions to the development needs of the LDCs represents, I suggest, the early stages of global socializing adaptation. The process so far has been modest, and there are contrary currents, e.g., the new protectionism and the current American subordination of North-South to East-West issues, both in the face of mounting balance-of-payments and debt problems of the LDCs and falling prices for many LDC primary products. Nevertheless, there is reason to believe that GSA has been proceeding successfully.

Overall economic growth and development of the less developed economies since World War II has been considerably better than most had come to expect. LDC income per person increased by almost 3 percent per annum during the third quarter of the twentieth century.[33] This considerably exceeds the growth rate achieved by the presently developed economies during their industrializations; from mid-nineteenth to mid-twentieth centuries, their per capita growth rate was generally less than 2 percent per annum. The growth in LDC output has generally been accompanied by economic modernization. In virtually all the LDCs, industrial sectors have grown most rapidly, and many of these countries manufacture technologically sophisticated machinery and equipment. The LDCs have been increasing exports of manufactured goods, both absolutely and as a percentage of world exports of manufactures, and have been diversifying their exports generally. There have been substantial improvements in their infrastructures, in skills, in the functioning of complex modern institutions, and in other aspects of their economies.

LDCs have also improved upon broader aspects of the quality of life. The proportion of primary-school-age children actually in school increased from 32 to 52 percent between 1960 and 1975 for the low-income group of the LDCs, and from 79 to 97 percent for the "middle-income" LDCs. Other educational activities showed similar gains. The quality of life improved in other ways; the data show expanding literacy, declining infant mortality, increasing life expectancy, widening access to safe water and sewer systems, and improving nutrition.[34]

The South's relatively good performance was caused partially by the ebullient functioning of world capitalism and partially by changes within the LDCs. It was also promoted, I suggest, by global socializing adaptation. Consider foreign aid, the most readily quantifiable form of GSA. Aid from OECD members, 1950–1980, has exceeded $350 billion (in constant 1977 prices).[35] Aid programs, of course, have been subject to many shortcomings, failures, and dysbenefits. (The most sweeping criticisms of such programs, however—that they impose a capitalist development pattern and preclude the choice of a [superior] socialist alternative—are not relevant to the issue being discussed here, namely, whether, given a capitalist process, GSA contributed to a more rapid rate of development.) Despite all the waste, corruption, and errors, however, it is difficult to believe that the $350 billion had a marginal productivity of zero or less. When one considers that a gradually increasing proportion of OECD aid (one-third in the most recent years) was funneled through the World Bank and other multilateral agencies, the view that it contributed to growth is reinforced. The World Bank loaned its money carefully, much of it for projects deemed self-liquidating or bankable, i.e., adjusted to have a positive payoff when assessed in quite conservative terms. In addition, it is a reasonable judgment that some contribution to LDC development has also been made by the numerous United Nations aid and assistance programs, the international trade preferences for LDCs, the operations of the World Bank, the International Monetary Fund, and other international organizations, and other forms of socializing adaptation.

It is worth remarking again that this judgment does not necessarily imply that GSA did a good or even a decent job in promoting development. It simply says that within world capitalism as it is, with all its protectionist, monopolistic, and other development-retarding political and economic tendencies, LDC development has proceeded better than it would have in the absence of the activities and institutions that GSA comprises.

The improved development performance of the "third world" since World War II has another implication for global socializing adaptation. That performance, regardless of its causes, helps to explain why GSA has not proceeded more vigorously. After the immediate postwar defections, the overall record of world capitalism suggests that, despite significant disaffection and some setbacks, it has functioned effectively enough to sustain its own viability. An intensification of GSA would be called for only if faltering performance by the capitalist international economic order should threaten "third world" adherence to that order.

I have been arguing that GSA, taking the form of collective actions for the purpose of assisting LDCs, has contributed to the relatively successful overall performance of the South since World War II, and, moreover, that the improved performance has limited the extent of GSA so far. A further submission: the trend toward GSA, minor fluctuations aside, is virtually irreversible. Southern power in the world system has been growing. Concurrently, the North's commitment to assist the development of the South has been gradually broadening. The adaptation process is ratchet-like; concessions to the LDCs, once made, are extremely difficult to recall. Moreover, pressure inexorably increases for further concessions. In a world of great income contrasts, development is never rapid enough in the LDCs. Even if the ruling elites and the economically fortunate should be satisfied, most of the population is not. For them, the Marxist exit from the capitalist economic order ever beckons.

3. Issues for the Developing Countries

Assuming that the thesis so far presented is valid and that GSA promotes Southern development, a major issue that remains for LDCs is the choice between some form of GSA-assisted capitalism and some form of socialism.

While this article is no place to attempt a thorough discussion of capitalism versus socialism, the main lines of the argument for the socialist alternative should be sketched. The socialist argues that the capitalist international economic order has not performed as well as humankind can reasonably expect. Although overall Southern development since World War II has been rather good, the poorest LDCs are generally the slowest growing. In countries with half the "third world" population (excluding China), per capita income, 1950–1975, has grown at less than 2 percent per annum. Despite the enormous gap between them and the MDCs, they are growing at a slower percentage rate than the MDCs did during the preceding century, and their absolute increases in income are pitifully tiny.[36] The relative as well as the absolute income gap is widening between the poorest LDCs and the other countries of the world. Most of the world's increase in income is going to the few most affluent countries. Similarly, within most capitalist LDCs, whether we consider the middle-income or the low-income group of countries, most of the incremental income is going to a disproportionately small elite, and income inequality is increasing.

Moreover, hundreds of millions of people live under conditions of absolute poverty, i.e., "at the very margin of subsistence—with inadequate food, shelter, education, and health care."[37] The World Bank estimates that there were 770 million such people in the capitalist "third world" economy in 1975, 37 percent of the population in that economy. These were not all in the poorest countries; 140 million were in the mid-income LDCs, or 16 percent of the population of those countries.[38] Although absolute poverty is partially a matter of inadequate aggregate income, it is also a matter of the distribution of income between nations and within nations.

One could continue with an extensive catalogue of searing problems, but this would serve little purpose. Let us turn instead to the socialist contention that, even if capitalist performances should prove adequate by past standards, the "third world" would be better off if it chose a socialist route. China's development record lends credence to that argument. In the past few years, there has been broad recognition of what a World Bank-sponsored study calls "China's success in development."[39]

China's economic growth rate for the period 1950–75 was outstanding (although subsequent growth appears to have slowed substantially). Average income and output increased 4.2 percent per annum for China, compared to 3.0 percent for all other LDCs, including the oil-rich countries.[40] Thus China's economic growth for the quarter-century was 40 percent greater than that of the rest of the "third world." If we compare the records of the most populous LDCs on the ground that their development problems differ from those of smaller nations, China's record is even more outstanding. China's 4.2 percent growth rate was well over twice the 1.9 percent average for the next seven most populous countries.[41]

A number of studies have indicated that rapid growth has usually reduced not only the relative income share of the very poor, but also the absolute level of income, i.e., has caused absolute impoverishment. These studies have been disputed; the data on income distribution are meager, unreliable, and subject to varying interpretations. However, it is clear that China's record on this score was a good one. "Among the most populous countries, only in China and possibly in Mexico does it seem to be agreed that there has been no large-scale absolute impoverishment among the poor." In the other large countries the issue is in dispute. Depending on how the disputed cases are read, it is possible that the greater part of the world's very poor outside of China have become absolutely poorer during the third quarter of this century.[42]

A broader indicator of how well an economy has performed is life expectancy.[43] On this count, too, China has done well. Between 1950 to 1955 and 1965 to 1970, China's life expectancy at birth increased from 48 to 60 years, while for all LDCs it increased from 42 to 49 years. China's life expectancy was higher than that of the other LDCs, and its increase was greater.[44]

To sum up, this article suggests that a broad, long-run process of global socializing adaptation is under way in the world capitalist economy, and that this process promotes Southern development. If one compares LDCs with MDCs at their earlier stages, the GSA-assisted capitalist development can be considered satisfactory. But a more pertinent comparison for LDCs in this era is to development under a socialist alternative. Here, at this intersection of the great East-West and North-South issues, is a sensible place to wind up this presentation of the GSA hypothesis.

Notes

The author wishes to thank Eileen Applebaum, David Good, Robert Heilbroner, Gerald Helleiner, Jay Mandle, Richard L. Sklar, and Milica Zarkovic for helpful comments.

1. In Marx's terms, the conflict between "the material forces of production in society" and "the existing relations of production . . . [i.e.,] the property relations." Marx sets forth this conflict in summing up the "general conclusion" he reached in his early study of political economy, "which, once reached, continued to serve as the leading thread in my studies." Karl Marx, *A Contribution to the Critique of Political Economy* (Chicago: Charles H. Kerr, 1904), pp. 11–12.

2. Presented here is an exposition of the fundamental incongruity and not an attempt to build a solid case for the validity of the concept. The latter would be a major task and is not essential for the purpose of this article. That purpose is to present a conception of world capitalist development which arose out of my understanding of the fundamental incongruity concept, but the reader could accept the concept and reject my hypothesis, or vice versa (or, of course, could reject or accept both).

3. One can see Marx's social-private contradiction as a counter-principle to Adam Smith's invisible hand, with the pattern of individuals acting for their own private ends causing anarchy of production (Marx) rather than harmony (Smith). There is a further parallel. Smith expected private ends-seeking or atomism (in the form of competition) to guide the invisible hand beneficently, but his vision proved deficient partially because atomistic competition was overridden by monopolistic tendencies. Similarly, Marx expected atomism in the economy (in the form of private control over the means of production) to generate capitalist breakdown, but his vision proved deficient because atomistic control was overridden by state control over the productive system.

4. The movement toward increasingly socialized decision-making proceeds on a private as well as a public level, as reflected in tendencies toward concentration, merger, consolidation, and multinationality.

5. Sometimes, of course, the measures adopted have more far-reaching effects than were foreseen.

6. See, e.g., Robert L. Heilbroner, "Inflationary Capitalism," *The New Yorker*, 8 October 1979, p. 121ff.

7. In Marxist terminology, socializing adaptation represents a partial resolution of the contradiction between the social nature of production (thesis) and the private nature of control (antithesis) through a synthesis involving some government or social controls over production.

8. The foregoing discussion of socializing adaptation does not address the question of whether it will continue to be effective in maintaining the viability of capitalism. This major issue is beyond the scope of this paper.

9. The degree to which development-retarding conditions within the "third world" have been internally and externally generated is not dealt with in this article.

10. Capital-intensive technology developed in, and appropriate for, the advanced economies; such technology employs relatively fewer workers and thus exacerbates unemployment in the less developed countries.

11. Pricing of goods traded between national subsidiaries of a multinational corporation in a way that artificially reduces the book profits of one of the subsidiaries.

12. As multinational corporations often have large holdings of many national currencies, it is prudent for them to sell currencies that appear likely to decline in value. The increase in the supply of the suspect currency, however, tends to bring about and intensify the anticipated decline.

13. Zbigniew Brzezinski, "The World According to Brzezinski" (James Reston interview of Zbigniew Brzezinski), *New York Times Magazine*, 31 December 1978, p. 10ff.

14. Robert Heilbroner, *An Inquiry into the Human Prospect* (New York: Norton, 1974), pp. 42–45.

15. For a contrary view, see Geoffrey Barraclough, "Waiting for the New Order," *New York Review of Books,* 26 October 1978, pp. 45–58; and his "The Struggle for the Third World," *New York Review of Books,* 9 November 1978, pp. 47–58.

16. World Bank, *World Development Report 1978* (New York: Oxford University Press, 1978), p. 13.

17. Ibid., p. 68.

18. While "it is true that the [N]orth holds most of the cards" in North-South negotiations, nevertheless, warns *The Economist,* the North's "sense of self-interest should remind it of what is at stake in the [S]outh's development." See *The Economist,* 17 February 1979, p. 85.

19. Bahram Nowzad, "Differential Trade Treatment for LDCs," *Finance and Development* 15, 1 (1978):16–21.

20. Harry Magdoff, speaking of "[t]he changes advocated by the New International Economic Order, even if by some miracle they were adopted," in "The Limits of International Reform," *Monthly Review* 30, 1 (1978):1–11 (quoted from p. 11).

21. System-threatening problems arose in relations among MDCs at an earlier time, and earlier adaptations were undertaken. The Bretton Woods order was primarily a way of dealing with North-North problems caused by the narrowness of the decision-making system in the interwar period relative to the degree of interdependence of the world's productive system. However, this article confines itself to North-South issues.

22. The terminology of the early post-World War II years.

23. Post-World War II decolonization was perhaps the first major act of GSA. On the surface, decolonization may appear to involve increased dispersion rather than socialization of decision-making, in that economic decisions formerly made by the imperial power were thereafter made or shared by many new countries. I suggest, however, that the opposite was the case. Decolonization represented a limited extension of social control in that economic processes in the colonies, previously carried out largely on the basis of private interests modified by metropolitan government concerns, became subject to broader control by the emerging of new governments. The weight of the colonial peoples (or various groups of them) in the decision-making process was increased.

24. Nowzad, "Differential Trade," p. 17.

25. Jyoti Shankar Singh, *A New International Economic Order* (New York: Praeger, 1977), p. 44. Ways in which the IMF has been aiding LDCs include allocations of some gold-sale profits to LDCs, provision of highly concessional loans to assist oil-importing LDCs, significant enlargement of borrowing authorizations, substantial expansion of "compensatory financing" authorizations (for loans to compensate for temporary shortfalls in export receipts arising from price fluctuations or other causes). See William R. Cline, *International Monetary Reform and the Developing Countries* (Washington, DC: Brookings Institution, 1976), pp. 5–7, 89–90; Singh, *New International Economic Order,* pp.

45, 145; and Edward M. Bernstein, "The International Monetary Fund," in Richard N. Gardner and Max F. Millikan (eds.), *The Global Partnership: International Agencies and Economic Development* (New York: Praeger, 1968), pp. 131–151 (esp. pp. 140–141).

26. A shift was made in 1965 from uniform interest rates to rates based on ability to pay. Loan durations and repayment-free grace periods have been gradually extended and are commonly twenty and twenty-five years, respectively, at the present time.

27. Fifty-year maturities, 10-year grace periods, elimination of interest charges entirely, or a substitution of a small annual service charge of 0.75 percent.

28. The Third Window is to provide subsidized loans on terms falling between IDA and regular World Bank terms.

29. The absolute amount of North-South aid has remained about constant for the past 15 years, hovering around $15 billion per annum (measured in United States dollars at 1977 prices). As a percentage of donor-country GNP, of course, it declined continuously, never reaching an early one percent target level and falling far short of even the reduced target level (accepted by the European Economic Community but not the United States) of 0.7 percent. United States aid fell from 0.53 percent of GNP in 1960 to 0.22 percent in 1977.

30. Such assistance amounts to less than 4 percent of total official aid to LDCs. In addition, a host of United Nations agencies which do not provide aid undertake operations specifically concerned with assisting LDCs.

31. By mid-1977, most MDCs had put into effect non-reciprocal trade concessions for LDCs on tropical products. The Lomé Convention of 1975 provided for favorable treatment by the EEC of the exports of 46 LDCs. Most MDCs participate in the GSP, each with its own national scheme specifying its own pattern of preferential treatment for the industrial exports of LDCs. LDCs generally benefit from the reciprocal trade concessions made between MDCs, for these are automatically extended to the LDCs even though the latter, operating under the principle of non-reciprocity, offer nothing in return. The Tokyo Round of multilateral trade negotiations of 1978 and 1979 was a disappointment for the LDCs, however. It was expected to produce further favorable arrangements for the LDCs, but by and large these did not materialize. On LDC expectations see, e.g., S.J. Anjaria, "The Tokyo Round of Multilateral Trade Negotiations," *Finance and Development* 15, 1 (1978):14–15; Isaiah Frank, "Reciprocity and Trade Policy of Developing Countries," *Finance and Development* 15, 1 (1978):20–23; and Nowzad, "Differential Trade." On LDC disappointment, see the evaluation by *The Economist*, 21 April 1979, p. 95: that LDCs as well as MDCs benefit in balance from the Round, but the complaint "that the talks have not produced new and special benefits for the poor . . . is true. The rich countries have not fulfilled all they promised" at the beginning of the talks.

32. See Albert Fishlow, "A New International Economic Order: What Kind?" in Fishlow et al., *Rich Nations and Poor Nations in the World Economy* (New York: McGraw-Hill, 1978), pp. 11–86, esp. p. 63; and Robert E. Baldwin and

T. Murray, "MFN Tariff Reductions and LDC Benefits under the GSP," *Economic Journal* 87, 345 (1977):30–46.

33. This statistic and all data on the LDCs as a group in this paper exclude China, Cuba, and other centrally planned economies. The centrally planned economies are not included in most international data sources. The data cited in this paragraph and the next are from World Bank, *World Development Report 1978*, pp. 3–11, 76–79. There are additional data in World Bank, *World Development Report 1979*, also *World Development Report 1980* (New York: Oxford University Press, 1979, 1980); and in World Bank, *World Tables*, 2d ed. (Washington, DC: World Bank, 1980), which is a convenient treasure trove of world economic and related statistics.

34. I have not taken the time or space to present the statistics.

35. Author's estimate, based on data in World Bank, *World Development Report 1978*, pp. 98–99; and in Organisation for Economic Co-operation and Development, *Development Co-operation, 1978 Review* (Paris: OECD, 1978) and earlier publications of the same or similar titles.

36. On the other hand, it can be argued that this group of the poorest LDCs has nevertheless experienced an acceleration of growth rates compared to past stagnation, and that historical processes inevitably require time, even though this is agonizing to those who suffer and those who feel compassion.

37. World Bank, *World Development Report 1978*.

38. Ibid., p. 33.

39. David Morawetz, *Twenty-Five Years of Economic Development 1950 to 1975* (Baltimore: Johns Hopkins University Press, 1977), p. 9. The study lists eight countries with populations of at least one million that had faster growth rates (Libya, Iraq, Taiwan, South Korea, Iran, Hong Kong, Jamaica, and Israel), but their combined 1975 population was 106 million, compared to China's 820 million, and special circumstances helped explain their rapid growth in at least several of these cases (p. 15).

40. Ibid., pp. 12–13.

41. Ibid., p. 15. The countries are, in order of population, India, Indonesia, Brazil, Bangladesh, Nigeria, Pakistan, Mexico. The 1.9 percent figure is a population-weighted average.

42. Ibid., pp. 42–43.

43. Increases in life expectancy "provide one of the strongest available indications" of broad improvement "because the increases in life expectancy were more the result of general improvements in living conditions than more closely defined medical improvements." Ibid., pp. 48–49.

44. Ibid., p. 48.

CHAPTER EIGHT

International Capital and National Development: Comments on Postimperialism

JEFF FRIEDEN

The problems of political and economic development in the "third world" present great analytical and practical challenges to contemporary social analysis. Yet few students of the less developed countries (LDCs) are satisfied with current theories of development, and inadequate theories are indicative of the paucity of solid analysis. This theoretical and analytical deficiency has become more and more painful as the LDCs themselves come to look less and less like the stereotypes imbedded in prevailing schools of thought. The postimperialism approach, first set forth by Richard L. Sklar in 1976, attempts to clear the cobwebs of conceptual confusion from development studies.

The cogency of postimperialism is demonstrated by Sklar and David G. Becker in their joint chapter in this volume as well as in their individual contributions. What is unquestionably refreshing and compelling about postimperialism is that, unlike most "dependency" and "mainstream" approaches to the problem of development, it takes seriously the dynamic of class formation *within* the LDCs. Sklar charges in his chapter that "it is a singular failing of many 'radical,' including Marxist, analyses of such countries to underestimate the strength and historic importance of bourgeois class formation as well as the nationalist integrity of that class."[1] The task postimperialism has set for itself is to remedy this failing.

The postimperialism approach thus postulates a national bourgeoisie in the LDCs whose leading stratum is a "managerial bourgeoisie" that is part of a nascent transnational bourgeoisie; the national managerial and corporate international bourgeoisies are linked by ties of mutual interest in which the concerns of international capital—for access to LDC markets and factors of production—match those of the LDCs (embodied in their state apparatuses as well as their private sectors)—to industrialize. In this view, multinational corporations (MNCs) are not forces *against* the nation but, rather, forces that can adapt themselves to the nations in which they are operating. Sklar calls the tendency of foreign corporations to submit themselves to the rule of local law "the doctrine of domicile." The political effect of foreign investment in the LDCs, then, is *not* to undermine the national integrity of the developing nations. Instead, foreign investment's impact is felt through its specific effects on class relations in the developing societies. The presence of multinational corporations is a stimulus to the rise of the managerial bourgeoisie to a position of local class dominance; aided by association with foreign capital, which neither "denationalizes" nor weakens the managerial bourgeoisie, this class becomes ever more capable—technically, politically, and socially—of reproducing and improving its dominant position within the developing nation.

The postimperialism approach is unusual and extraordinarily useful in its focus upon differentiated classes in place of undifferentiated nations. As Sklar observes in the conclusion of his chapter, "The fate of the bourgeoisie—corporate and managerial—will probably be determined by domestic struggles, not by anti-imperialist struggles that pit insurgent nations against foreign powers."[2] Thus, *politics remains primarily a national matter, despite the internationalization of investment and finance.* This view, which I share, is an optimistic one, for it implies that individuals and groups within nations indeed can have an impact on the processes of economic, social, and political development. The all-too-common assumption that economic integration at the global level has eliminated the possibility of national-level political action clearly is refuted by theoretical and case-study work undertaken from a postimperialist standpoint.

The position set forth by Sklar and Becker has met with an ever more favorable reception among those "third world" scholars who are fed up with endless sterile debates about "dependency." By the same token, the postimperialist position on multinational corporations now has come to be far more widely accepted than would have seemed possible ten years ago. A broad spectrum of people now believe, with Sayre Schatz, that assertive pragmatism in the use of foreign direct investments is the best possible road for both socialist and capitalist LDCs. In Schatz's words, "The pragmatic approach favors active host-government bargaining with and regulation of [MNCs] in order to improve the cost-benefit mix."[3] The experience of many nations, including many postrevolutionary states, seems to indicate that it is possible to develop working relations with MNCs in such a way that national sovereignty is not compromised or national goals undermined. This is not to say, of course, that multinational corporations are always and

everywhere to be welcomed, only that allowing foreign direct investment in a developing nation is not *necessarily* the kind of abject surrender to the evils of imperialism that many believed it to be in the 1960s
and 1970s. Whether the political and economic management of a developing nation are "surrendered" to imperialism depends almost entirely upon the domestic class dynamic in the nation in question and
very little, if at all, upon national acceptance or rejection of foreign investment per se.

The postimperialism approach is a significant, unified, exciting
step forward in our theoretical understanding of LDC development.
Postimperialism is both a major theoretical advance and a refreshing
example of how class analysis, once freed from doctrine, can enlighten
our understanding of social life. In what follows I will raise certain specific and general questions about the postimperialism approach, and I
will make several critical, questioning comments. Nothing that I say
should be taken to detract from the value of the approach. I remain
agnostic, as some of the following comments will indicate, yet I have no
doubt that postimperialism will be a central part of the ongoing debate
about LDC development for the next decade at least. My comments
simply are meant to encourage and clarify discussion of the issues that
postimperialism raises. I begin with three comments on issues raised by
postimperialism, then voice two cautions about the approach and its
applications, and finally raise a question about the future of postimperialism.

Three Critical Comments on the
Theory of Postimperialism

A first comment has to do with the contradiction, which the postimperialism school has gone far in clarifying, between the national and
the international. As Schatz phrases this contradiction, "Productive
interdependence becomes more thoroughly international, but the
means of state control remain national."[4] In the postimperialism approach, the dialectical interaction between national social actors and
international, or foreign, actors is explained primarily by focusing on
the role of the managerial (or corporate national) bourgeoisie. The
managerial bourgeoisie attenuates the conflict between national and
international concerns by mediating between foreign and national
bourgeois interests. As the managerial bourgeoisie increases in numbers, power, self-confidence, and technical expertise, and as foreign
corporations adhere more rigorously to the doctrine of domicile
(which implies respect for the national political systems and values of

countries in which these corporations invest), tension between the national development of particular countries and developments in the international system declines. As Becker and Sklar put it, "Postimperialism implies the beginning of a new postnationalist age."[5]

This position is similar in some ways to that advanced by Karl Kautsky nearly seventy years ago. For Kautsky, conflict *between* national imperialisms would decline as the processes of productive and financial internationalization continued to accelerate.[6] Lenin, of course, gave a different answer to a set of questions about the possible evolution of capital beyond the bounds of the nation-state, arguing that before international capitalism became truly international its internal contradictions would lead to its self-destruction. Postimperialism's explanation of this set of issues depends on the link between the managerial bourgeoisie and the rest of the national bourgeoisie in the developing country itself. For according to the postimperialist school, the managerial bourgeoisie mitigates national-international conflict, and serves, in Becker's terms, as "the economic and political hinge . . . between local societies and the metropoli."[7] His description follows Sklar, for whom "the managerial bourgeoisie is the ruling stratum of the national bourgeoisie. . . . The action which, more than any other, sets this subclass apart from the bourgeoisie as a whole is its tendency to coalesce with bourgeois elements at comparable levels of control in foreign countries."[8]

Class formation and intra-class conflict are dynamic processes. There is nothing in developments in the most advanced LDCs to suggest that the managerial bourgeoisie *necessarily* will continue to grow in importance and hegemony without undergoing far-reaching changes in its class character, while other strata of the national bourgeoisie decline relatively. Indeed, Sklar's original statement of the postimperialism thesis leaves open the possibility that the opposite may be the case. "In the long run," Sklar says, "if capitalism in [a given newly industrializing] country is preserved, the corporate bourgeoisie may be expected to supersede the managerial bourgeoisie as the ruling class."[9] This process seems to be taking place in several of the more developed LDCs. In countries such as Brazil, Argentina, Mexico, South Korea, and the Philippines, large segments of that part of the corporate national bourgeoisie based in private capital not only have increased their competence and power. They also have come into more or less direct conflict with the state-centered part, with which they had previously shared power. Alternatively, as Becker describes in Chapter 3, the two bourgeois elites—state-corporate and private-corporate—may fuse, resulting in a corporate national bourgeoisie with a distinctive class character and set of interests. In either case it is not at all certain that rising and assertive elements of the national bourgeoisie will pursue policies of collaboration rather than conflict with the Western-based corporate international bourgeoisie. The role of the national bourgeoisie in developing countries has long been one of the most controversial questions in the entire development literature. Although postimperialism clarifies the position of the local capitalist class by explaining the development of a managerial bourgeoisie, this approach does not yet lay the ghost of Lenin to rest. In order to do so, it may be necessary to pay closer attention to conflicts *within* the managerial (or corporate national) bourgeoisie.

A second, and not unrelated, comment has to do with the conscious volition of social classes in the postimperialism approach. Postimperialist authors appear to believe that class structures in the "third world" are determined more by power relations than by relations of production as such. The very definition of the managerial bourgeoisie set forth by Becker and Sklar emphasizes the "common class interest in the relations of political power and social control that are intrinsic to the capitalist mode of production."[10] I see no inherent theoretical or logical problem with this formulation. Yet it does at times lead to a blurring of the line between economic and ideological interest. It is important in any theory of social life to distinguish between the result of the conscious actions of conscious actors and the result of underlying, and perhaps unrecognized, socioeconomic trends in the nation in question. We must not simply replace economic determinism with what might be called political determinism—the notion that all social developments can be explained by the political actions of politically conscious groups or individuals. Becker asserts, for example, that "the attainment by the Peruvian government of its principal bargaining aims [in a negotiation with a large resource MNC] . . . was due primarily to the knowledge and expertise of its negotiators and their staffs."[11] But a variety of other explanations for Peruvian success might be advanced, among them the peculiar nature of extractive industries, the vulnerable bargaining position in which those who had invested in Peru found themselves, and the state of Peru's diplomatic relations with the firm's home country, the United States.

Becker's assertion that "in a postimperialist world, capital's access to the 'periphery' is secured by ideological and political means"[12] is similarly ambiguous. If all he means is that ideology and politics serve an important role in giving capital access to the "periphery," this is self-evident. If, however, Becker means to suggest that capital relies *solely* upon ideology and politics to maintain its access to the periphery, his statement is surely misleading. Metropolitan capital is able to maintain access to the periphery at least in part because it has certain economic, technical, and managerial benefits to offer social classes in the periphery. The challenge is to specify and understand how economics, politics, and ideology interact in the overseas investment process, not simply to affirm that they do interact.

In fact, the different attitudes within the developing world toward foreign direct investment—which Sayre Schatz usefully separates into "acceptance," "rejection," and "pragmatism"[13]—might be explained on purely economic grounds *without* falling back upon ideological or cultural explanations. One might argue, for instance, that opposition to foreign direct investment is strong where there are local business-people who are, or might be, in direct competition with MNCs and who feel that they are incapable of competing on a more or less equal basis. This most generally would be the case in countries at a medium level of development and in sectors in which large concentrations of capital or expertise are necessary for success. On the other hand, one might expect a much more accepting (or "pragmatic") approach to foreign direct investment where local entrepreneurs believe that MNCs will not enter into direct competition with them or else that they are powerful enough to confront MNC competition. This characteristically would be the case in both the least developed countries and the most developed countries; in sectors where concentrations of capital and expertise are relatively unimportant; and, perhaps, where knowledge of the local market (also, possibly, familiarity with local politicians) is of great significance.

It would be self-contradictory if an approach that began with an unabashed call for class analysis were to fall back upon arguments that do not rely on the self-interested actions of social classes to explain social phenomena, as seems to be the case with at least some of these assertions. So I find myself wishing that authors who subscribe to the postimperialist idea would more clearly emphasize class-analytical considerations—such as the material interests of social classes in the LDCs in extracting benefits from MNCs and the way in which these interests are expressed. Far more can be explained by the self-interested actions of individuals who collectively make up social classes than by the notion of ideological action alone. Ideology *is* important, but only (from a class-analytical perspective) insofar as it is related unambiguously to the material interests that it seeks to justify.

A third set of comments has to do with the question of democracy. Although the main premise of postimperialist thought—the emergence of a transnationally dominant class—is inherently oligarchic, the fate of national movements for political democracy is neither sealed nor predetermined. However, it is not clear to me whether for Sklar and Becker the national bourgeoisie is inherently pro-democratic or authoritarian. This question is relevant particularly to the managerial and corporate national incarnations of that class. Sklar answers in one manner, saying that the managerial bourgeoisie "has shown a marked disposition to take refuge in various forms of political monopoly, such as the one-party state and the 'caesarist' military regime."[14] Becker, on the other hand, when speaking of "leading strata" that have evolved into a corporate national bourgeoisie, claims that "as their dominance is not narrowly self-serving, it does not need to rest on coercive force and can coexist with formal democracy."[15] He begins his discussion of democracy in the context of postimperialism by noting that "the wave of authoritarianism has spent its force and is receding" and points out that "the correlation between direct foreign investment and the potential for capitalist democracy thus turns out to be positive."[16] Becker's point is essentially that as the managerial (or corporate national) bourgeoisie gains in self-confidence and effectiveness, it has less need for authoritarian, repressive means of maintaining its control.

Yet there are other ways of interpreting contemporary political developments in the LDCs. There undoubtedly has been a dramatic rebirth of democracy in many of the more advanced developing countries; one need only look at democratization in Brazil, Argentina, Uruguay, and Peru for examples. In virtually all of these cases, however, it seems that it has been only a part of the managerial (or corporate national) bourgeoisie which has stood most strongly for formal democracy. Specifically, in many cases it is corporate executives in the private sector who have felt that their interests require them to struggle against the overweening power of the state and its officialdom. In that intra-bourgeois battle, the demand for formal democratization has become a powerful weapon for rallying public support. The ongoing process of Latin American democratization appears to have pitted officials of the state and parastatal management corps, who have close ties to foreign capital, against more nationally oriented business leaders, including corporate executives in the private sector, who want the economy to dispense with some of its ties (political as well as economic) to overseas capital. More recently, protests and debates over LDC austerity programs adopted in response to the international financial crisis have served to split the allegiances of the corporate national bourgeoisie: its domestically oriented parts have allied with the broader national bourgeoisie and the working class against some important interests of the state management and of foreign capital.

Brazil's dramatic democratization during the late 1970s and early 1980s is a good example. Much of the impetus for liberalization came from the national bourgeoisie. In 1978, on the eve of a new president's inauguration, eight of the country's most influential businessmen issued a call for a more concerted commitment to democracy. "We believe," they wrote, "that economic and social development as we conceive it can only be possible within a political framework that permits the broad participation of all. Only democracy is capable of promoting the full expression of interest and opinions, and has sufficient flexibility to absorb tensions without transforming them into an undesirable class conflict."[17] This unexpected and forceful statement of national-bourgeois belief in formal democracy was one of the most important causes of the military regime's decision in 1979 to undertake an accelerated democratization of the political system. As the economic crisis deepened, private-sector corporate executives became a more and more powerful opposition voice and played a leading role in gaining and consolidating power for a new civilian government in 1985. However one may want to read these events, far more investigation is needed before we can draw specific conclusions about the relationship between the managerial and national bourgeoisies, on the one hand, and formal democracy in the developing countries, on the other.

On all three points—the relationship between national and international class formation and interaction; the conscious volition of classes; and the relationship between class formation and political development—the postimperialism approach offers suggestive ideas but does not yet give conclusive answers. This is more a sign of the novelty of the effort than of an inherent failing on the part of the theory or its practitioners. Further research and elaboration undoubtedly will help clarify these and related issues. It is in this light that I shall go on to present two more specific cautionary remarks concerning some of the empirical bases and applications of postimperialism.

Two Cautionary Notes on the Scope of Postimperialist Theory

As scholars proceed to test and flesh out the postimperialism approach, they should keep in mind that the cases that thus far have been analyzed in depth are neither sectorially nor geographically representative. The work of Sklar and Becker has dealt almost exclusively with extractive industries and has been conducted in very few countries. Therefore, it is possible that the cases cited to support Sklar and Becker's version of the postimperialism thesis may be exceptional in the context of the LDCs as a whole.

The first concern should be to achieve greater sectorial diversification in the cases studied. Virtually all the specific studies relied upon to launch and project the postimperialism approach revolve around the mining industry. But conclusions drawn from studies of the mining sector may not be applicable to other industries. Mining is a very pecu-liar industry. As Becker himself notes, "Without doubt it is over ques-tions of minerals investment where 'third world' host countries have become most assertive and, on the whole, most successful in their deal-ings with transnational firms; the transnationals, for their part, have not generally opposed host-country aims to the bitter end."[18] Foreign mining investment has characteristics that make it inherently more subject to national policies in the host country than foreign investment in most other industries. Mining activities generally demand very large investments, are of considerable size, and are tied to a particular geo-graphic location; they require government backing to ensure the avail-ability of supporting infrastructure such as water, electric power, and transportation to and from port cities; and they are peculiarly visible in the usually isolated areas where they are concentrated. Mining, espe-cially in those sectors where MNCs are particularly active, is also an im-portant component of national exports. In fact, although mining and petroleum combined account for only 3 percent of Latin America's gross product, nonfuel minerals account for 26 percent of Latin American exports and petroleum for another 22 percent.[19] Thus, the extractive industries are some fifteen times more important in Latin American exports than they are in the Latin American economies in general. It is to be expected that, regardless of nationality, firms in an industry so important in earning foreign exchange would come under close national scrutiny.

Foreign-owned extractive industries are visible, concentrated, large-scale, export-oriented elements of LDC economies. These indus-tries are usually among the first in LDCs to be closely regulated, and they are also usually among the first to be nationalized. One sample of several hundred examples of LDC expropriation of foreign firms showed that although extractive industries constituted only 15 percent of foreign direct investment in the LDCs, they accounted for 35 per-cent of all such actions.[20] U.S. direct investment in the extractive indus-tries actually declined in real terms in the 1960s and 1970s, even as U.S. direct investment in manufacturing and other sectors rose very substantially.

Thus, it is important to separate the specific sectorial characteris-tics of the mining sector from the characteristics of foreign direct in-vestment in the LDCs more generally. The response of LDCs to foreign corporations varies widely by sector. The treatment accorded foreign-owned public utilities, for example, is similar to that received by foreign-owned mining firms but is quite different from that to which foreign firms in the capital goods industries have been subjected; nor is it evident that similar outcomes, when found, stem from similar causes.

The postimperialism approach therefore must go beyond the extractive industries and look at the class effects of manufacturing, finance, services, and other foreign investments in the LDCs.

A second concern should be to achieve more geographical diversity in cases studied. The two deepest national applications to date are those of Sklar in Zambia and Becker in Peru. Both countries, apart from being unusually dependent upon copper exports, are somewhat unrepresentative even of their respective regions—not to speak of their enormous differences from East Asian LDCs. In his discussion of Peruvian "bonanza development," Becker refers to "the appearance in the host country of a stable capitalist order. . . . Bonanza development allows a dominant class to enjoy the fruits of an administratively strong and capable state without paying for them out of its own pockets in higher taxes on enterprise profits and personal income."[21] One might question the applicability of these remarks to the *current* Peruvian scene; and the trend to which Becker points is far from universal even in those countries whose industrial development depends on the exploitation of a mineral "bonanza." We need to ask to what extent these tendencies are universal; to what extent they define the evolution of social reality in the LDCs; and to what extent they are simply several among many, often contradictory, cross-cutting political, economic, and social developments in the contemporary "third world."

What is more, some of the trends considered by the postimperialist school now seem to be moving in a direction opposite to the one practitioners of the approach appear to have anticipated. In the more developed LDCs the trend has been *away* from foreign direct investment during the last fifteen years. More and more of the local economy is coming under local control. In many cases, as I have shown in my own contribution to the case studies collected in this volume,[22] this increased local control of economic activity is financed overseas by borrowing on international financial markets.

Whatever the contours of the shift, it is undeniable that the relative share of foreign corporations in virtually all of the rapidly industrializing LDCs has been declining for quite some time. In Brazil, for example, foreign firms accounted for 42 percent of the sales and for 20 percent of the capital of the country's 200 largest firms in 1972; foreign firms now account for approximately 23 and 8 percent respectively. Similar trends are clear in virtually all of Latin America.[23] Although those trends do not invalidate a research emphasis on the formation of a dominant, autonomous national bourgeoisie linked to foreign corporations and including both managerial (in Sklar's sense) and domestic corporate elements, their presence calls for further investigation of the interaction of these two frequently conflicting class elements. Becker finds that "the mining-bourgeois class element is well placed to be part of the politically and ideologically leading stratum of the national bourgeoisie."[24] He also points out, however, that the bourgeoisie as a whole is made up of

> self-interested individuals for whom the competitive pursuit of parochial interests is the most salient and immediate fact of economic and social life. The class is therefore divided into strata and interest groups that differ with respect to what they produce, their market role and orientation, their preferences in regard to state action in the economy, their domestic or international focus, etc. In a pluralist bourgeois democracy, these groups compete for influence within the overall system of power.[25]

How are "these groups" to be defined and described? How have they responded to the decline in the relative importance of MNCs in many developing countries? The further development of the postimperialism approach will require investigation of this issue in the context of postimperialism's conception of the managerial (or corporate national) bourgeoisie. For that it is essential to expand the universe of cases to include examples from Asia, North Africa, and the Middle East as well as countries with important industrial bases—the so-called newly industrializing countries (NICs), such as South Korea and Brazil.

A Final Question for Postimperialist Theorists

One reason for scholars to pay attention to the development of postimperialist thought is that it holds extraordinary promise as a new theoretical approach to economic and political development. In fact, the most pressing task confronting adherents of postimperialism is to take what is essentially a series of theoretical and analytical observations and, by thinking them through and applying them, to turn postimperialism into a full-blown theory of development. Becker and Sklar insist in Chapter 1 that "*postimperialism is not a theory of economic development per se,*"[26] but there are enough predictive elements in the approach that it practically cries out for further theoretical elaboration.

Thus, as Becker and Sklar write, "postimperialism implies the beginning of a new postnationalist age."[27] That conclusion is clearly in line with the overall thrust of the postimperialism approach; but the authors will forgive me if I infer from their claim that if postimperialism is not a theory of development, it will have to become one to fulfill its potential. Otherwise we will have little basis on which to accept, or even to evaluate, some of the assertions imbedded in the analysis as well as some of the predictions that flow from it.

The broadest such prediction runs suggestively like a thread through many of the chapters in this volume. International investment in a postimperialist era is blurring the lines between the "third" and "first worlds"; or, in the more precise words of Becker and Sklar, "the current global division between developed and less developed territories is fluid rather than fixed."[28] But precisely because postimperialism is not, or is not yet, a theory of development, this assertion remains empirically compelling and analytically suggestive rather than theoretically convincing. If the works of Becker, Schatz, Sklar, and others have shown quite clearly that foreign direct investment can lead to industrial development in the LDCs, they leave unanswered whether this industrial development will continue at such a pace as to bring some of the contemporary LDCs into the ranks of the advanced industrial world. Becker believes that it will, that "some 'third world' countries may one day attain metropolitan status . . . without contravening the fundaments of the international order."[29] However, the admission of this possibility raises analytical issues requiring the elaboration of more far-reaching theoretical relationships than postimperialism currently offers, especially with respect to the contours and strength of the international economic system as it currently is constituted. Does the contemporary international economic system operate in and of itself to maintain a hierarchy in the international political and economic order? If so, is the hierarchy fixed as to membership, so that no nation can obtain a "promotion"? Is it fixed as to size of the various ranks, so that one nation's "promotion" depends upon another's "demotion"? Or, in another possible variant, are there internal structural differences between developed and developing societies that make it virtually impossible for the latter to catch up? If so, how, if at all, are these differences related to the international economic system?

This extraordinarily complex set of issues demands empirical research and theoretical breakthroughs as called for by the postimperialism manifestoes. The explanatory power of postimperialism is demonstrated convincingly by the works of Becker and Sklar in this volume and by their discussion of related work on LDC economic and political development in Chapter 1. There are two obvious next steps that the approach must take: empirical broadening and theoretical deepening. Further application of the tools of postimperialist analysis to other societies and other economic sectors will help strengthen the theory's explanatory power and will provide fuel for further elaboration. At the same time, the incorporation of diverse national and sectorial experiences into the theory will lead to further insights as to postimperialism's predictive power. These steps will lead to important advances in our thinking about the problems of "third world" development.

Notes

1. Richard L. Sklar, ch. 2, p. 28.
2. Ibid., p. 32.
3. Sayre P. Schatz, ch. 5, p. 112.
4. Ibid., p. 114.
5. David G. Becker and Richard L. Sklar, ch. 1, p. 14.
6. Karl Kautsky, *Der Weg zur Macht* (Berlin, 1910); and "Akkumulation und Imperialismus," *Neue Zeit* 32, 2 (1914):908–922. Relevant extracts of both works are reprinted in Patrick Goode (ed. and trans.), *Karl Kautsky: Selected Political Writings* (New York: St. Martin's, 1983), pp. 75–89. It may be noted that for Kautsky, internationalized capitalism remains imperialistic—thus his appelation "ultra-imperialism." Although postimperialism joins with Kautsky in opposition to Lenin's notion of "inter-imperialist" conflict, it differs from Kautsky in that it does not regard today's international capitalism as imperialist in any sense. This position does not imply that no imperialism exists in the modern world—only that the expansion of capitalism as such is not in itself imperialist in character. Neither does postimperialism deny that capitalist imperialism was a feature of an earlier historical epoch.
7. David G. Becker, ch. 3, p. 53.
8. Sklar, ch. 2, p. 30.
9. Ibid., p. 32.
10. Becker and Sklar, ch. 1, p. 7.
11. David G. Becker, ch. 4, p. 52.
12. Becker, ch. 3, p. 100.
13. Schatz, ch. 5.
14. Sklar, ch. 2, p. 27.
15. Becker, ch. 4, pp. 66–67.
16. Becker, ch. 3, pp. 46, 49.
17. As cited in *Senhor,* August 17, 1983, p. 25.
18. Becker, ch. 4, p. 67.
19. Inter-American Development Bank (IDB), *Economic and Social Progress in Latin America: Natural Resources* (Washington, DC: IDB, 1983), p. 106.
20. Stephen J. Kobrin, "Foreign Enterprise and Forced Divestment in LDCs," *International Organization* 34, 1 (1980):65–88; esp. p. 76.
21. Becker, ch. 4, p. 69.
22. Jeff Frieden, ch. 6.
23. Specifically, Becker notes elsewhere that these trends are in evidence in Peru. See David G. Becker, "Peru after the 'Revolution': Class, Power, and Ideology," *Studies in Comparative International Development* 20, 3 (1986):3–30.
24. Becker, ch. 4, p. 87.
25. Becker, "Peru after the 'Revolution,'" p. 19.
26. Becker and Sklar, ch. 1, p. 13 (emphasis in original).
27. Ibid., p. 14.
28. Ibid., p. 13.
29. Becker, ch. 3, p. 54.

CHAPTER NINE

Postimperialism and the Great Competition

SAYRE P. SCHATZ

In the course of joint work on the introductory chapter of this book, it became clear that there were ways in which my conception of postimperialism differed from that of David G. Becker and Richard L. Sklar; and it has seemed best to write a separate note on these differences. I will deal with three points: the degree of conflict between the more and the less developed countries; the role of the world contest between capitalism and socialism (the Great Competition) in bringing about mutuality between these two groups of countries; and, most importantly, the role of that competition in shaping the nature of the postimperialist era. These points all relate to the part of the world that is capitalist or in which capitalism is still in contention (which I will refer to as the "capitalist sphere").

The forces that engender a mutuality of interests between the more and the less developed countries (as represented by their ruling classes), and that give rise to a tendency toward class coalescence, have been discussed in Chapter 1. That chapter also is quite clear about the coexistence of conflict regarding distribution of gains. It is my suggestion, however, that the conflict may be deeper than indicated there. In particular, I suggest that the processes of world capitalist development that foster mutuality also create the foundation and impetus for more effective assertion of conflicting interests.

Becker and Sklar observe in Chapter 1 that transnational corporate investment and related processes have abetted organizational revolutions in the "third world" and have fostered the ascendance of the managerial bourgeoisies and their control of the state. My point here is that this control, in turn, has provided the managerial bourgeoisies with an independent power base that enables them to assert their own interests in a historically new and effective way. Beginning from a weak position, the less developed countries benefited from a catch-up period during which they enhanced their bargaining strength and succeeded in winning substantial concessions, often relatively easily.

Indigenization of ownership has been a key area of conflict. It involves a head-on collision of interests (although concurrence by the transnational corporation may represent the only prudent course of action). Indigenization is an effective move in a zero-sum game[1]; the managerial bourgeoisies capture some of the income (and other benefits) that previously accrued to the parent company and the home country.[2]

Indigenization also provides a base for continuing conflict; it creates an ongoing rivalry between the parent company and those whose primary stake is in the subsidiary. The parent gets all of its own profits and other gains but only a portion of those accruing to its partially owned subsidiary. Thus, the parent transnational corporation has a strong incentive to adopt policies—such as exploitative transfer pricing—that aggrandize it at the expense of its subsidiary.

There are also the usual conflicts of interest regarding international trade, debt, investment, and the like. In such matters, impersonal market forces do not specify the exact division of gains, and there are not many universally accepted rules of the game. Within wide limits, the division is determined by the economic strength and bargaining power of the two sides.

Thus, two opposite tendencies arise in the relations between the managerial bourgeoisies and the dominant classes in the more developed countries. On the one hand, linkages through the transnational corporations promote mutuality, and this mutuality grows stronger as transnational corporate expansion provides an expanding flow of income, wealth, prestige, and power. On the other hand, managerial-bourgeois control of the state gives rise to conflict, and this conflict grows stronger as the managerial bourgeoisie tightens its control over an increasingly capable state apparatus.

Such conflict is viewed in Chapter 1 as relatively superficial competition for distribution of rewards rather than as fundamental antagonism. That is, the conflict between the managerial bourgeoisies of the developing countries and the dominant classes of the developed countries is said to be a kind of clash that does not override the common class interest in sustaining the viability of capitalism. Although I concur with this distinction between superficial and fundamental conflict, I suspect that in the absence of other forces the collision of interests delineated previously might be sufficiently powerful to obscure and render nugatory for a considerable period the underlying mutuality.

However, mutuality does prevail in the postimperialist era. It is saved by another major factor: the threat of socialism in the "third world." This decisively tips the balance toward mutuality (among ruling classes). The dominant classes in both the "first" and "third worlds" have a common interest in nurturing capitalism and warding off socialism. This draws them together in joint efforts in spheres ranging from the purely economic to the military.

The Great Competition is important also in determining the basic nature of the contemporary era. It is my thesis that the character of postimperialism will depend upon the relative merits of capitalism and socialism.[3] In order to explain this point, I will review briefly three aspects of the economic and political position of the less developed countries in the capitalist sphere.

1. Economically, the "third world" has developed under capitalism and continues to develop. This point has been made in several contributions to this volume, and the evidence is clear by now—contrary to the predictions of Paul Baran (whose analysis was powerful even though, with hindsight, we can see some fundamental errors),[4] and to the assertions of some of his followers (who do not appear to see the evidence). During the third quarter of the twentieth century, real income per capita of the less developed countries increased at an annual rate of almost 3 percent, a rate considerably in excess of the growth of more developed countries either contemporaneously or during their comparable early industrialization periods. Even after "the international environment had become less favorable to developing countries in the period after 1973 . . . because of the slowdown in industrial-country growth," growth rates of the less developed countries continued to be good. Their average aggregate growth rate was 5.2 percent per annum for the period 1973–1980, almost double the 2.8 percent rate of the industrial market economies. There was inevitably a substantial slowdown during the severe world recession of 1980–1983, but even then less-developed-country growth was almost double that of the more developed countries.[5] Broader indicators of development, such as proportion of children in school, literacy rates, infant mortality, life expectancy, availability of safe water, and others also show continuing improvement since 1980.[6]

As development proceeds in the less developed countries, the normal mutual-gain parameters of capitalist economic interaction assert themselves. These interactions have constituted a positive-sum game, with gains normally accruing to both sides. Although there is conflict, possibly intense, about division of the gain, such conflict is secondary as long as the situation is structured so that both players normally benefit.

Moreover, the developing countries, aided by their stance of assertive pragmatism and by the industrialized countries' pattern of global socializing adaptation, have made many gains in the distribution of benefits from international economic relationships.[7] This is reflected in the relatively high growth rates of LDCs since 1950. Furthermore, there is strong reason to believe LDCs will enhance their bargaining strength as they catch up educationally, scientifically, and technologically.

2. Politically, the degree of domination of less by more developed countries, in historical terms, is fading rapidly (leaving aside the issue of socialism, to be discussed shortly). It is no longer a matter—as it was under colonialism—of the more developed countries being the decision-making power in the "third world." Nor can the former dictate or shape the policies of the independent "third world" countries as they did just a few decades ago. Compare the U.S. "big stick" policy in Latin America before World War II with the difficulty the United States has today in trying to impose even basic orientations, let alone specific policies. As has been said in Chapter 1, domination in the capitalist sphere is being replaced by mutuality of interests and class coalescence.

Even a government as utterly dependent upon external support, past and present, as the Mobutu regime in Zaïre has considerable autonomy.

> Mobutu has shown a Machiavellian flair for establishing and manipulating shifting coalitions of support, both internally and externally. Other states and business interests within them, international organizations, such as the IMF and the World Bank, private international banks, transnational corporations, and groups such as the Catholic Church all have complex, shifting, and often competing sets of economic, politico-strategic, and normative interests to pursue in the Zaïrian arena. The interstices created by these multiple sets of interests often permit some room for maneuver, some autonomy for the ruler and his political aristocracy. Thus Mobutu and his ruling class have maintained a significant degree of relative autonomy; external influence clearly has its limits.[8]

3. The economic, social, and political improvements in the status of the less developed countries do not result necessarily in harmony in the capitalist sphere. Some less developed countries and, in virtually all such countries, some movements espouse socialism. However, pro-socialist strivings often encounter active external opposition. The more developed capitalist countries tend to react to serious pressures for socialism in LDCs—whether exerted by indigenous forces (which might be acting alone or might be bolstered by outside support) or by external forces—by employing economic, political, quasi-military, or

military measures, either to buttress friendly governments or to support opposition to anti-capitalist governments. The more developed countries are prepared to use their considerable economic, political, and military resources to ensure that the national economies of the less developed countries remain or become capitalist.

Returning now to my thesis that the character of the contemporary era depends upon the superiority of either capitalism or socialism for the "third world," I will consider the alternative assumptions of general capitalist and of general socialist superiority. (I refer here to superiority for present "third world" development tasks. Whether socialism will be more desirable at some future time, perhaps after the less developed countries have reached a "higher stage," is not relevant.) Other assumptions are possible—neither might be generally or clearly superior; each might be superior for some countries and not others; there might be convergence—but the limited purposes of this chapter do not necessitate an exploration of those other assumptions.

Under the assumption of capitalist superiority, all citizens of the less developed countries would have a common interest in their societies remaining (or becoming) capitalist. The more developed countries, in supporting capitalism, would not be attempting to impose a less desirable mode of production upon the less developed countries. Although political and economic conflicts would continue, the fundamental mutuality between North and South described in Chapter 1 increasingly would manifest itself. The postimperialism described in that chapter—which, I suggest, is based implicitly on the capitalism-superior assumption—would characterize the current era.

Let us turn to the alternative assumption of socialist superiority. Despite the successes of capitalist development, it also has produced profound problems. It has given us the Marcoses, Duvaliers, Mobutus, and Pinochets. Most of the world's poorest countries are capitalist in orientation, and these countries are the slowest growing, falling ever farther behind. Capitalist development's performance in the areas of welfare and income distribution often has been poor. The World Bank estimated that in 1975, 37 percent of the population involved in the capitalist "third world" economy lived in conditions of absolute poverty.[9] Because of the shortcomings of capitalism, many believe that some form of socialism would be superior. In consequence, socialist movements constitute a political force to be reckoned with. It is difficult to judge the developmental merits of socialism, partly because of dispute about whether any present LDCs are really socialist[10]; partly because even if we accept the existing "third world" socialisms at their word, there are few of them, and they exist under difficult and specialized conditions; and partly because it is not easy to assess the contrasting scholarly appraisals that have been made.[11] However, for the purposes of this chapter there is no need to appraise the developmental merits of socialism. It is sufficient that socialism is an alternative that cannot be ignored.

On the assumption of socialist superiority, the relationship between "first" and "third worlds" in the capitalist sphere would *not* be one of increasing mutuality; it would be one of conflict. In their efforts to promote capitalism, the more developed countries would be trying to impose an inferior mode of production upon the less developed countries. Intra-capitalist harmony between these two groups, based upon mutuality of ruling-class interests, would be overridden by this more fundamental divergence.

I ask at this point: How should one characterize this state of affairs? Does it mean, with its continuing domination of the less by the more developed countries, that the current era is a continuation of imperialism, or is this era postimperialist? If the latter, what is the nature of this postimperialism?

If one shaped one's definition of imperialism appropriately— defining it as support for, and imposition of, (inferior) capitalism upon less developed countries—one could characterize the situation just depicted as an era of imperialism. However, such a use of the term obscures rather than informs or enlightens. It misses the differences between the present era (under the socialism-superior assumption) and the previous era. Moreover, the term carries with it a large suitcase of meanings, associations, and connotations, and this intellectual baggage tends to mystify rather than clarify. At the least, I submit, one should recognize explicitly that such "imperialism" is substantially different from imperialism as it usually is understood.

Let us compare three attributes of the current era as they are usually understood within the context of imperialism and as they would be described under the socialism-superior assumption. If imperialism is the starting point, (1) the continuing existence of capitalism is not in question. (2) Within the framework of that economy, less developed countries are subject to continuing external control or domination, which has persisted and will persist throughout the imperialist era. (3) The processes of the world capitalist economy systematically are damaging (in the view of most writers who share this understanding of imperialism) to the less developed countries.

Thus, conflicts between industrialized and less developed countries (or colonies) in the imperialist age are not about the possible replacement of capitalism by some socialist alternative. Rather, these conflicts take the form of efforts by the LDCs to diminish or terminate political domination and economic exploitation, thereby leaving the continuation of capitalism unquestioned.[12]

Under the socialism-superior assumption, these three attributes of the contemporary era would be turned around. (1) Conflict between industrialized and less developed countries is about precisely what previously was taken for granted: the continuation of capitalism. The overriding issue is *not* continued control and economic damage within the framework of capitalism but is that of the Great Competition—the possible replacement of capitalism by socialism. (2) If we leave aside the issue of capitalism versus socialism and turn instead to relations within the capitalist fold, the LDCs are not subject to persisting control and domination. On the contrary, the degree of domination of less developed countries by industrialized ones is diminishing. "Third world" capitalist countries—strengthened by class coalescence; by their position as "first world" allies in the Great Competition; and by tightening managerial-bourgeois control over an increasingly capable state apparatus—move ever closer to parity in their relations with the "first world." (3) Similarly, economic interrelations that are damaging to the "third world" tend to give way to mutually beneficial positive-sum activities.[13] Although there is conflict about division of gains, this conflict does not take the form of a structured relation of exploitation between national societies.

Because the characteristics of the present era under the socialism-superior assumption are so different from those of imperialism as usually understood, it seems preferable to characterize the era as one of postimperialism. This is not a semantic matter. The point is that the pattern of relationships between the developed countries and the LDCs differs fundamentally from that of the preceding imperialist era and that one should not use the same term to describe both periods.

However, the postimperialism of the socialism-superior assumption differs from that described in Chapter 1. In contradistinction to what seems to be suggested there, nationalist and ideological conflict in the capitalist sphere would not cease or abate. They also would continue, although in forms different from those of the imperialist era. They would also merge. The major collisions between more and less developed countries within the capitalist sphere would tend increasingly to be about socioeconomic systems or modes of production. Thus, the conflicts would be both national and ideological. This merging of national and ideological conflict is illustrated by the current clash between the governments of Nicaragua and the United States.

Thus, under either the capitalism-superior or the socialism-superior assumption, the present era is postimperialist. In the former case, the postimperialism is that of Chapter 1, characterized by basic mutuality between the less and the more developed countries, although with competition for the division of benefits. In the latter case, fundamental conflict takes place between "first" and "third worlds," but it is postimperialist conflict about the mode of production.

I conclude that postimperialism is a valuable and significant concept and that it can be accepted without subscribing in all its particulars to the thesis set forth in Chapter 1. The task now is to proceed with the research and analysis needed to test the concept and to make use of it in explaining the present world order and its continuing development.

Notes

My indebtedness to Richard L. Sklar is evident. I also have benefited greatly from extensive and valuable comments by David G. Becker and have used some of his formulations. Stubbornness and wrongheadedness are my own.

1. If indigenization and associated policies reduce profitability, the game would be a negative-sum game.

2. David Becker has a different view. In his book, *The New Bourgeoisie and the Limits of Dependency* (Princeton: Princeton University Press, 1983), he suggests (p. 329) that indigenization is undertaken voluntarily by some transnational corporations as a cost-cutting measure. Compare my discussion of indigenization in Nigeria in Schatz, *Nigerian Capitalism* (Berkeley and Los Angeles: University of California Press, 1977).

3. The proper definition of socialism is a controversial issue. As a recent major survey points out, "There is much disagreement and indecisiveness among the radicals" about what countries, if any, are socialist, and about a whole series of propositions concerning the characteristics of a socialist country. Keith Griffin and John Gurley, "Radical Analyses of Imperialism, the Third World, and the Transition to Socialism: A Survey Article," *Journal of Economic Literature* 23, 3 (1985):1089–1143; see p. 1136. It would be far beyond the scope of this chapter—and not required by its purposes—to enter into this complex and not very fruitful controversy.

4. Paul A. Baran, *The Political Economy of Growth* (New York: Monthly Review Press, 1957).

5. World Bank, *World Development Report 1984* (New York: Oxford University Press, 1984), pp. 11, 23.

6. World Bank, *World Tables*, 3d ed., vol. 1 (Washington, DC: World Bank, 1983); and *World Development Report 1978* (New York: Oxford University Press, 1978).

7. See chs. 5 and 7.

8. Thomas M. Callaghy, "The Political Economy of African Debt: The Case of Zaire," in John Ravenhill (ed.), *Africa in Economic Crisis* (New York: Columbia University Press, forthcoming).

9. World Bank, *World Development Report 1978* (fn. 6), pp. 32–33.

10. Griffin and Gurley, "Radical Analyses," pp. 1126–1136.

11. Ibid.

12. Lenin, the originator of the conventional Marxist view of capitalist imperialism, did not expect "third world" movements for national liberation to establish socialism. He supported them because he reasoned that any movement in opposition to capitalist exploitation weakened the world capitalist system.

13. Positive-sum, that is, for the local dominant class, but not (under the socialism-superior assumption) for the subordinate classes.

CHAPTER TEN

Postimperialism:
A First Quarterly Report

DAVID G. BECKER

Richard L. Sklar's original essay on postimperialism appeared in print in 1976.[1] It was a perplexing paper on first reading, the impressive breadth of its scholarship notwithstanding, for it broke cleanly with much received wisdom. Sklar's broadening of the concept of class beyond ownership of the means of production was difficult to reconcile with the Marxian literature. The routine flagellation of capitalist exploitation expected in avowedly progressive writing on development was missing. His choice of the term *managerial bourgeoisie,* although a sound rhetorical device in principle, turned out in practice to have been somewhat infelicitous; many readers promptly misinterpreted it as denoting a class of managers. Moreover, the paper did not fall from the sky into a world breathlessly awaiting a new theory of development. Much to the contrary, it appeared at an unpropitious moment when development theory was on the verge of premature closure.

"Modernization theory," the development studies orthodoxy of the 1950s and 1960s, already had become obsolete by 1976, its demise hastened by events. Those events—the radicalization of the Cuban Revolution, the failure of the Alliance for Progress, the deepening U.S. involvement in Vietnamese "nation-building"—had claimed other victims as well: the dream of a value-free social science, for one; the myth of a uniquely benevolent U.S. imperialism, for another. Hence the search for a new theory of development had started off in the opposite direction—which is to say, leftward. A theory was wanted that would be explicitly progressive and critical; that would expose the evils of Western imperialism without exculpating the North American variant; that would overcome ethnocentrism by incorporating the viewpoints and insights of scholars and intellectuals from the "third world." Angry advocacy writing[2] achieved, for a time, an unaccustomed academic respectability. Afterward the quest paused at the gates of "dependency theory" in its several guises: "ECLA structuralism"[3]; "unequal exchange"[4]; the "Monthly Review school"[5]; the "structure of dependence"[6]; and, of course, the "development of underdevelopment."[7] Still later, as the decade was drawing to a close, seekers converged upon Fernando Henrique Cardoso's notion of "dependent development."[8]

Times have changed, and the rush to closure has been replaced by a willingness to pause and reflect. Cuba and Vietnam have faded into the gray penumbra of authoritarian "socialism," while radical nationalism has been stripped of its allure by the excesses repeatedly committed in its name. The glory days of OPEC are behind us, along with the myth of "third world" solidarity; the New International Economic Order seems more than ever a Utopian dream. For better or worse, today's angry advocates are read mainly by each other. "Dependency theory" has lost most of its adherents, thanks to its ideological excesses and its inability either to account for observations or to guide a meaningful political praxis. Those who want a progressive theory of development have been left with two contenders: what Peter Evans has called "Cardoso's 'historical-structural method'"[9]—and postimperialism.

Of the four contributors to this book, only two of us—Sklar and Becker—thus far have worked self-consciously within the framework of postimperialist theory. Jeff Frieden has described himself as "agnostic," and Sayre Schatz would be content with the same label. Still, each of them, in his own way and motivated by his own scholarly concerns, has been led to a position that fits comfortably within this framework. One reason for publishing the present collection is the strong suspicion that Frieden and Schatz are not alone in upholding that position.

As postimperialism encounters a wider audience, it becomes the object of more careful criticism. We are encouraged, not only by the growing number of published critiques but also, and far more importantly, by their steadily increasing depth and quality. Postimperialism ought not to ossify into doctrine; the odds that the theory will be perfected—or replaced by something better—improve in proportion as its deficiencies are revealed and answered.

I will address criticisms received from two quarters. The first is represented by Peter Evans, a self-professed "Cardosian" who, in collaboration with Theda Skocpol and others, wishes to "bring the state back in" to the study of capitalist development.[10] The second is represented by the two "agnostic" positions set forth in this book.

Further Pitfalls of "Cardosianism"

Evans believes that "what comes next" in development studies "will be very much in the tradition of the dependency approach but without the dependency label," which is "too closely associated with simplistic hypotheses of external domination." In a recent review article he sets forth four propositions that he considers basic to the "dependency tradition" as exemplified by Cardoso.

1. The economic forces of capitalist development are not socially transformatory in a progressive sense. Transnational corporations can coexist "in comfortable harmony with a state dominated by the landed oligarchy, taking advantage of tax incentives to fill corporate coffers in the United States rather than expanding capacity" in the host country. "The local private bourgeoisie in dependent countries will not and cannot play the economically 'revolutionary' role that is assigned to it by theories based on the supposed history of industrialization in currently advanced countries."

2. Consequently, "a more active, more 'relatively autonomous' state is an essential element in moving the development of dependent countries forward."

3. Rather than being united by common concerns, "global profit makers" and "those primarily interested in national development" are separated by "fundamental differences."

4. Capitalist development in today's less developed countries results in "levels of inequality that are extreme in comparison to those found in developed countries."[11]

Evans claims that my study of mining in Peru[12] supports each of these propositions.[13] Consequently, there are no significant differences between the postimperialist framework of my study and the Cardosian version of dependency.

There are, in truth, parallels between the two. Both attempt to replace "systemic logic" with systematic method; both regard development as an interaction between particularities of the local scene and the influence of a dynamically evolving international capitalism[14]; both focus upon the conflictual aspects of socioeconomic and political change; and both agree that today's capitalist development cannot possibly replicate the earlier experience of the West. Even so, the differences between them are far greater than the similarities. These differences were documented in Chapter 1; in essence they lie in the fact that the postimperialist approach is consistently class analytical, whereas the foundation and inspiration of Cardoso's "historical-structural method" are national-populist.

Capitalist Development and Social Change

As determined by the logic of the interests at stake and by observation of the available cases, landed-oligarchic domination invariably means a static internal market, little promotion of local industry, and a predominantly agro-export economy.[15] Transnational corporations active in natural resources or the processing of agricultural products sometimes can profit for a while in such an environment, although few manufacturing transnationals can.[16] The latter, however, enjoy other options—they can choose among the more dynamic "third world" domestic markets and bypass the static ones. In Latin America, landed-oligarchic domination persists mainly in some of the Central American countries; in Asia it is most prominent in the Philippines (although this may now be changing). Both areas have low per capita foreign direct investment by regional standards despite historically close political relationships with the United States.[17] Apart from Panama and Costa Rica, which are not under landed-oligarchic domination, Central America also has received little indirect foreign investment in per capita terms (the Philippines has done better, thanks to security-motivated U.S. assistance).

What of those transnationals that do invest where landed oligarchies rule? Corporate managements are disposed ideologically (the doctrine of domicile) to conduct their business in harmony with the policies of every state in which their subsidiaries are located, so long as their right to earn profits is respected. Transnational subsidiaries coexist with avowedly socialist states such as China and Angola; with radical nationalist states such as Libya; with interventionist capitalist states such as Brazil and South Korea; with minimalist states such as Hong Kong—and with a few landed-oligarchic states, such as El Salvador. Coexistence rests on a promise of "good corporate citizenship." However, it remains for local authorities to determine how a "good citizen" must behave. If neither official policy nor the transnational's profit strategy for the local market encourages expansion of capacity, none will be forthcoming. On the other hand, if the local authorities define "good citizenship" in terms of expansion *and* adopt policies that create new market opportunities, foreign firms revise their perspectives accordingly—or are replaced by more willing rivals.

Evans's arguments about corporate behavior, like those of the "dependency tradition" he claims as his own, are populist despite their class-analytical vocabulary. Business corporations, especially foreign ones, are "malefactors of great wealth." They are measured against idealistic standards of social responsibility—in this instance the standard requires them to invest only where there are social orders of which a progressive can approve—and always are found wanting. As we know from the history of North American social criticism, populist muckraking performs an important service by exposing abuses of corporate power. We also know, however, that such muckraking is incapable of the more radical critique that consists in analyzing the institutional character of the corporation and its role in the system of class domination.

Postimperialism, in contrast, substitutes analysis for wishful thinking and counterfactual comparisons. Although transnational corporations dictate neither the form and class content of the host-country state nor the local development model, the political effects of their presence are enormous. But the effects are just hinted at by short-term corporate decision-making and by policy and bargaining outcomes. Instead, most of the impact of foreign investment is long term and is felt through its influence on local and transnational processes of class formation. These processes result in time in the transformation or replacement of local dominant classes and in the rise of new constellations of class forces. The newly emergent dominant classes, in turn, overhaul state institutions so that the interest of these classes in political power and social control is better served. Subordinate classes, too, are reshaped in a fashion that makes them more effective politically. Their transformation is part and parcel of capitalist development, an inseparable element of its dialectic. As such the transformation poses new problems for the reformed system of domination. The working out of this dialectic is capitalist development, whether in the world periphery or anywhere else.[18]

When he criticizes "third world" bourgeoisies for their apparent developmental passivity, Evans compares their record with the "*supposed* history of industrialization" in the developed countries. The adjective is required, for recent historiography decisively has undermined the notion of a "heroic" bourgeoisie and has shown that, with the partial exception of Britain, industrialization always has depended on stimuli provided by a state apparatus acting on behalf of a dominant class with an interest in industrial development. Alexander Gerschenkron, writing well before the word "dependency" had become legal tender for U.S. academicians, demonstrated convincingly that late development has been associated consistently with a high level of state economic intervention.[19] A class interest in industrialization is not incompatible with a tendency toward risk-averse investment behavior.

"Relative Autonomy" and State Intervention

Postimperialism has little quarrel with Evans's second proposition. However, the proposition is not unique to the dependency tradition and applies with equal force to all capitalist development.

Every state is, in a sense, "relatively autonomous." In capitalist societies the actions of state institutions are never confined to slavish obeisance; nor, conversely, can government officials run these institutions like private fiefdoms. State officials and parastatal managers constitute a distinct functional group within the bourgeois class and have their own parochial interests, which they pursue by all available means. Where these functionaries differ from every other such group is in the fact that their institutional position carries with it the responsibility for projecting (ideological) universality and managing consensus in a society rent by class conflict. A private bourgeois institution like a business corporation can opt to ignore subordinate-class interests altogether, at least in the short run. If the corporation's self-serving actions are opposed strenuously, it can call upon another institution—the state—to pacify, overcome, or suppress the opposition and can regard the cost of doing so as an externality without relevance for the corporate balance sheet. The state can do no such thing. Whenever the actions of the authorities are consequential in terms of class interests (which is most of the time), the range of feasible action alternatives is constrained by the possible responses that each such alternative is likely to engender. Thus, even if every contending class is not physically represented within the state, *class struggle* always is present within it and serves as another limitation on the state's independent power. This limitation applies both to the self-interested behavior of state officials and to the institutional interests of the state itself.

Finally, every state is constrained by an international environment over which none has full control. (Environmental limitations of geography, population, resource endowment, and the like are not even controllable in principle.) The import of this set of constraints varies tremendously, both in time and from one state to another. For that reason it always is possible to array states on a continuum ranging from very strong to very weak,[20] but it always is arbitrary to divide them into "core" and "periphery" on any criterion other than geographical location (and, perhaps, age). *Dependencistas,* good populists that they are, want absolute sovereignty; it simply cannot be had.

State nurturing of capitalist development and of local bourgeois domination, a process aided by foreign investment, is a principal theme in postimperialist case studies of development.[21] States nurture capitalist development because it is in the interest of ruling elite strata; or, under landed-oligarchic domination, because the oligarchs have *some* concern with capitalism and are not free to pick and choose which aspects of it they will accept. Provided that class membership is defined on the basis of a common interest in political power and social control, these ideas—the unambiguously bourgeois class membership of the state officialdom; its interest in furthering a capitalist form of class domination; the scope and limits of state action—flow directly and naturally from the definition and from the basic structure of capitalist society. "Relative state autonomy" becomes a mere truism, a description of a reality inherent in the capitalist system. The term's separate conceptual status is needed only insofar as one hews to a doctrinaire insistence on economic determinism; *then* a special concept has to be invented in order to explain why the state is more than the "executive committee for managing the affairs of the whole bourgeoisie."[22]

Transnational Corporations Versus National Development

By "fundamental differences" Evans seems to be referring to a hypothesized zero-sum contest to divide the spoils of capitalist development.[23] Differences of this sort sometimes arise; they may run deep, but they remain differences about *immediate interests,* of exactly the same order as between corporate managers who want interest rates kept low and financiers who want them high. With regard to the maintenance of bourgeois class power and social control, transnational corporations, local dominant classes, and capitalist host governments are as one. Nothing in Evans's superb analysis of Brazilian development[24] indicates otherwise. To be sure, one might attempt to argue that local dominant classes and host governments are not interested in national development. However, arguments for *entreguismo* in the current age fly in the face of the facts and, besides, have been disputed by Evans himself.

In my view, a more cogent counterargument is Sayre Schatz's, presented in Chapter 9 of this book—that the apparent mutuality of interest between transnational corporate managements and local dominant classes derives mainly from their mutual fear of socialism. I will take up this counterargument separately.

Capitalist Development and the Question of Equity

Evans's final point seems to imply that every theory of development that stands outside of the dependency tradition unequivocally praises capitalist development and finds it in the interest of the common people of the less developed countries. This misconception is the inevitable outcome of conceiving development in terms of nations rather than classes. Let me clarify what is at stake by posing the issue in this way—all the people who constitute a national society obtain a *potential* benefit when the society's material productivity increases due to capitalist industrialization, under transnational corporate aegis or under any other. However, for the vast majority whose claim on the social product is not secured "automatically" by class privilege, the actualization of this potential depends upon the distribution of the expanded product.

In state-socialist systems where market forces have been suppressed, state elites can impose a fairly equitable distributional profile by fiat if they so desire. They generally do—partly out of principled belief, but partly because of the evident advantages for regime legitimation.[25] State-socialist models apart, no one has proven that the inequities of development in the "third world" of today are historically unique. Indeed, a growing volume of recent studies points in the opposite direction.[26] Time-series data for the United States indicate that income inequality rose throughout the 1920s, a period of corporate consolidation, and then began a slow decline that leveled off in the early postwar years.[27] Less complete data for other Western countries reveal similar trends. The timing of these shifts in income distribution lends strong support to the hypothesis that as economic power becomes concentrated in corporate hands, inequality increases; and later, as working classes become better organized and more politically adept, that inequality decreases in response to their pressures. Working-class formation, of course, is itself an outcome of capitalist development, and *in this sense* it could be said that Western capitalist development "produced" a relative distributional equity. But the memories of the countless men and women who have trod picket lines and fought for their rights against the modern state's panoply of coercive means are served poorly by that phrasing.

Postimperialist theory, although class analytical, has rejected the narrow economic determinism typical of orthodox currents in Marxian thought. Only in this way is it possible to come to terms with the nature of class formation and action in a transformed "late" capitalism where market forces are not everywhere dominant. Insofar as oligopoly (from above) and popular pressures (from below) restrict the operation of the market as an allocative device, a space is opened up in which *ideologically motivated* class action can occur. "Corporate liberalism," the prevailing ideology of the international bourgeoisie,[28] includes an important humanitarian component that justifies *in capitalist terms* some deviation from market strictures in order to redistribute wealth toward the world's poorest. Plainly, it is in the interest of the international bourgeoisie to be perceived as humane. Quite apart from the fact that corporate managers so perceive themselves, the successful projection of bourgeois humanitarianism—which must be backed up with *some* reference to reality—helps in multifarious ways to stabilize the system of class domination. Moreover, modern industrial bourgeoisies cannot afford to forget that workers also serve the economy as consumers; hence, limited redistribution actually furthers capital accumulation in the long run.[29]

Furthermore, postimperialism understands that the processes that give rise to the new international oligarchy simultaneously reinforce the working classes of the newly industrializing countries in numbers, knowledge, experience, and organizing capability.[30] Without denying the harsh realities of poverty and inequality in today's less developed countries, postimperialism intimates that these realities are better understood and combatted for what they are, rather than by reference to conditions that may or may not have existed elsewhere and long ago.

More Thoughts on the Bourgeoisie and Development

Instead of trying to fit postimperialism into the Procrustean bed of an outworn ideology, Jeff Frieden, in Chapter 8, confronts it "agnostically" but in its own terms. He is concerned that postimperialist class analysis be perfected—an endeavor that should reveal the weaknesses in its fundamental assumptions about social reality. In particular, he wonders whether Sklar and Becker have dealt sufficiently with intra-bourgeois conflict and whether Becker's treatment of ideology and class action threatens to lose sight of the conception of class action as interest based. He also asks about the connection between development and democracy. This is a question that every prospective theory of development should be made to answer.

The Role of Intra-Bourgeois Conflict

Frieden advises that future case studies "pay closer attention to conflicts *within* the managerial (or corporate national) bourgeoisie [his emphasis]." The advice is sound; its applicability, however, would appear to depend on what one is trying to learn. Intra-bourgeois conflicts are most relevant to studies of institutional behavior and policy outcomes. Few policy debates, on the whole, involve class interests unambiguously[31]; most often the interests immediately engaged are parochial ones belonging to functional groups or institutions controlled by them, regardless of whether the outcome has an impact in class terms. Even when the debate affects popular interests centrally, it is in the nature of capitalist politics that the "popular" side actually be carried by a bourgeois functional group with coincident concerns.[32]

On the other hand, studies aimed directly at questions of class formation or action would do well *not* to overemphasize the roles of various bourgeois functional groups or "fractions." Here one must avoid slipping into elite analysis and therefore must conceive of classes always as socially comprehensive entities whose interests lie with political power and social control.[33]

Action, Consciousness, and Ideology

Frieden cautions against what he fears may be a tendency in postimperialist thought to explain "all social developments . . . by the political actions of politically conscious groups or individuals"; he warns of the need to take account of "the result of underlying, and perhaps unrecognized, socioeconomic trends in the nation in question." I would differ not with the warning but with the fear that prompted it. Postimperialist class analysis attempts to explain social developments as products of the interplay between politically self-conscious actions of subjects (individuals or groups) and the socioeconomic structures and political institutions constituting the environment within which actions take place. This is, in my opinion, the only way that class analysis can be practiced in a nondeterministic manner.

The bargaining episode to which Frieden refers illustrates the point nicely. I sought to describe skilled Peruvian bargaining that interacted with structural conditions—the state of the international copper industry, the institutional character of the Southern Peru Copper Corporation, the past history of its dealings with the Peruvian government, and so forth—in a way that translated their *potentially* favorable significance into a correspondingly favorable outcome. As bargaining skill also demands explanation, I attempted to trace it to a further interaction between the Peruvian mining bourgeoisie's efforts to accumulate capital and a similar set of structural conditions.

Ideology should not be reduced to consciousness. The underlying thesis of postimperialism is that transnational corporate access to the periphery rests on shared interests. Still, the existence of an objective commonality of interest provides no guarantee that the subjects will in every instance act "properly" to secure the common interest over the long haul. Ideology operates to ensure that actions *do* serve long-term class interests most of the time. It does so, as I argued in Chapter 3, by arranging matters such that the context of action is one in which class interests are *already present,* imbedded in the sham-universalist image of reality that ideology projects. Thus, ideology does indeed help to secure—that is, to protect—transnational corporate access to the periphery. The fact may seem intuitively self-evident, but it merits demystification and elucidation nevertheless.

Ideology and Development

My studies of ideology cause me to disagree both with Frieden's tentative hypothesis that countries at intermediate levels of development are most likely to adopt a "rejectionist" stance[34] toward foreign investment and with his contention that local business executives' attitudes toward foreign investment are shaped mainly by competitive concerns. It frequently has been commented that attacks on foreign investment tend to awaken fears among local business executives, who may detect therein an assault upon the prerogatives of private capital per se.[35] The Latin American executives whom I have interviewed know that they face a dilemma—how to counter the competitive pressures of technologically superior foreign firms without giving aid and comfort to anticapitalist forces. The solution they prefer is not "rejection" but an "assertive pragmatism" that seeks to control foreign investment without banning it altogether.

Secondly, Frieden's critical comments about "bonanza development" merit a brief response. The concept was formulated in order to show how and why an otherwise anti-developmental landed oligarchy was able to accept a form of industrial development that ultimately led to its demise. Bonanza development propitiated the rise of Peru's corporate national bourgeoisie and was the particular, historically conditioned form that local class formation happened to take. In the process bonanza development became an integral part of the Peruvian developmental ideology. If, however, capitalist development in Peru is to retain its present legitimacy, its ideology will have to *transcend* bonanza development and embrace themes of sacrifice and hard work. Ideology also will have to create the image of sacrifice equitably shared. Impressive obstacles stand in the path, but they are not insurmountable. *Dependencismo* helps by shifting the blame for developmental shortcomings beyond the national frontiers. Peru's new president, Alan García Pérez, has been masterful at this kind of ideological projection, in which he enjoys the full support of the country's business community.

The Bourgeoisie and Democracy

Frieden, citing Sklar, evinces doubts about the democratic bona fides of the managerial bourgeoisie. The citation is incomplete, however. Sklar does argue that "[t]he most common device for dominant-class *consolidation* in Africa has been authoritarian government [emphasis added]" and that in Latin America "military regimes usually 'represent' the dominant class" before it is able to make its dominance hegemonic. But he goes on to highlight the reemergence of limited government once the process of class consolidation is farther along.

> Limited government implies a commitment to political freedom. Its reappearance on a grand scale . . . also betokens the existence of dominant social classes, whose members are confident of their ability to manage the affairs of society. Liberal governments are far more stable and less susceptible to revolutionary upheaval than dictatorships that serve the interests of privileged classes in an oppressive and demeaning manner.[36]

Inasmuch as corporate liberalism entails the idea of a "divided establishment"[37] and rests on the private sector's interest in retaining its entrepreneurial freedom of action, bourgeois classes in countries with strong private sectors are probably the ones with the greatest likelihood of opting for democratic political alternatives. They are also the ones that are most likely to succeed when they bring pressure to bear in favor of democratization. Certainly, a caveat is in order—the bourgeois interest in democracy holds only so long as challenges to the system of domination can be countered within a democratic framework and democratic institutions function reasonably smoothly from a bourgeois standpoint.[38] I continue to believe that the recent spread of democracy in Latin America is largely a product of organizational revolutions propelled forward with the aid (often indirect and almost always unintended) of foreign investment. If bourgeois support for democracy is contingent, there can be no guarantees about its future. The same is true, however, of the fate of bourgeois democracy in the developed countries.

On Socialism and Conflict

Sayre Schatz, in Chapter 9, is concerned about the relative neglect of socialism in current postimperialist writing. His chapter manifests the spirit of progressive thought since Marx—that a critical theory of capitalism must portray it as a historically bounded system and must attempt to reveal the mechanisms or processes by which it may be transcended. He likewise partakes of the Marxian tradition's strong interest in conflict as the chief precipitator of social change, and therefore he wonders whether postimperialism threatens to wave away much of the conflict that presently characterizes "North-South" relations. His inquiry has led him to take issue with three points in the exposition by Sklar and Becker that introduced this collection. The first is our stress on the mutuality of interests between the dominant classes of developed and less developed countries at the present stage of world capitalist development; the second is our failure to deal with the Great Competition between capitalism and socialism as a source of this mutuality; and the third is our apparent insinuation that capitalist development is better for "third world" societies than socialist development would be.

Mutuality Versus Conflict

Schatz believes that conflict between the developed and the less developed countries "might be sufficiently powerful to obscure and render nugatory for a considerable period the underlying mutuality." This choice of words concedes the existence of a tendency toward mutuality, yet suggests that it may not be realized in practice.

We live in an anarchic system of sovereign states that is ordered imperfectly and incompletely by economic interdependence and international class formation. In such a system the absence of external guarantees of security necessarily results in conflict. Students of international relations and those responsible for foreign policy formulation know all too well that a classification of policy objectives into neat conceptual categories, although essential for analysis after the fact, is unimaginable in the hurly-burly of daily practice. The "real world" actions of any state are motivated by an intimate melding and (con)fusion of security concerns, political concerns, economic concerns, and so forth. Hence, when development is conceived *fundamentally* in terms of nations (or national blocs) rather than in terms of class, not only is one type of conflict—interstate conflict—accentuated; in addition, the character of the conflict is hopelessly obscured.

Postimperialism still lacks a class analysis of the developed countries; the germ of one lurks in Chapter 2, but it has not yet been worked out. Let me tentatively adumbrate what such an analysis might reveal about the nature of the conflict that Schatz is addressing.

In the developed countries are found national bourgeois strata whose members participate only indirectly in the international economy—or do so occasionally or from positions of relative competitive weakness.[39] These individuals may come to believe that their international concerns can only be secured with the assistance of home-state politico-military power. As the developed countries are democracies, the interests of such strata can be well served by Right-populist political strategies aimed at forging alliances with susceptible popular sectors.[40] If I am right, the greatest threat to corporate-international bourgeois dominance in the developed countries is populism, not socialism. Reaganism and Thatcherism exemplify the sort of populism I have in mind.

In Chapter 1 we speculated briefly and inconclusively about a future world order characterized by a more-or-less uncontested international bourgeois domination. There are tendencies in this direction, and the logic of postimperialism would lead one to presume that the corporate international bourgeoisie has the economic clout it needs to fend off populist challenges—but in the long haul and subject to the proviso that (temporary) resurgences of developed-country populism do not precipitate ruinous wars that might restructure the international order in unpredictable ways. Thus, severe North-South conflict is possible in the short run, and such conflict could have deleterious consequences for the world order on which the idea of postimperialism is based. Nevertheless, in this very tentative analysis the odds remain on the side of the corporate international bourgeoisie.

It is essential that postimperialism direct its attention to the class structures of the developed countries in order to resolve issues such as these. Schatz is to be applauded for having placed them on the agenda.

The "Danger" of Socialism

In the class-analytical model of capitalist development, conflict is ever present. All bourgeois class action occurs in its shadow and therefore is directed in major part toward confronting—or, wherever possible, toward anticipating and heading off—challenges from below to the system of domination. To the degree that popular-class practice is socialist, then, the model implicitly incorporates the Great Competition.[41] What is more, if all bourgeois class action entails a confrontation with an actual or potential socialism, it is inherently impossible to disentangle action motivated by this confrontation from that motivated by anything else.

However, I suspect that Schatz has in mind a far more self-conscious fear of socialism on the part of the local bourgeoisies of the "third world."[42] Is the fear well founded?

Dependencistas have long assumed, in effect, that the "third world" would soon erupt in socialist revolution were it not for liberal applications of coercive force and, in extremis, the military might of the United States. Although any number of vanguards would offer themselves as proof, and although a few of them conceivably could prevail in armed struggle against weak or corrupt states, this ultra-Leftist scenario is sheer fantasy. Even abortive social-revolutionary outbreaks in the less developed countries are surprisingly rare in light of the poverty and deprivation found there; to provoke one seems to require an extraordinary measure of incompetence and selfishness on the part of the rulers—a standard to which only a select few, such as Ferdinand Marcos and Anastasio Somoza, have been able to measure up. My studies of mine labor (often the most radical of all working-class elements) in Peru found few signs of a class practice that reasonably could be called socialist.[43] Until additional case studies indicate otherwise, it appears to me that the weight of the evidence is against Schatz on this point.

To be sure, local bourgeoisies might misperceive popular demands for elementary justice and minor wage gains as "socialism"; bourgeois paranoia is hardly unknown. The existence and scale of such fear in the absence of an identifiable threat would appear to be an empirical matter open in principle to investigation. But, as with many attitudinal studies in less developed countries, research design poses daunting problems—not the least of which is the uncertain relationship between such attitudes and class action.

A Pro-Capitalist Bias?

In raising this question, Schatz has put his finger on the biggest reason why many progressives have had difficulty in fully appreciating the postimperialism idea. Most of us have come to the study of development out of what are, at bottom, normative concerns. We have been moved by the hunger, disease, poverty, gross inequality, and apparent lack of progress of "third world" societies that we have known; we want to help put an end to these things; and we perceive readily a relationship between them and the exploitative aspects of capitalist development.

Yet it remains the case that one cannot comprehend either the longevity of capitalism or its ability to renew and extend itself on a world scale in response to class struggle and other pressures if one concentrates on its exploitative aspects to the exclusion of all else. This is the approach taken by Leninist (not Marxist) orthodoxy[44] and by the dependency standpoint, both of which hold capitalist development responsible for every real and imagined evil in the "third world." It may be that in its effort to counter this distorted and unidimensional view, postimperialism on occasion has overstressed the other side of the coin. If Schatz is warning us that balance now demands more attention to the actual and potential crisis points of capitalist development, the warning is well taken.[45]

Postimperialism also represents an effort to inject a new realism into the study of development. Realistically speaking, the question of socialist development's superiority over the capitalist variety is moot; for nowhere in the world have the socialist ideals of democratic participation in political life and the absence of class domination in all of its forms been achieved. If socialism were truly on the agenda, it would be there because *real social forces at work in the world* embody the socialist ideal in their class practices. However, class analysis has not succeeded in turning up signs that such forces exist. It would appear, therefore, that the only presently viable alternative to capitalist development is coercive "primitive accumulation" of the Stalinist sort, which is, at best, a perversion of socialism. My personal view is that the human costs of Stalinist autarky are too high to be contemplated by those of us who lack the sense of certainty and mission that only ideological or religious fervor can provide.

The Truly Radical Alternative

Nothing in postimperialism implies unawareness of capitalism's historicity and consequent impermanence. Nothing in postimperialism forecloses a critique of capitalism's failings. On the contrary, postimperialism is radical in the fullest sense of the word. For it "goes to the root" of worldwide capitalist domination as it refocuses attention on class, rather than national, "contradictions." That radical analysis also exposes the sources of capitalism's capacity to endure and renew itself is a strength, not a weakness; in theory as in political practice, there is no room for wishful thinking.

One of the consequences of analyzing capitalism holistically, as postimperialism does, is acknowledgment of the fact that the basic forces and mechanisms of capitalism are the same everywhere; what differs is how these forces and mechanisms are embodied in historically shaped institutions and in the actions of real people in various parts of the world. The implication is that socialism in the "third world" may be achieved after a considerable prior experience of capitalist development. The same realism convinces me that postimperialism—not dependency, not Cardoso's "historical-structural method," not anything "in the tradition of the dependency approach but without the dependency label"—is the better guide for people in developing countries who seek a unity of theory and practice that can orient progressive political action.

Notes

Special thanks are due to Sanford G. Thatcher for having stimulated the conception of this chapter and to Richard L. Sklar, whose comments and criticisms provided material assistance at its birth.

1. See ch. 2 of this volume.

2. See, for example, Frantz Fanon, *The Wretched of the Earth*, trans. Constance Farrington (New York: Grove Press, 1963); Walter Rodney, *How Europe Underdeveloped Africa* (Dar es Salaam: Tanzania Publishing House, 1972); Susanne J. Bodenheimer, *The Ideology of Developmentalism: The American Pardigm-Surrogate for Latin American Studies*, Sage Professional Papers in Latin American Studies 2 (Beverly Hills, CA: Sage Publications, 1971). I hasten to add that even if much of this writing must be adjudged poor social science, some of it—notably Fanon's, among the three samples cited here—unquestionably excels as personal testament and as literature.

3. See, e.g., Raúl Prebisch, *Towards a Dynamic Development Policy for Latin America* (New York: United Nations, 1963); and Celso Furtado, *Economic Development of Latin America: A Survey from Colonial Times to the Cuban Revolution*, trans. Suzette Macedo (Cambridge: Cambridge University Press, 1970). ECLA is the United Nations Economic Commission for Latin America, which Prebisch headed for many years; his influence on Latin American and other "third world" students of development, particularly economists, has been profound.

4. Arghiri Emmanuel, *Unequal Exchange, A Study of the Imperialism of Trade* (New York: Monthly Review Press, 1969).

5. Its best-known effort at constructing a comprehensive theory of development is Paul A. Baran, *The Political Economy of Growth* (New York: Monthly Review Press, 1957).

6. Theotonio Dos Santos, "The Structure of Dependence," *American Economic Review* 60, 2 (1970):231–236.

7. André Gunder Frank, *Capitalism and Underdevelopment in Latin America: Historical Studies of Chile and Brazil*, rev. ed. (New York: Monthly Review Press, 1969); and Samir Amin, *Accumulation on a World Scale: A Critique of the Theory of Underdevelopment*, trans. Brian Pearce (New York: Monthly Review Press, 1974).

8. Cardoso's writings had been known to Latin Americanists since the 1960s. The first of his theoretical works to come to the attention of a wider audience was his article "Dependency and Development in Latin America," *New Left Review*, 74 (1972):83–95. Later on he was praised for warning against attempts, then much in fashion, to construct a "general theory of dependency." See Cardoso, "The Consumption of Dependency Theory in the United States," *Latin American Research Review* 12, 3 (1977):7–24. His star reached its zenith after the publication of a superb English-language translation of the book, *Dependencia y desarrollo en América Latina*; see Fernando Henrique Cardoso and Enzo Faletto, *Dependency and Development in Latin America*, trans. Marjory Mattingly Urquidi (Berkeley and Los Angeles: University of California Press, 1979).

9. Peter Evans, "After Dependency: Recent Studies of Class, State, and Industrialization," *Latin American Research Review* 20, 2 (1985):149–160.

10. See Peter B. Evans, Dietrich Rueschemeyer, and Theda Skocpol (eds.), *Bringing the State Back In* (Cambridge: Cambridge University Press, 1985), esp. the contributions by Evans himself (alone and in collaboration with Rueschemeyer).

11. Evans, "After Dependency."

12. David G. Becker, *The New Bourgeoisie and the Limits of Dependency: Mining, Class, and Power in "Revolutionary" Peru* (Princeton: Princeton University Press, 1983).

13. In regard to his third proposition, Evans adduces from my book the case of Utah International's Marcona mine, which shifted profits from Peru to a Panamanian shipping subsidiary and which was eventually nationalized; also "the refusal of even the cooperative Asarco to yield" to Peruvian demands regarding the building of a copper refinery (ibid., pp. 39–43, 118, 125). However: (1) The Marcona operation was due for automatic, no-cost transfer to full state ownership in the early 1980s; its hasty nationalization in 1975 was undertaken for domestic political reasons, and most analysts affiliated with the Peruvian Left now agree that the expropriation was an economic disaster for the host country. (2) Peru acquired a refinery anyway and, having done so, forced Asarco's local subsidiary to patronize it despite the fact that refining charges, set until 1981–1982 by state fiat, were considerably higher than those of equivalent facilities in the United States and Europe.

14. The appellation "*post*imperialism" implies the prior existence of capitalist imperialism. Only with the postwar appearance of a truly interdependent world economy and a correspondingly international business institution—the transnational corporation—do we enter the postimperialist age. Admittedly, these institutional changes, profound though they are, have not altered the underlying mechanisms of capitalist accumulation and exploitation. It would seem to follow that if today's capitalism has no structural "need" to exploit by way of imperialism, then capitalism never had such a need; in other words, the concept of postimperialism embodies a Hobsonian rather than Leninist appreciation of capitalism's imperialist phase. As is suggested in ch. 3, I cheerfully accept this assessment; faithfulness to received doctrine is not a valid test of a theory of development.

15. The internal market is static because the landed class depends on coerced peasant labor; thus, much of the population remains outside the money economy. Local industry is promoted only when there are difficulties in acquiring manufactured goods through trade (as happened in Latin America during the Depression and war years) because the usual means of promotion entail higher costs for oligarchic consumers; also, widespread industrialization carries with it the dangers of labor mobility and new opportunities for popular-class political organization. Agro-exports obviously enrich the oligarchy directly.

16. Even export-platform industrialization requires, at a minimum, a disciplined, industrious, and (usually) literate workforce. Such a workforce is utterly incompatible with landed-oligarchic domination, which rests economically on coercive (overt or disguised) labor control and frequently is plagued by political disorder and instability. In the very few cases where oligarchs thought they could attract transnationals for export-platform industrialization on the basis of fiscal incentives alone, their efforts have been largely unavailing. El Salvador is a case in point.

17. For the Philippines, the total stock of direct foreign investment (DFI) amounted to $28.60 per capita in 1975 versus $57.70 per capita for all of "capitalist developing East Asia" (Philippines plus Hong Kong, Indonesia, Korea, Malaysia, Singapore, Taiwan). The net inflow of DFI in 1975–1980 per capita of 1975 population was $16.90 for the Philippines and $42.90 for "capitalist developing East Asia" (now including Thailand and excluding Taiwan). Because the UN's tabulated data on DFI stocks include no entries for Central America, only a DFI inflow comparison is possible. The net DFI inflow in 1975–1980 per capita of 1975 population was $46.80 for "oligarchic Central America" (El Salvador, Guatemala, Honduras, Nicaragua) versus $72.80 for all of Latin America excluding Cuba; the figures for nonoligarchic Costa Rica and Panama are $277.00 and $63.80 respectively. Computed by the author from data in UN Commission on Transnational Corporations, *Transnational Corporations in World Development: A Re-examination* (New York: United Nations, 1978), E/C.10/38, pp. 254–257; and World Bank, *World Tables*, 3d ed., vol. 1 (Washington, DC: World Bank, 1983). Note that *World Tables* defines tabulated DFI (p. xii) as "investment . . . sufficient to give the nonresident a lasting interest and an effective voice in the management of the enterprise."

18. Consequently, the theories and tools of class analysis are as applicable to the less developed countries as they are to the developed countries—provided, naturally, that the appropriate contingencies and specificities are factored in.

19. Alexander Gerschenkron, *Economic Backwardness in Historical Perspective* (Cambridge: Belknap Press, Harvard University Press, 1962). The first chapter of Gerschenkron's book was published separately ten years earlier.

20. I grant that superpower status, conveyed mainly by possession of a large-scale nuclear deterrent capability, is a category apart.

21. In this volume see chs. 4 and 6. Also see Richard L. Sklar, *Corporate Power in an African State: The Political Impact of Multinational Mining Companies in Zambia* (Berkeley and Los Angeles: University of California Press, 1975); and

Sayre P. Schatz, *Nigerian Capitalism* (Berkeley and Los Angeles: University of California Press, 1977).

22. Evans's own recent writings on the state do not differ significantly from the view presented here. In his "Transnational Linkages and the Economic Role of the State: An Analysis of Developing and Industrial Nations in the Post-World War II Period," in Evans et al., *Bringing the State Back In*, pp. 192–225, he offers an analysis that closely parallels Jeff Frieden's in ch. 6 of this volume except for the emphasis on direct rather than indirect foreign investment. His analysis is a telling refutation of Immanuel Wallerstein's conception of a "world-economy" structured rigidly into three zones on the basis of state capabilities as well as levels of development. Rueschemeyer and Evans, "The State and Economic Transformation: Toward an Analysis of the Conditions Underlying Effective Intervention," in Evans et al., pp. 44–77, discuss the role of the state and the relationship between foreign investment and state effectiveness in a way that fits quite comfortably within a postimperialist framework.

One of the dangers in overstressing "relative state autonomy" is that in the hands of *dependencistas* the concept seems to allow for eating one's cake and having it, too. The state is said to be "relatively autonomous" of the local dominant class (whose existence thus need not be denied) so that the state can serve more readily the "anti-national" interests of foreign capital. Naturally, these attempted feats of gustatory and conceptual legerdemain can only be brought off with the ample aid of smoke and mirrors. Either the state is "relatively autonomous" of class forces—including those outside the national territory—or it is not.

23. Evans cannot mean the "fundamental differences" implied by "development of underdevelopment" or other simplistic versions of capitalist imperialism; these he has rejected soundly. He may have in mind an ideological definition of "national development" according to which it is incompatible a priori with the interests of "global profit makers"; that approach, alas, is not uncommon in development studies.

24. Peter Evans, *Dependent Development: The Alliance of Multinational, State, and Local Capital in Brazil* (Princeton: Princeton University Press, 1979).

25. Significantly, however, not one has dispensed for very long with differential material rewards, whose beneficiaries are mostly the same managerial cadres who do well in capitalist systems. The few ultra-radical experiments in dictated equality—Cuba in the 1960s, China during the Cultural Revolution, Kampuchea under Pol Pot—have been costly failures.

26. Felix Paukert, "Income Distribution at Different Levels of Development: A Survey of Evidence," *International Labour Review* 108, 2–3 (1973):97–125, shows that income inequality always and everywhere has gotten worse when capitalist development has reached an intermediate stage; the historical data for the presently developed countries prior to the Great Depression are quite comparable to those for most of today's newly industrializing countries. (Interestingly, Paukert's analysis reveals that this concentration of wealth does not contract the lowest quintile's income share; the losers, rather, are the middle quintiles.) Peter H. Lindert and Jeffrey G. Williamson, "Reinterpreting Britain's Social Tables, 1688–1913," *Explorations in Economic History* 20, 1

(1983):94–109, find that in 1867 the top quintile of the British (England and Wales) income distribution captured 63.3 percent of the national income—one of the highest maldistributions ever recorded.

27. Bureau of the Census, *Historical Studies of the United States, Colonial Times to 1970*, 2 vols. (Washington, DC: U.S. Government Printing Office, 1975), 1:201–202.

28. On corporate liberalism see Martin J. Sklar, *The Corporate Reconstruction of American Capitalism, 1890–1916: The Market, the Law, and Politics* (Cambridge: Cambridge University Press, 1987), esp. chs. 1, 6.

29. These assertions deliberately fly in the face of conventional Marxist imagery that paints business executives as vicious exploiters. Under early, free-market capitalism, generalized competition made it difficult or impossible for capitalists to take a longer view of the accumulation process; it left them little choice but to squeeze out of their workers the maximum amount of surplus value *on a day-to-day basis*. Those conditions have changed radically, however; oligopolistic competition allows businesspeople far more flexibility in their strategies of capital accumulation. The image of the rapacious capitalist may retain some value as political propaganda, but it has none as theory; Ebenezer Scrooge and Robert McNamara belong to different centuries. To be sure, capitalist exploitation continues unabated. But Marx contended that exploitation inheres in the capitalist labor contract and consists in the appropriation of surplus value; under present-day conditions this appropriation is entirely consistent with a humane attitude toward the worker and the generalized poor as individuals and, indeed, is facilitated thereby.

It may be added that its appreciation of these factors causes postimperialist theory to take a direct interest in ideological class action and to try incorporating within itself a theory of ideology. As always, ideology justifies interests—in this case, the bourgeois interest in system stability and hegemonic (i.e., noncoercive) domination. The bourgeois humanitarianism of "late" capitalism is hardly as bizarre as it may seem; it is merely the *noblesse oblige* that every successful dominant class projects. Too, not every "noble" feels himself *obligé*. In those instances where the demands of *noblesse oblige* conflict with the core interests of the class, the latter will prevail.

30. Also, residential patterns, lifestyle commonalities, and economic interchange—specifically, the interchange between workers and the "informal sector," which provides them with many basic commodities and services—tend to create a broader popular solidarity. For one case study, see Evelyne Huber Stephens, "The Peruvian Military Government, Labor Mobilization, and the Political Strength of the Left," *Latin American Research Review* 18, 2 (1983):57–93.

31. For one of two reasons, depending on the nature of the political institutions: (1) In authoritarian systems, those who might challenge the core interests of the dominant class are forcibly excluded from the debate. (2) In democratic systems, class dominance takes the form, as argued in ch. 3, of ideological hegemony. Ideology operates to structure "reality"; to determine, inter alia, "common sense"—what is thinkable and what, quite literally, unthinkable. Ideology thereby tends to confine policy debate to the realm of the

thinkable, in bourgeois terms. Dominant class interests are not challenged fundamentally because such challenges belong to the realm of the unthinkable.

32. Among the reasons why this is so are the preponderantly bourgeois character of the relevant expertise; the corresponding tendency to define policy options wherever possible in highly technical terms; bourgeois control of the media of mass communication; and, by no means least, the recognition by some bourgeois elites that they can prevail and strengthen their claims to class leadership if they can enlist popular allies in the intra-bourgeois conflict.

33. Cf. Sklar's handling of these issues in his studies of bourgeois class formation by the "fusion of elites": Richard L. Sklar, "The Nature of Class Domination in Africa," *Journal of Modern African Studies* 17, 4 (1979):531–552.

34. Schatz's terminology—see ch. 5.

35. Not because local businesspeople are innately sympathetic toward the claims of foreign investors but because they understand that foreign investment is, in most less developed countries, the most politically vulnerable form of private capital. Businesspeople tend to be less fearful of successful frontal assaults on all forms of capital (which they consider highly improbable) than of flanking attacks against "soft spots," which intend to chip away gradually at class privileges.

36. Sklar, "The Nature of Class Domination in Africa" (quoted from pp. 540, 542). For his remark on Latin America Sklar cites José Nun, "The Middle-Class Military Coup," in Claudio Véliz (ed.), *The Politics of Conformity in Latin America* (London: Oxford University Press, 1967), pp. 66–118.

37. Richard L. Sklar, "Notes for a UCLA Colloquium on Postimperialism," May 1984 (unpublished draft). Also see his discussion of countervailing power in ch. 2.

38. In the recent history of Latin America, the 1973 overthrow of Chile's Salvador Allende is the only instance in which the bourgeoisie precipitated a military coup d'état out of fear of an imminent socialist takeover; and even there, the breakdown of order and Allende's inability to show himself in control of events were contributing factors. In every other case the bourgeoisie turned against populist regimes that seemed persistently to have mismanaged the economy.

39. In the context of the current argument, indirect participation is to be understood as including foreign competition in the participant's home market.

40. This is nothing more than an updated, class-analytical version of Hobson's argument; I have shown already how in a hegemonic order intra-bourgeois conflict frequently takes the form of a competitive search for popular allies.

41. If popular-class action is nonsocialist, the whole issue is irrelevant except for the possible existence of "bourgeois paranoia," which will be touched upon subsequently.

42. In portraying the fear as a mutuality, Schatz is saying that the corporate international bourgeoisie feels it, too. His assumption, however, does not seem to be borne out by experience. Many transnational firms do business with socialist states, and corporate spokespeople generally have responded unenthusiastically to Reagan's policies of confrontation. On the other hand, one

presumes that the international bourgeoisie would not want socialism to spread widely throughout the "third world" and that this bourgeoisie would lend support (if it could do so without risking its interests) to a local bourgeoisie that it respected and perceived as truly threatened. It seems to me that replacing Schatz's original assumption with this weaker and, perhaps, more realistic version actually strengthens his overall argument.

43. Becker, *New Bourgeoisie,* pp. 279–319; and Becker, "The Workers of the Modern Mines in Southern Peru: Socio-Economic Change and Trade-Union Militancy in the Rise of a Labor Elite," in Thomas Greaves and William Culver (eds.), *Miners and Mining in the Americas* (Manchester, Eng.: Manchester University Press, 1985), pp. 226–256.

44. See Bill Warren, *Imperialism, Pioneer of Capitalism* (London: New Left Books, 1980).

45. Still, I would caution against the *dependencista* and conventional Marxist tendency to find socialism's entering wedge in every economic crisis. See Tom Bottomore, *Theories of Modern Capitalism* (London: George Allen & Unwin, 1985), pp. 14–21, for a discussion of this point. To my mind it is praiseworthy—and symptomatic of a new openness in some Marxian circles—that Bottomore bases his argument on a sympathetic rereading of that Leninist bête noir, Hilferding's *Finanzkapital* (recently republished in English translation as Rudolf Hilferding, *Finance Capital: A Study of the Latest Phase of Capitalist Development,* trans. Tom Bottomore [London: Routledge & Kegan Paul, 1981]).

Bibliography

Abdel-Malek, Anouar. *Egypt: Military Society.* Trans. C.L. Markman. New York: Random House, 1968.

Adamson, Walter L. *Hegemony and Revolution: Antonio Gramsci's Political and Cultural Theory.* Berkeley and Los Angeles: University of California Press, 1980.

Almeida Magalhães, João Paulo de. *Modelo brasileiro de desenvolvimento.* Rio de Janeiro: Record, 1976.

Amin, Samir. *Accumulation on a World Scale: A Critique of the Theory of Underdevelopment.* Trans. Brian Pearce. New York: Monthly Review Press, 1974.

————. *Unequal Development: An Essay on the Social Formations of Peripheral Capitalism.* Trans. Brian Pearce. New York: Monthly Review Press, 1976.

————. "Expansion or Crisis of Capitalism?" *Third World Quarterly* 5, 2 (1983):361–380.

Ammour, Kader; Leucate, Christian; and Moulin, Jean-Jacques. *La voie algérienne: Les contradictions d'un developpement national.* Paris: Maspero, 1974.

Angell, Alan, and Thorp, Rosemary. "Inflation, Stabilization and Attempted Redemocratization in Peru, 1975–1979." *World Development* 8, 11 (1980):865–886.

Anjaria, S.J. "The Tokyo Round of Multilateral Trade Negotiations." *Finance and Development* 15, 1 (1978):14–15.

Aronson, Jonathan David (ed.) *Debt and the Less Developed Countries.* Boulder, CO: Westview Press, 1979.

Arrighi, Giovanni, and Saul, John S. "Socialism and Economic Development in Tropical Africa." *Journal of Modern African Studies* 6, 2 (1968):141–169.

Bachrach, Peter. *The Theory of Democratic Elitism: A Critique.* Boston: Little, Brown, 1967.

Baldwin, Robert E., and Murray, T. "MFN Tariff Reductions and LDC Benefits under the GSP." *Economic Journal* 87, 345 (1977):30–46.

Ball, George W. "Cosmocorp: The Importance of Being Stateless." In Courtney C. Brown (ed.). *World Business: Promise and Problems,* pp. 330–338. New York: Macmillan, 1970.

Bamat, Thomas. "Relative State Autonomy and Capitalism in Brazil and Peru." *The Insurgent Sociologist* 7, 2 (1977):74–84.

Baran, Paul A. *The Political Economy of Growth.* New York: Monthly Review Press, 1957.

Baran, Paul A., and Sweezy, Paul M. "Notes on the Theory of Imperialism." *Monthly Review* 17, 10 (1966):15–33.

Barber, Richard J. *The American Corporation.* New York: Dutton, 1970.

Barnet, Richard J. *Roots of War.* New York: Atheneum, 1972.

Barnet, Richard J., and Müller, Ronald E. *Global Reach: The Power of the Multinational Corporations.* New York: Simon & Schuster, 1974.

Barraclough, Geoffrey. "The Struggle for the Third World." *New York Review of Books,* 9 November 1978, pp. 47–58.

―――. "Waiting for the New Order." *New York Review of Books,* 26 October 1978, pp. 45–58.

Barratt-Brown, Michael. *The Economics of Imperialism.* Harmondsworth, Eng.: Penguin Books, 1976.

Becker, David G. "Modern Mine Labour and Politics in Peru since 1968." *Boletín de estudios Latinoamericanos y del Caribe,* 32 (1982):35–60.

―――. *The New Bourgeoisie and the Limits of Dependency: Mining, Class, and Power in "Revolutionary" Peru.* Princeton: Princeton University Press, 1983.

―――. "Peru after the 'Revolution': Class, Power, and Ideology." *Studies in Comparative International Development* 20, 3 (1986):3–30.

―――. "The Workers of the Modern Mines in Southern Peru: Socio-Economic Change and Trade-Union Militancy in the Rise of a Labor Elite." In Thomas Greaves and William Culver (eds.) *Miners and Mining in the Americas,* pp. 226–256. Manchester, Eng.: University of Manchester Press, 1986.

Beek, David C. "Commercial Bank Lending to the Developing Countries." *Federal Reserve Bank of New York Quarterly Review* 2, 2 (1977):1–8.

Behrman, Jack N. *National Interests and the Multinational Enterprise: Tensions Among the North Atlantic Countries.* Englewood Cliffs, NJ: Prentice-Hall, 1970.

Bell, Daniel. *The Coming of Post-Industrial Society: A Venture in Social Forecasting.* New York: Basic Books, 1973.

Bergsman, Joel. *Brazil: Industrialization and Trade Policies.* London: Oxford University Press, 1970.

Bergsten, C. Fred; Horst, Thomas; and Moran, Theodore H. *American Multinationals and American Interests.* Washington, DC: Brookings Institution, 1978.

Berle, Adolf A., Jr. *Power Without Property.* New York: Harcourt, Brace, 1959.

―――. *The Twentieth Century Capitalist Revolution.* New York: Harcourt, Brace, 1954.

Berle, Adolf A., Jr., and Means, Gardiner C. *The Modern Corporation and Private Property.* New York: Macmillan, 1932.

Bernstein, Edward M. "The International Monetary Fund." In Richard N. Gardner and Max F. Millikan (eds.) *The Global Partnership: International Agencies and Economic Development,* pp. 131–151. New York: Praeger, 1968.

Bettelheim, Charles. *India Independent.* Trans. W.A. Caswell. New York: Monthly Review Press, 1969.

Bill, James. "Class Analysis and the Dialectics of Modernization in the Middle East." *International Journal of Middle East Studies* 3, 4 (1972):417–434.

―――. *The Politics of Iran: Groups, Classes, and Modernization.* Columbus, OH: Merrill, 1972.

Bill, James A., and Hardgrave, Robert L., Jr. *Comparative Politics: The Quest for Theory.* Columbus, OH: Merrill, 1973.

Bodenheimer, Susanne J. "Dependency and Imperialism: The Roots of Latin American Underdevelopment." In K.T. Fann and Donald C. Hodges (eds.) *Readings in U.S. Imperialism,* pp. 155–181. Boston: Porter Sargent, 1971.

————. *The Ideology of Developmentalism: The American Pardigm-Surrogate for Latin American Studies.* Sage Professional Papers in Latin American Studies 2. Beverly Hills, CA: Sage Publications, 1971.

Bonilla, Heraclio. *Guano y burguesía en el Perú.* Lima: Instituto de Estudios Peruanos, 1974.

————. *El minero de los Andes: una aproximación a su estudio.* Lima: Instituto de Estudios Peruanos, 1974.

Bossio Rotundo, José C. "Cambios en la política minero-metalúrgica." In Ernst-J. Kerbusch (ed.), *Cambios estructurales en el Perú,* pp. 121–144. Lima: Instituto Latinoamericano de Investigaciones Sociales, 1976.

Bottomore, Tom. *Theories of Modern Capitalism.* London: George Allen & Unwin, 1985.

Bourque, Susan C., and Palmer, David Scott. "Transforming the Rural Sector: Government Policy and Peasant Response." In Abraham F. Lowenthal (ed.) *The Peruvian Experiment: Continuity and Change under Military Rule,* pp. 197–219. Princeton: Princeton University Press, 1975.

Bourricaud, François. *Poder y sociedad en el Perú contemporáneo.* Buenos Aires: Editorial Sur, 1967.

Brenner, Robert. "The Origins of Capitalist Development: A Critique of Neo-Smithian Marxism." *New Left Review,* 104 (1977):25–92.

Brewer, Anthony. *Marxist Theories of Imperialism: A Critical Survey.* London: Routledge & Kegan Paul, 1980.

Brundenius, Claes. "The Anatomy of Imperialism: The Case of Multinational Mining Corporations in Peru." *Journal of Peace Research* 9, 3 (1972):189–206.

Bureau of the Census. *Historical Studies of the United States, Colonial Times to 1970.* 2 vols. Washington, DC: U.S. Government Printing Office, 1975.

Burnham, James. *The Managerial Revolution.* New ed. Bloomington: Midland Books, Indiana University Press, 1960.

Callaghy, Thomas M. "The Political Economy of African Debt: The Case of Zaíre." In John Ravenhill (ed.) *Africa in Economic Crisis.* New York: Columbia University Press, forthcoming.

Caporaso, James A. "Dependence, Dependency, and Power in the Global System: A Structural Analysis." *International Organization* 32, 1 (1978):13–43.

Caporaso, James A., and Zare, Behrouz. "An Interpretation and Evaluation of Dependency Theory." In Heraldo Muñoz (ed.) *From Dependency to Development: Strategies to Overcome Underdevelopment and Inequality,* pp. 43–56. Boulder, CO: Westview Press, 1981.

Cardoso, Fernando Henrique. "Dependency and Development in Latin America." *New Left Review,* 74 (1972):83–95.

————. "Associated-Dependent Development: Theoretical and Practical Implications." In Alfred Stepan (ed.) *Authoritarian Brazil: Origins, Policies, and Future,* pp. 142–176. New Haven: Yale University Press, 1973.

————. "The Consumption of Dependency Theory in the United States." *Latin American Research Review* 12, 3 (1977):7–24.

Cardoso, Fernando Henrique, and Faletto, Enzo. *Dependency and Development in Latin America*. Trans. Marjory Mattingly Urquidi. Berkeley and Los Angeles: University of California Press, 1979.

Castells, Manuel. "Class, State and Dependency in Latin America: Some Theoretical Guidelines." Paper presented at the Joint Meeting of the African Studies Association and the Latin American Studies Association, Houston, November 1977. Mimeographed.

Catlin, George E. Gordon. *Systematic Politics: Elementa Politica et Sociologica*. Toronto: University of Toronto Press, 1962.

Cavarozzi, Marcelo. "Elementos para una caracterización del capitalismo oligárquico." *Revista Mexicana de Sociología* 40, 4 (1978):1327–1352.

Chaliand, Gérard, and Minces, Juliette. *L'Algérie indépendante*. Paris: Maspero, 1972.

Chenery, Hollis B., and Keesing, Donald B. "The Changing Composition of Developing Country Exports." World Bank Staff Working Paper no. 314. Washington, DC: World Bank, 1979. Mimeographed.

Chudson, Walter. "Africa." In H.R. Hahlo, J. Graham Smith, and Richard W. Wright (eds.) *Nationalism and the Multinational Enterprise: Legal, Economic, and Managerial Aspects,* pp. 136–161. Dobbs Ferry, NY: Oceana, 1973.

Clegg, Ian. *Workers' Self-Management in Algeria*. New York: Monthly Review Press, 1971.

Clement, Norris, and Green, Louis. "The Political Economy of Devaluation in Mexico." *Inter-American Economic Affairs* 32, 3 (1978):47–75.

Cleveland, Harold van B., and Brittain, W.H. Bruce. "Are the LDCs in Over Their Heads?" *Foreign Affairs* 55, 4 (1977):732–750.

Cline, William R. *International Monetary Reform and the Developing Countries*. Washington, DC: Brookings Institution, 1976.

Cohen, Benjamin J. *The Question of Imperialism: The Political Economy of Dominance and Dependence*. New York: Basic Books, 1973.

————. *Multinational Firms and Asian Exports*. New Haven: Yale University Press, 1975.

Connor, John. *The Market Power of Multinationals*. New York: Praeger, 1977.

Cotler, Julio. "The Mechanics of Internal Domination and Social Change in Peru." In David Chaplin (ed.) *Peruvian Nationalism: A Corporatist Revolution,* pp. 35–71. New Brunswick, NJ: Transaction, 1976.

————. *Clases, Estado y nación en el Perú*. Lima: Instituto de Estudios Peruanos, 1978.

————. "State and Regime: Comparative Notes on the Southern Cone and the 'Enclave' Societies." In David Collier (ed.) *The New Authoritarianism in Latin America,* pp. 255–282. Princeton: Princeton University Press, 1979.

Dahrendorf, Ralf. *Class and Class Conflict in Industrial Society*. Stanford, CA: Stanford University Press, 1959.

Deutsch, Karl W. *The Nerves of Government: Models of Political Communication and Control*. New York: Free Press, 1966.

Díaz Alejandro, Carlos F. "Direct Foreign Investment in Latin America." In Charles P. Kindleberger (ed.) *The International Corporation*, pp. 319–344. Cambridge: MIT Press, 1970.

Djilas, Milovan. *The New Class: An Analysis of the Communist System*. New York: Praeger, 1957.

Dominguez, Jorge. "National and Multinational Business and the State in Latin America." Paper presented at the Annual Meeting of the American Political Science Association, Washington, DC, September 1979.

Dos Santos, Theotonio. "The Structure of Dependence." *American Economic Review* 60, 2 (1970):231–236.

Drucker, Peter F. "Multinationals and Developing Countries: Myths and Realities." *Foreign Affairs* 53, 1 (1974):121–134.

Dumont, René. *False Start in Africa*. 2d ed., rev. Trans. Phyllis Nauts Ott. New York: Praeger, 1969.

Dunning, John H. "The Multinational Enterprise: The Background." In John H. Dunning (ed.) *The Multinational Enterprise*, pp. 15–48. London: Allen & Unwin, 1971.

Easton, David. *A Framework for Political Analysis*. Englewood Cliffs, NJ: Prentice-Hall, 1965.

————. *A Systems Analysis of Political Life*. New York: Wiley, 1965.

Edwards, Anthony. *The New Industrial Countries and Their Impact on Western Manufactures*. London: The Economist Intelligence Unit, 1979.

Einaudi, Luigi R. "Revolution from Within? Military Rule in Peru since 1968." In David Chaplin (ed.) *Peruvian Nationalism: A Corporatist Revolution*, pp. 401–427. New Brunswick, NJ: Transaction, 1976.

Einaudi, Luigi R., and Stepan, Alfred C., III. *Latin American Institutional Development: Changing Military Perspectives in Brazil and Peru*. R-586-DOS. Santa Monica, CA: RAND Corporation, 1971.

Emmanuel, Arghiri. *Unequal Exchange, A Study of the Imperialism of Trade*. New York: Monthly Review Press, 1969.

Epstein, Edwin M. *The Corporation in American Politics*. Englewood Cliffs, NJ: Prentice-Hall, 1969.

Espinosa Uriarte, Henrique, and Osorio, José. "Dependencia y poder económico: caso minería y pesquería." In Henrique Espinosa Uriarte et al. *Dependencia económica y tecnológica: Caso peruano*, pp. 69–230. Lima: Centro de Investigaciones Sociales, Universidad Nacional Federico Villarreal, 1971.

Evans, Peter. *Dependent Development: The Alliance of Multinational, State, and Local Capital in Brazil*. Princeton: Princeton University Press, 1979.

————. "After Dependency: Recent Studies of Class, State, and Industrialization." *Latin American Research Review* 20, 2 (1985):149–160.

————. "Transnational Linkages and the Economic Role of the State: An Analysis of Developing and Industrial Nations in the Post-World War II Period." In Peter B. Evans, Dietrich Rueschemeyer, and Theda Skocpol (eds.) *Bringing the State Back In*, pp. 192–225. Cambridge: Cambridge University Press, 1985.

Fanon, Frantz. *The Wretched of the Earth.* Trans. Constance Farrington. New York: Grove Press, 1963.

Farrah, A. "La Necessité de planification." *Révolution africaine,* 783 (1979):18–19.

Femia, Joseph V. "The Gramsci Phenomenon: Some Reflections." *Political Studies* 27, 3 (1979):472–483.

Fields, Gary S. "Who Benefits from Economic Development? A Reexamination of Brazilian Growth in the 1960s." *American Economic Review* 67, 4 (1977):570–582.

Figueroa, Adolfo. *Capitalist Development and the Peasant Economy in Peru.* Cambridge:·Cambridge University Press, 1984.

Fishlow, Albert. "A New International Economic Order: What Kind?" In Albert Fishlow et al. *Rich Nations and Poor Nations in the World Economy,* pp. 11–86. New York: McGraw-Hill, 1978.

FitzGerald, E.V.K. *The State and Economic Development: Peru since 1968.* Cambridge: Cambridge University Press, 1976.

————. *The Political Economy of Peru, 1956–78: Economic Development and the Restructuring of Capital.* Cambridge: Cambridge University Press, 1979.

Flores Galindo, Alberto. *Los mineros de la Cerro de Pasco, 1900–1930 (un intento de caracterización social).* Lima: Departamento Académico de Ciencias Sociales, Pontificia Universidad Católica del Perú, 1974.

Frank, André Gunder. "The Development of Underdevelopment." *Monthly Review* 18, 4 (1966):17–31.

————. *Capitalism and Underdevelopment in Latin America: Historical Studies of Chile and Brazil.* Rev. ed. New York: Monthly Review Press, 1969.

————. *Lumpenbourgeoisie: Lumpendevelopment: Dependence, Class, and Politics in Latin America.* Trans. Marion Davis Berdecio. New York: Monthly Review Press, 1973.

Frank, Charles; Kim, Kwang Suk; and Westphal, Larry. *Foreign Trade Regimes and Economic Development: South Korea.* New York: Columbia University Press, 1975.

Frank, Isaiah. "Reciprocity and Trade Policy of Developing Countries." *Finance and Development* 15, 1 (1978):20–23.

Franko, Lawrence G., and Seiber, Marilyn (eds.) *Developing Country Debt.* New York: Pergamon, 1979.

Friedman, Irving. *The Emerging Role of Private Banks in the Developing World.* New York: Citicorp, 1977.

Furtado, Celso. *Economic Development of Latin America: A Survey from Colonial Times to the Cuban Revolution.* Trans. Suzette Macedo. Cambridge: Cambridge University Press, 1970.

Galbraith, John Kenneth. *The New Industrial State.* Boston: Houghton Mifflin, 1967.

Galtung, Johan. "A Structural Theory of Imperialism." *Journal of Peace Research* 8, 2 (1971):81–117.

García de Romana, Alberto. "Comportamiento gremial y político de los empresarios industriales, 1968–73." Lima: Taller de Estudios Urbano-

Industriales, Pontificia Universidad Católica del Perú, 1975. Mimeographed.

Gerschenkron, Alexander. *Economic Backwardness in Historical Perspective.* Cambridge: Belknap Press, Harvard University Press, 1962.

Gerth, H.H., and Mills, C. Wright. "A Marx for Managers." *Ethics* 52, 3 (1942):200–215.

Gilpin, Robert. *U.S. Power and the Multinational Corporation: The Political Economy of Foreign Direct Investment.* New York: Basic Books, 1975.

Girvan, Norman. "Multinational Corporations and Dependent Development in Mineral Export Economies." *Social and Economic Studies* 19, 4 (1970):490–526.

Gold, David A.; Lo, Clarence Y.H.; and Wright, Erik Olin. "Recent Developments in Marxist Theories of the Capitalist State." *Monthly Review* 27, 5 (1975):29–43; 27, 6 (1975):36–51.

Goodsell, Charles T. *American Corporations and Peruvian Politics.* Cambridge: Harvard University Press, 1974.

Gould, Stephen Jay. *The Panda's Thumb.* New York: Norton, 1980.

Gouldner, Alvin W. *The Future of Intellectuals and the Rise of the New Class.* New York: Seabury Press, 1979.

Gramsci, Antonio. *Selections from the Prison Notebooks.* New York: International Publishers, 1971.

———. *Letters from Prison.* New York: Harper & Row, 1973.

Green, Reginald Herbold. "Political Independence and the National Economy: An Essay on the Political Economy of Decolonisation." In Christopher Allen and R.W. Johnson (eds.) *African Perspectives: Papers in the History, Politics, and Economics of Africa Presented to Thomas Hodgkin,* pp. 273–324. Cambridge: Cambridge University Press, 1970.

Green, Rosario. *El endeudamiento público externo de México 1940–1973.* Guanajuato: El Colegio de México, 1976.

Gregor, A. James. *Italian Fascism and Developmental Dictatorship.* Princeton: Princeton University Press, 1979.

Griffin, Keith, and Gurley, John. "Radical Analyses of Imperialism, the Third World, and the Transition to Socialism: A Survey Article." *Journal of Economic Literature* 23, 3 (1985):1089–1143.

Grimaud, Nicole. "Les Finances publiques de l'Algérie." *Maghreb-Machrek,* 56 (1973):30–37.

———. "Une Algérie en mutation à l'heure de la charte nationale." *Maghreb-Machrek,* 73 (1976):70–77.

Grupo de Economía Mexicana-CIDE. "México: devaluación, petróleo y alternativas de desarrollo." *Economía de América Latina,* 2 (1979):171–187.

Gutiérrez R., Roberto. "La balanza petrolera de México, 1970–1982." *Comercio Exterior* 29, 8 (1979):839–850.

Hacker, Andrew. "Politics and the Corporation." In Andrew Hacker (ed.) *The Corporation Take-Over,* pp. 239–262. New York: Harper & Row, 1964.

Halpern, Manfred. *The Politics of Social Change in the Middle East and North Africa.* Princeton: Princeton University Press, 1963.

Harding, Colin. "Land Reform and Social Conflict in Peru." In Abraham F. Lowenthal (ed.) *The Peruvian Experiment: Continuity and Change Under Military Rule*, pp. 220–253. Princeton: Princeton University Press, 1975.

Harringer, Reinhold. "The Development of International Debt." *Aussenwirtschaft* (March-June 1978):13.

Heilbroner, Robert L. *An Inquiry into the Human Prospect*. New York: Norton, 1974.

———. "Inflationary Capitalism." *The New Yorker*, 8 October 1979, p. 121ff.

Helleiner, Gerald K. "Transnational Enterprises in the Manufacturing Sector of the Less Developed Countries." *World Development* 3, 9 (1975):641–650.

———. "Transnational Enterprise, Manufactured Exports and Employment in Less Developed Countries." *Economic and Political Weekly* 11, 5–7 (1976):289.

———. "International Technology Issues: Southern Needs and Northern Responses." In Jagdish N. Bhagwati (ed.) *The New International Economic Order*, pp. 295–316. Cambridge: MIT Press, 1977.

Henfrey, Colin. "Dependency, Modes of Production, and the Class Analysis of Latin America." *Latin American Perspectives* 8, 3–4 (1981):17–54.

Herman, Edward S. *Corporate Control, Corporate Power*. Cambridge: Cambridge University Press, 1981.

Hewlett, Sylvia Ann. "The State and Brazilian Economic Development: The Contemporary Reality and Prospects for the Future." In William H. Overholt (ed.) *The Future of Brazil*, pp. 149–210. Boulder, CO: Westview Press, 1978.

Hilferding, Rudolf. *Finance Capital: A Study of the Latest Phase of Capitalist Development*. Trans. Tom Bottomore. London: Routledge & Kegan Paul, 1981.

Hobson, John A. *Imperialism: A Study*. Rev. ed. London: Allen & Unwin, 1938.

Holsen, John, and Waelbroeck, Jean. "LDC Balance of Payments Policy and the International Monetary System." World Bank Staff Working Paper no. 226. Washington, DC: World Bank, 1976. Mimeographed.

Horowitz, Irving Louis. "Capitalism, Communism, and Multinationalism." In Abdul A. Said and Luiz R. Simmons (eds.) *The New Sovereigns: Multinational Corporations as World Powers*, pp. 120–138. Englewood Cliffs, NJ: Prentice-Hall, 1975.

Hunt, Shane. "Growth and Guano in the Nineteenth Century in Peru." Working paper, Woodrow Wilson School of Public and International Affairs. Princeton: Princeton University, 1973. Mimeographed.

Huntington, Samuel P. "Transnational Organizations in World Politics." *World Politics* 25, 3 (1973):333–368.

Hymer, Stephen. "The Multinational Corporation and the Law of Uneven Development." In Jagdish N. Bhagwati (ed.) *Economics and World Order from the 1970s to the 1990s*, pp. 113–140. New York: Macmillan, 1971.

Hyneman, Charles S. *The Study of Politics: The Present State of American Political Science*. Urbana: University of Illinois Press, 1959.

Ilett, J. "Inducements for Industrial Development: When Are They Worthwhile?" *Yorkshire Bulletin of Economic and Social Research* 19, 2 (1967):105.

Inter-American Development Bank (IDB). *Economic and Social Progress in Latin America 1976 Report.* Washington, DC: IDB, 1977.

————. *Economic and Social Progress in Latin America: Natural Resources.* Washington, DC: IDB, 1983.

Jessop, Bob. "Capitalism and Democracy: The Best Possible Political Shell?" In Gary Littlejohn et al. (eds.) *Power and the State,* pp. 10–51. New York: St. Martin's, 1978.

————. *The Capitalist State.* New York: New York University Press, 1982.

Jo, Sung-Hwan. "The Impact of Multinational Firms on Employment and Income: The Case Study of South Korea." World Employment Programme Research Working Paper 12. Geneva: International Labour Organisation, 1976. Mimeographed.

Jodice, David A. "Sources of Change in Third World Regimes for Foreign Direct Investment, 1968–1976." *International Organization* 34, 2 (1980):177–206.

Johnson, Harry. *International Economic Questions Facing Britain, the United States and Canada in the Seventies.* London: British-North American Research Association, June 1970.

Jones, Leroy P. *Public Enterprise and Economic Development: The Korean Case.* Seoul: Korea Development Institute, 1975.

Kahl, Joseph A. *Modernization, Exploitation, and Dependency in Latin America: Germani, González Casanova, and Cardoso.* New Brunswick, NJ: Transaction, 1976.

Kautsky, Karl. "Akkumulation und Imperialismus." *Neue Zeit* 32, 2 (1914):908–922. Extracts reprinted in Patrick Goode (ed. and trans.) *Karl Kautsky: Selected Political Writings,* pp. 75–89. New York: St. Martin's, 1983.

————. *Der Weg zur Macht.* Berlin, 1910. Extracts reprinted in Patrick Goode (ed. and trans.) *Karl Kautsky: Selected Political Writings,* pp. 75–89. New York: St. Martin's, 1983.

Keesing, Donald B. "World Trade and Output of Manufactures: Structural Trends and Developing Countries' Exports." World Bank Staff Working Paper no. 316. Washington, DC: World Bank, 1979. Mimeographed.

Kidron, Michael. *Foreign Investments in India.* London: Oxford University Press, 1965.

Kilson, Martin. "African Political Change and the Modernization Process." *Journal of Modern African Studies* 1, 4 (1963):425–440.

King, Timothy. *Mexico: Industrialization and Trade Policies since 1940.* London: Oxford University Press, 1970.

Knight, Peter T. "New Forms of Economic Organization in Peru: Toward Workers' Self-Management." In Abraham F. Lowenthal (ed.) *The Peruvian Experiment: Continuity and Change under Military Rule,* pp. 350–401. Princeton: Princeton University Press, 1975.

Kobrin, Stephen J. "Foreign Enterprise and Forced Divestment in LDCs." *International Organization* 34, 1 (1980):65–88.

Koebner, Richard, and Schmidt, Helmut Dan. *Imperialism: The Story and Significance of a Political Word, 1840–1960.* Cambridge: Cambridge University Press, 1964.

Krueger, Anne O. *Studies in the Modernization of the Republic of Korea, 1945–1975: The Developmental Role of the Foreign Sector and Aid.* Cambridge: Harvard University Press, 1979.

Kruijt, Dirk, and Vellinga, Menno. *Labor Relations and Multinational Corporations: The Cerro de Pasco Corporation in Peru (1902–1974).* Assen, Neth.: Van Gorcum, 1979.

Laclau, Ernesto. "Feudalism and Capitalism in Latin America." *New Left Review,* 67 (1971):19–38.

Lall, Sanjaya. "Less-Developed Countries and Private Foreign Investment: A Review Article." *World Development* 2, 4–5 (1974):43–48.

Larson, Magali Sarfatti. *The Rise of Professionalism: A Sociological Analysis.* Berkeley and Los Angeles: University of California Press, 1977.

Larson, Magali Sarfatti, and Bergen, Adele Eisen. *Social Stratification in Peru.* Berkeley: Institute of International Studies, University of California, 1969.

Lasswell, Harold D., and Kaplan, Abraham. *Power and Society: A Framework for Political Inquiry.* New Haven: Yale University Press, 1950.

Latham, Earl. "The Body Politic of the Corporation." In Edward S. Mason (ed.) *The Corporation in Modern Society,* pp. 218–236. Cambridge: Harvard University Press, 1959.

Lenin, V.I. *Imperialism, the Highest Stage of Capitalism: A Popular Outline.* New York: International Publishers, 1939.

Lenski, Gerhard. *Power and Prestige: A Theory of Social Stratification.* New York: McGraw-Hill, 1966.

Leys, Colin. *Underdevelopment in Kenya: The Political Economy of Neo-Colonialism.* Berkeley and Los Angeles: University of California Press, 1974.

———. "African Economic Development in Theory and Practice." *Daedalus* 111, 2 (1982):99–124.

Lindert, Peter H., and Williamson, Jeffrey G. "Reinterpreting Britain's Social Tables, 1688–1913." *Explorations in Economic History* 20, 1 (1983):94–109.

Lissakers, Karin. *International Debt, the Banks and U.S. Foreign Policy.* Staff report prepared for the Subcommittee on Foreign Economic Policy of the Committee on Foreign Relations, U.S. Senate. Washington, DC: U.S. Government Printing Office, 1977.

Litvak, Isaiah A., and Maule, Christopher J. "The Multinational Firm: Some Perspectives." In Gilles Paquet (ed.) *The Multinational Firm and the Nation State.* Don Mills, Ont.: Collier-Macmillan, 1972.

Lofchie, Michael F. "The Political Origins of the Uganda Coup." *Journal of African Studies* 1, 4 (1974):464–496.

———. "Agrarian Socialism in the Third World: The Tanzanian Case." *Comparative Politics* 8, 4 (1976):479–499.

Looney, Robert E. *Mexico's Economy: A Policy Analysis with Forecasts to 1990.* Boulder, CO: Westview Press, 1978.

Macpherson, C.B. *The Real World of Democracy.* London: Oxford University Press, 1966.

Magdoff, Harry. "The Limits of International Reform." *Monthly Review* 30, 1 (1978):1–11.

Marcuse, Herbert. *Soviet Marxism: A Critical Analysis.* New York: Random House, 1961.

Markakis, John. *Ethiopia: Anatomy of a Traditional Polity.* Oxford: Oxford University Press, 1974.

Marx, Karl. *A Contribution to the Critique of Political Economy.* Chicago: Charles H. Kerr, 1904.

————. *The Eighteenth Brumaire of Louis Bonaparte.* New York: International Publishers, 1963.

————. *The Poverty of Philosophy.* New York: International Publishers, 1963.

McClintock, Cynthia. *Peasant Cooperatives and Political Change in Peru.* Princeton: Princeton University Press, 1981.

McConnell, Grant. *Private Power and American Democracy.* New York: Knopf, 1966.

Meillassoux, Claude. "A Class Analysis of the Bureaucratic Process in Mali." *Journal of Development Studies* 6, 2 (1970):97–110.

Mellos, Koula. "Developments in Advanced Capitalist Ideology." *Canadian Journal of Political Science* 11, 4 (1978):829–860.

Mepham, John. "The Theory of Ideology in Capital." In John Mepham and David-Hillel Ruben (eds.) *Marxist Philosophy Vol. III: Epistemology, Science, Ideology,* pp. 141–169. London: Harvester Press, 1978.

Middle East Research and Information Project (MERIP). *State Capitalism in Algeria.* Report no. 35. Washington, DC: MERIP, 1975.

Mikesell, Raymond F. "Conflict in Foreign Investor-Host Country Relations: A Preliminary Analysis." In Raymond F. Mikesell et al. *Foreign Investment in the Petroleum and Mineral Industries: Case Studies of Investor-Host Country Relations,* pp. 29–55. Baltimore: Johns Hopkins University Press, 1971.

————. *Foreign Investment in Copper Mining: Case Studies of Mines in Peru and Papua New Guinea.* Baltimore: Johns Hopkins University Press, 1975.

————. *The World Copper Industry: Structure and Economic Analysis.* Baltimore: Johns Hopkins University Press, 1975.

————. "Mining Agreements and Conflict Resolution." In Sandro Sideri and Sheridan Johns (eds.) *Mining for Development in the Third World: Multinational Corporations, State Enterprises and the International Economy,* pp. 198–209. New York: Pergamon, 1980.

Miliband, Ralph. *The State in Capitalist Society: An Analysis of the Western System of Power.* New York: Basic Books, 1969.

Miller, Richard W. *Analyzing Marx: Morality, Power and History.* Princeton: Princeton University Press, 1984.

Mills, C. Wright. *The Power Elite.* New York: Oxford University Press, 1956.

Minian, Isaac. "Rivalidad intercapitalista e industrialización en el subdesarrollo: notas para un estudio sobre la división internacional del trabajo." *Economía de América Latina,* 2 (1979):81–102.

Ministry of Finance and Public Credit (Mexico). "The First and Second Reports on the Public Debt Presented to the Congress of the Union." *Comercio Exterior de México* (English language edition) 24, 1 (1978):25.

Molteno, Robert, and Tordoff, William. "Independent Zambia: Achievements and Prospects." In William Tordoff (ed.) *Politics in Zambia,* pp. 363–401.

Berkeley and Los Angeles: University of California Press, 1974.

Moran, Theodore H. "Transnational Strategies of Protection and Defense by Multinational Corporations: Spreading the Risk and Raising the Cost for Nationalization in Natural Resources." *International Organization* 27, 2 (1973):273–287.

———. *Multinational Corporations and the Politics of Dependence: Copper in Chile.* Princeton: Princeton University Press, 1974.

Morawetz, David. *Twenty-Five Years of Economic Development 1950 to 1975.* Baltimore: Johns Hopkins University Press, 1977.

Müller, Ronald E. "The Multinational Corporation and the Underdevelopment of the Third World." In Charles K. Wilbur (ed.) *The Political Economy of Development and Underdevelopment,* pp. 124–151. New York: Random House, 1973.

Muñoz, Heraldo. "The Strategic Dependency of the Centers and the Importance of the Latin American Periphery." In Heraldo Muñoz (ed.) *From Dependency to Development: Strategies to Overcome Underdevelopment and Inequality,* pp. 59–92. Boulder, CO: Westview Press, 1981.

Myrdal, Gunnar. *Asian Drama: An Inquiry into the Poverty of Nations.* 3 vols. New York: Pantheon, Random House, 1968.

Nam, Duck-woo. "Mobilization of Domestic Resources." In *International Conference on Korean Futures,* p. 263. Seoul: Asiatic Research Centre, Korea University, 1975.

Neersø, Peter. "Tanzania's Policies on Private Foreign Investment." In Carl Widstrand (ed.). *Multinational Firms in Africa,* p. 194. New York: African Publishing, Holmes & Meier, 1975.

Neumann, Franz L. "Approaches to the Study of Political Power." *Political Science Quarterly* 65, 2 (1950):161–180.

North, Liisa, and Korovkin, Tanya. *The Peruvian Revolution and the Officers in Power, 1967–1976.* Montréal: Centre for Developing-Area Studies, McGill University, 1981.

Nowzad, Bahram. "Differential Trade Treatment for LDCs." *Finance and Development* 15, 1 (1978):16–21.

Nun, José. "The Middle-Class Military Coup." In Claudio Véliz (ed.). *The Politics of Conformity in Latin America,* pp. 66–118. London: Oxford University Press, 1967.

———. *Latin America: The Hegemonic Crisis and the Military Coup.* Berkeley: Institute of International Studies, University of California, 1973.

O, Won-chol. "Economic Development and Industrialization in Korea." In *International Conference on Korean Futures,* p. 289. Seoul: Asiatic Research Centre, Korea University, 1975.

O'Brien, Philip J. "A Critique of Latin American Theories of Dependency." In Ivar Oxaal, Tony Barnett, and David Booth (eds.) *Beyond the Sociology of Development: Economy and Society in Latin America and Africa,* pp. 7–27. London: Routledge & Kegan Paul, 1975.

O'Donnell, Guillermo A. *Modernization and Bureaucratic-Authoritarianism: Studies in South American Politics.* Berkeley: Institute of International Studies, University of California, 1973.

————. "Reflections on the Patterns of Change in the Bureaucratic-Authoritarian State." *Latin American Research Review 13*, 1 (1978):3–38.

————. "Tensions in the Bureaucratic-Authoritarian State and the Question of Democracy." In David Collier (ed.) *The New Authoritarianism in Latin America,* pp. 285–318. Princeton: Princeton University Press, 1979.

Organisation for Economic Co-operation and Development. *Development Co-operation, 1978 Review.* Paris: OECD, 1978.

Orren, Karen. *Corporate Power and Social Change: The Politics of the Life Insurance Industry.* Baltimore: Johns Hopkins University Press, 1974.

Ossowski, Stanislaw. *Class Structure in the Social Consciousness.* Trans. Sheila Patterson. New York: Free Press, 1963.

Palma, Gabriel. "Dependency: A Formal Theory of Underdevelopment or a Methodology for the Analysis of Concrete Situations of Underdevelopment?" *World Development 6*, 7–8 (1978):881–924.

Paukert, Felix. "Income Distribution at Different Levels of Development: A Survey of Evidence." *International Labour Review 108*, 2–3 (1973):97–125.

Payer, Cheryl. "Third World Debt Problems: The New Wave of Defaults." *Monthly Review 28*, 4 (1976):1–19.

Payne, James L. *Labor and Politics in Peru: The System of Political Bargaining.* New Haven: Yale University Press, 1965.

Pearson, David W. "The Comunidad Industrial: Peru's Experiment in Worker Management." *Inter-American Economic Affairs 27*, 1 (1973):15–29.

Pease García, Henry. *El ocaso del poder oligárquico.* Lima: DESCO, 1977.

Penrose, Edith. "'Ownership and Control': Multinational Firms in Less Developed Countries." In Gerald K. Helleiner (ed.). *A World Divided: The Less Developed Countries in the International Economy,* pp. 147–174. Cambridge: Cambridge University Press, 1976.

Perlmutter, Howard V. "The Tortuous Evolution of the Multinational Corporation." In Courtney C. Brown (ed.) *World Business: Promise and Problems,* pp. 66–82. New York: Macmillan, 1970.

Petras, James F. "State Capitalism and the Third World." *Journal of Contemporary Asia 6*, 4 (1976):432–443.

Philip, George. "The Soldier as Radical: The Peruvian Military Government, 1968–1975." *Journal of Latin American Studies 8*, 1 (1976):29–51.

Plamenatz, John. *On Alien Rule and Self-Government.* London: Longmans, 1960.

Poulantzas, Nicos. *Political Power and Social Classes.* London: New Left Books, 1973.

Prebisch, Raúl. *Towards a Dynamic Development Policy for Latin America.* New York: United Nations, 1963.

Purcell, John F.H. "The Perceptions and Interests of U.S. Business in Relation to the Political Crisis in Central America." In Richard E. Feinberg (ed.) *Central America: International Dimensions of the Crisis,* pp. 103–123. New York: Holmes & Meier, 1982.

Purser, W.F.C. *Metal-Mining in Peru, Past and Present.* New York: Praeger, 1971.

Radetzki, Marian. "LDC Policies Towards Foreign Mineral Investors." In Sandro Sideri and Sheridan Johns (eds.) *Mining for Development in the Third World:*

Multinational Corporations, State Enterprises and the International Economy, pp. 283–296. New York: Pergamon, 1980.

Reissman, Leonard. *Class in American Society.* Glencoe, IL: Free Press, 1960.

Robock, Stefan. *Brazil: A Study in Development Progress.* Lexington, MA: Lexington Books, 1975.

Rodney, Walter. *How Europe Underdeveloped Africa.* Dar es Salaam: Tanzania Publishing House, 1972.

Rueschemeyer, Dietrich, and Evans, Peter. "The State and Economic Transformation: Toward an Analysis of the Conditions Underlying Effective Intervention." In Peter B. Evans, Dietrich Rueschemeyer, and Theda Skocpol (eds.) *Bringing the State Back In,* pp. 44–77. Cambridge: Cambridge University Press, 1985.

Samamé Boggio, Mario. *Minería peruana: biografía y estrategia de una actividad decisiva.* 2d ed., 2 vols. Lima: Editorial Gráfica Labor, 1974.

Saul, John S. "African Socialism in One Country: Tanzania." In Giovanni Arrighi and John S. Saul (eds.) *Essays on the Political Economy of Africa,* pp. 237–335. New York: Monthly Review Press, 1973.

Savasini, José Augusto. *Export Promotion: The Case of Brazil.* New York: Praeger, 1978.

Schatz, Sayre P. "Crude Private Neo-imperialism: A New Pattern in Africa." *Journal of Modern African Studies* 7, 4 (1969):677–688.

———. *Nigerian Capitalism.* Berkeley and Los Angeles: University of California Press, 1977.

Schlagheck, James L. *The Political, Economic, and Labor Climate in Mexico.* Philadelphia: Industrial Research Unit, The Wharton School, 1977.

Schumpeter, Joseph A. *The Theory of Economic Development.* Cambridge: Harvard University Press, 1935.

———. *Capitalism, Socialism, and Democracy.* New York: Harper & Row, 1942.

Seidman, Anne (ed.). *Natural Resources and National Welfare: The Case of Copper.* New York: Praeger, 1975.

Semmel, Bernard. *Imperialism and Social Reform: English Social-Imperial Thought, 1895–1914.* Cambridge: Harvard University Press, 1960.

———. *The Rise of Free Trade Imperialism.* Cambridge: Cambridge University Press, 1970.

Shipler, David K. *Russia: Broken Idols, Solemn Dreams.* New York: New York Times Books, 1983.

Shivji, Issa G., et al. *The Silent Class Struggle.* Dar es Salaam: Tanzania Publishing House, 1973.

Sigmund, Paul. *Multinationals in Latin America: The Politics of Nationalization.* Madison: University of Wisconsin Press, 1980.

Singh, Jyoti Shankar. *A New International Economic Order: Toward a Fair Redistribution of the World's Resources.* New York: Praeger, 1977.

Skidmore, Thomas E. "Politics and Economic Policy Making in Authoritarian Brazil, 1937–71." In Alfred Stepan (ed.) *Authoritarian Brazil: Origins, Policies, and Future,* pp. 3–46. New Haven: Yale University Press, 1973.

Sklar, Martin J. "Woodrow Wilson and the Political Economy of Modern United States Liberalism." In James Weinstein and David W. Eakins (eds.) *For a New America: Essays in History and Politics from "Studies on the Left,"*

1959–1967, pp. 46–100. New York: Random House, 1970.

———. *The Corporate Reconstruction of American Capitalism, 1890–1916: The Market, the Law, and Politics.* Cambridge: Cambridge University Press, 1987. forthcoming.

Sklar, Richard L. "Contradictions in the Nigerian Political System." *Journal of Modern African Studies* 3, 2 (1965):201–213.

———. *Nigerian Political Parties: Power in an Emergent African Nation.* Princeton: Princeton University Press, 1963.

———. *Corporate Power in an African State: The Political Impact of Multinational Mining Companies in Zambia.* Berkeley and Los Angeles: University of California Press, 1975.

———. "Socialism at Bay: Class Domination in Africa." Paper presented at the Joint Meeting of the African Studies Association and the Latin American Studies Association, Houston, November 1977. Mimeographed.

———. "The Nature of Class Domination in Africa." *Journal of Modern African Studies* 17, 4 (1979):531–552.

———. "Democracy in Africa." Presidential address to the Twenty-Fifth Annual Meeting of the African Studies Association, Washington, DC, 5 November 1982. Mimeographed.

———. "On the Concept of Power in Political Economy." In Dalmas H. Nelson and Richard L. Sklar (eds.) *Toward a Humanistic Science of Politics: Essays in Honor of Francis Dunham Wormuth,* pp. 179–206. Lanham, MD: University Press of America, 1983.

———. "Lectures on Socialism and Development." Unpublished draft, n.d. Mimeographed.

Sklar, Richard L., and Whitaker, C.S., Jr. "The Federal Republic of Nigeria." In Gwendolen M. Carter (ed.) *National Unity and Regionalism in Eight African States,* pp. 7–150. Ithaca, NY: Cornell University Press, 1966.

Skocpol, Theda. "Wallerstein's World Capitalist System: A Theoretical and Historical Critique." *American Journal of Sociology* 82, 5 (1977):1075–1090.

Smith, Tony. "The Underdevelopment of Development Literature: The Case of Dependency Theory." *World Politics* 31, 2 (1979):247–288.

Sofer, Eugene F. "Recent Trends in Latin American Labor Historiography." *Latin American Research Review* 15, 1 (1980):167–176.

Soleye, O.O. "The Politico-Economic Position of Multinational Corporations: A Nigerian Example." In Carl Widstrand (ed.) *Multinational Firms in Africa,* pp. 199–205. New York: African Publishing, Holmes & Meier, 1975.

Solís, Leopoldo. "Desarrollo económico mexicano." In Edmar Bacha et al. *Estrategias de desarrollo económico en algunos paises de America Latina,* pp. 18–19. Bogotá: Fundación para la Educación y el Desarrollo, 1974.

Stepan, Alfred. *The State and Society: Peru in Comparative Perspective.* Princeton: Princeton University Press, 1978.

Stephens, Evelyne Huber. *The Politics of Workers' Participation: The Peruvian Approach in Comparative Perspective.* New York: Academic Press, 1980.

———. "The Peruvian Military Government, Labor Mobilization, and the Political Strength of the Left." *Latin American Research Review* 18, 2 (1983):57–93.

Strachey, John. *The End of Empire.* New York: Random House, 1960.

Streeten, Paul. "Costs and Benefits of Multinational Enterprises." In John H. Dunning (ed.) *The Multinational Enterprise*, pp. 240–258. London: Allen & Unwin, 1971.

―――. "The Multinational Enterprise and the Theory of Development Policy." *World Development* 1, 10 (1973):1–13.

―――. "Multinationals Revisited." *Finance and Development* 16, 2 (1979):39–42.

Streeten, Paul P., and Lall, Sanjaya. *Evaluation of Methods and Main Findings of UNCTAD Study of Private Overseas Investment in Selected Less Developed Countries.* TD/b/c.3/111. New York: United Nations, 1973.

Sunkel, Osvaldo. "National Development Policy and External Dependence in Latin America." *Journal of Development Studies* 6, 1 (1969):23–48.

―――. "Big Business and 'Dependencia': A Latin American View." *Foreign Affairs* 50, 3 (1972):517–531.

―――. "Transnational Capitalism and National Disintegration in Latin America." *Social and Economic Studies* 22, 1 (1973): 132–176.

Suzigan, Wilson. "As empresas do governo e o papel do Estado na economia brasileira." In Fernando Rezende et al. *Aspectos da participação do governo na economia.* Rio de Janeiro: IPEA/INPES, 1976.

Sweezy, Paul M. "The Nature of Soviet Society." *Monthly Review* 26, 11 (1974):1–16; 27, 1 (1975):1–15.

Sweezy, Paul M., and Bettelheim, Charles. *On the Transition to Socialism.* New York: Monthly Review Press, 1971.

Sweezy, Paul M., and Magdoff, Harry. "Notes on the Multinational Corporation." *Monthly Review* 21, 5 (1969):1–13; 21, 6 (1969):1–13.

―――. *The Dynamics of U.S. Capitalism.* New York: Monthly Review Press, 1972.

Szentes, Tamas. "Socioeconomic Effects of Two Patterns of Foreign Capital Investments, with Special Reference to East Africa." In Peter C.W. Gutkind and Immanuel Wallerstein (eds.) *The Political Economy of Contemporary Africa*, pp. 261–290. Beverly Hills, CA: Sage, 1976.

Szymanski, Albert. "Capital Accumulation on a World Scale and the Necessity of Imperialism." *The Insurgent Sociologist* 7, 2 (1977):35–53.

Therborn, Göran. "The Travail of Latin American Democracy." *New Left Review,* 113–114 (1979):71–109.

Todaro, Michael P. *Development in the Third World.* London: Longmans, 1977.

Trotsky, Leon. *The Revolution Betrayed.* Trans. Max Eastman. Garden City, NY: Doubleday, 1937.

Truman, David B. *The Governmental Process: Political Interests and Public Opinion.* 2d ed. New York: Knopf, 1971.

United Nations. *Multinational Corporations in World Development.* ST/ECA/190/1. New York: United Nations, 1973.

―――. *Summary of the Hearings Before the Group of Eminent Persons to Study the Impact of Multinational Corporations on Development and on International Relations.* ST/ESA/15. New York: United Nations, 1974.

United Nations Commission on Transnational Corporations. *Transnational Corporations in World Development: A Re-examination.* E/C.10/38. New York: United Nations, 1978.

U.S. Industry and Trade Administration. *Foreign Economic Trends and Their Implications for the United States: Algeria.* Washington, DC: U.S. Department of

. Commerce, 1979.

Vaitsos, Constantine V. "Power, Knowledge and Development Policy: Relations between Transnational Enterprises and Developing Countries." In Gerald K. Helleiner (ed.) *A World Divided: The Less Developed Countries in the International Economy*, pp. 113–146. Cambridge: Cambridge University Press, 1976.

Vernon, Raymond. *Sovereignty at Bay: The Multinational Spread of U.S. Enterprises*. New York: Basic Books, 1971.

———. "Storm over the Multinationals: Problems and Prospects." *Foreign Affairs* 55, 2 (1977):243–262.

———. *Storm over the Multinationals: The Real Issues*. Cambridge: Harvard University Press, 1977.

Villa M., Rosa Oliva. *Nacional Financiera: banco de fomento del desarrollo económico de México*. México, D.F.: Nacional Financiera, 1976.

Villanueva, Víctor. *El CAEM y la Revolución de la Fuerza Armada*. Lima: Instituto de Estudios Peruanos, 1972.

Villarreal, René. "Del proyecto de crecimiento y sustitución de importaciones al de desarrollo y sustitución de exportaciones." *Comercio Exterior* 25, 3 (1975):315–323.

Wachtel, Howard. *The New Gnomes: Multinational Banks in the Third World*. TNI Pamphlet no. 4. Washington, DC: Transnational Institute, 1977.

Wallerstein, Immanuel. "Dependence in an Interdependent World: The Limited Possibilities of Transformation within the Capitalist World-Economy." *African Studies Review* 17, 1 (1974):1–26.

———. *The Modern World-System: Capitalist Agriculture and the Origins of the European World-Economy in the Sixteenth Century*. New York: Academic Press, 1974.

———. "The Rise and Future Demise of the World Capitalist System: Concepts for Comparative Analysis." *Comparative Studies in Society and History* 16, 4 (1974):387–415.

———. "Trends in World Capitalism." *Monthly Review* 26, 5 (1974): 12–18.

———. "Nationalism and the World Transition to Socialism: Is There a Crisis?" *Third World Quarterly* 5, 1 (1983):95–102.

Warren, Bill. "Imperialism and Capitalist Industrialization." *New Left Review*, 81 (1973):3–44.

———. *Imperialism, Pioneer of Capitalism*. London: New Left Books, 1980.

Watson, Paul. *Debt and the Developing Countries: New Problems and New Actors*. Development Paper 26, NIEO Series. Washington, DC: Overseas Development Council, 1978.

Weinstein, James. *The Corporate Ideal in the Liberal State, 1900–1918*. Boston: Beacon Press, 1968.

Westphal, Larry. "The Republic of Korea's Experience with Export-Led Industrial Development." *World Development* 6, 3 (1978):349–374.

Whyte, William H., Jr. *The Organization Man*. New York: Simon & Schuster, 1956.

Wiarda, Howard J. "Toward a Framework for the Study of Political Change in the Iberic-Latin Tradition: The Corporative Model." *World Politics* 25, 2 (1973):206–235.

Wilkie, John W., and Reich, Peter (eds.) *Statistical Abstract of Latin America Vol. 20.* Los Angeles: UCLA Latin American Center, 1980.

Wilkins, Mira. *The Maturing of Multinational Enterprise: American Business Abroad from 1914 to 1970.* Cambridge: Harvard University Press, 1974.

Williame, Jean-Claude. *Patrimonialism and Political Change in the Congo.* Stanford, CA: Stanford University Press, 1972.

Wionczek, Miguel (ed.) *LDC External Debt and the World Economy.* Mexico City: El Colegio de México, 1978.

World Bank. *World Debt Tables 1979.* 2 vols. Washington, DC: World Bank, 1979.

———. *World Development Report 1978.* New York: Oxford University Press, 1978.

———. *World Development Report 1979.* New York: Oxford University Press, 1979.

———. *World Development Report 1980.* New York: Oxford University Press, 1980.

———. *World Development Report 1984.* New York: Oxford University Press, 1984.

———. *World Economic and Social Indicators 1980.* Washington, DC: World Bank, 1980.

———. *World Tables.* 2d ed. Washington, DC: World Bank, 1980.

———. *World Tables.* 3d ed., 2 vols. Washington, DC: World Bank, 1983.

Zeitlin, Maurice. "Corporate Ownership and Control: The Large Corporation and the Capitalist Class." *American Journal of Sociology* 79 (1974):1073–1119.

Zeitlin, Maurice, and Norich, Samuel. "Management Control, Exploitation, and Profit Maximization in the Large Corporation: An Empirical Confrontation of Managerialism and Class Theory." In Paul Zarembka (ed.) *Research in Political Economy,* pp. 33–62. Vol. 2. Greenwich, CT: JAI Press, 1979.

Zonis, Marvin. *The Political Elite of Iran.* Princeton: Princeton University Press, 1971.

Zorn, Stephen. "Recent Trends in LDC Mining Agreements." In Sandro Sideri and Sheridan Johns (eds.) *Mining for Development in the Third World: Multinational Corporations, State Enterprises and the International Economy,* pp. 210–228. New York: Pergamon, 1980.

"El sector externo de México en 1978 y sus perspectivas." *Comercio Exterior* 29, 3 (1979):263–270.

"La stratégie du developpement socialiste." *Révolution africaine,* 819 (1979):39–54.

"Las relaciones económicas con el exterior en 1979." *Comercio Exterior* 30, 5 (1980):442–447.

About the Authors

David G. Becker is assistant professor of government at Dartmouth College. He is author of *The New Bourgeoisie and the Limits of Dependency*, a study of postimperialist development in Peru, and is currently engaged in a comparative study of democratic capitalist development in three South American countries.

Jeff Frieden is assistant professor of political science at the University of California, Los Angeles. He has written a number of articles on the politics of international monetary and financial relations and is writing a book on the subject.

Sayre P. Schatz is professor of economics at Temple University. He is author of three books on African economic development, the most recent being *Nigerian Capitalism*.

Richard L. Sklar is professor of political science at the University of California, Los Angeles, and recent past president of the African Studies Association. His publications include *Nigerian Political Parties*, *Corporate Power in an African State*, and numerous articles on postcolonial political development in Africa.

Index